GOLF WAR$

GOLF WAR$

LIV AND GOLF'S BITTER BATTLE FOR POWER AND IDENTITY

IAIN CARTER

BLOOMSBURY SPORT
LONDON • OXFORD • NEW YORK • NEW DELHI • SYDNEY

BLOOMSBURY SPORT
Bloomsbury Publishing Plc
50 Bedford Square, London, WC1B 3DP, UK
29 Earlsfort Terrace, Dublin 2, Ireland

BLOOMSBURY, BLOOMSBURY SPORT and the Diana logo are trademarks of
Bloomsbury Publishing Plc

First published in Great Britain 2024

A catalogue record for this book is available from the British Library

Library of Congress Cataloguing-in-Publication data has been applied for

ISBN: HB: 978-1-3994-1016-8; eBook: 978-1-3994-1019-9; ePdf: 978-1-3994-1020-5

2 4 6 8 10 9 7 5 3 1

Typeset in Adobe Garamond Pro by Deanta Global Publishing Services, Chennai, India
Printed and bound in Great Britain by CPI Group (UK) Ltd., Croydon, CR0 4YY

To find out more about our authors and books visit www.bloomsbury.com
and sign up for our newsletters

For Sarah and Ollie

CONTENTS

PROLOGUE

This was golf, but louder. And for the players it did not involve a penny or cent of prize money, never mind an appearance or signing-on fee.

It was bedlam and we were only eight holes in; not even halfway round the course. They were perhaps the most dramatic eight holes I had ever witnessed. Television commentators were calling it the best Ryder Cup contest they had ever seen. America against Europe, a golf match in its most raw and captivating form and it was bringing the very best out of its two lead protagonists.

The crowd were thirsting for home success. 'U-S-A! U-S-A! U-S-A!' Every letter throatily and aggressively emphasised for maximum effect. No limit on volume control. The chant was as unimaginative and predictable as it was passionately delivered. They were roaring for 'Captain America' while Europe's isolated talisman was trying to prove why he should be considered the world's best player. Both were desperate to win. Neither wanted to give an inch. And both were inspired.

In the red corner, for the home team was Patrick Reed: arrogant, brash, bold, pugnacious. And often controversial. In the blue corner, Northern Ireland's Rory

McIlroy: supremely talented, the $10m man who had just won America's most valuable competition, the Tour Championship. Outspoken, forthright and savvy, but yet to become the darling of the establishment.

Between these two golfing gladiators lay plenty of mutual respect. They had been sent out first by their respective captains because they were the most likely to land a crucial win to set the tone for the final day of the 2016 Ryder Cup.

On the first tee, beneath his bright white cap emblazoned with the letters 'U', 'S' and 'A', Reed revved the crowd. America was ahead, but as a golfing nation it was hurting. Europe had beaten them in the previous three Ryder Cups, the last US success was way back in 2008. It was a must-win contest for the home team. The raucous hordes, fuelled by beer and burgers, accepted nothing less.

Both players shared a warm mid-morning handshake, McIlroy giving a sporting tap on the back of his opponent before first balls were struck. And from that moment ignited a spectacular display of golfing fireworks. By the time the players marched to the eighth tee they had traded almost exclusively in eagles and birdies to stand all square. Both of them were pumped, gesticulating to the baying crowds. I share that march; headphones clamped to both ears, volume turned to the max, I'm defying health and safety regs, but still unable to hear our BBC radio coverage or the commands of the production team above a seemingly endless din.

Relative silence then descends as the players hit tee shots to this uphill short hole. Reed shows better distance control but puts it comfortably left of the flag. McIlroy's tee shot creeps on to the front left of the green. The flag is back right. A pair of incongruously average tee shots. The European is miles away. It is marginally advantage America as the players stomp to the green.

There are thousands upon thousands of people standing on the banked surrounds. They yell abuse at McIlroy, chant their 'U-S-A's, remind him of his failed romance with tennis star Caroline Wozniacki and implore Reed to 'Kill the fucker!'

Golf getting louder.

Then silence.

McIlroy has dispassionately stalked his putt, there are acres of Minnesota real estate to be negotiated. Knock it close enough for Reed to concede a relatively stress-free par. That can be his only objective. Surely? The European leader gives his ball a firm rap up the hill. It is good for pace, looks decent for line. Very decent on both counts. It continues to travel in sure-footed fashion. The ball disappears into the hole. Suddenly, minority European voices erupt; the Americans are silenced.

Astonished.

McIlroy puts his right hand to his ear. He's gone ballistic. He is almost levitating. Every muscle in his body is flexed. 'C'mon!' He roars. 'I can't hear you!'

Reed offers a sardonic smile. Gets to work.

A golf hole measures 4¼ inches in diameter. In the past hour, to these players this target has seemed the size of a bucket. Reed decides the line. He's probably 25 feet away. The putt is struck firmly, confidently. With no deviation or deceleration it unerringly races. And disappears into the cup. It is another sensational half; a pair of birdies among the most extraordinary to have ever been witnessed in the long history of the royal and ancient game. One experienced hack later says: 'It was as good as golf could get, maybe in your lifetime.'

Hazeltine explodes.

Reed wags his right index finger while McIlroy's machismo slowly, reluctantly melts. He cannot stop himself smiling. They touch knuckles and amid the cacophony head to the ninth tee.

This was the high point.

Behind them, I'm marching, body shaking and yelling an account of the extraordinary scenes into my tremulous microphone. To this day, I have no recollection of what I said. But I can still feel the heart rate, and the electricity. This truly was what is meant when sport is described as pulsating. Photographer Matthew Harris hurries alongside me, amid a massive media throng. Looks of disbelief cross the faces of some of the longest-serving watchers of the game. 'Have you ever seen anything like this?' Matthew asks as we yomp to our next vantage point. A breathless 'No,' is all I can muster.

'Unbelievable.'

This was September 2016 at Hazeltine National Golf Club near Minneapolis. Understandably, neither player could sustain the brilliance of those first eight holes for the entire round, but it remained an engrossingly tight affair. Reed went on to win by a single hole, sealing it with a deft approach to the final green for a closing birdie. Again, he celebrated as if his life and the future of his nation depended on it.

This victory reinforced his status as a hero of American golf. He had done his job spectacularly well, paving the way for his country to win back a precious trophy that continues to stir golfing emotions like no other. 'We mocked each other a little bit,' McIlroy admitted to reporters. 'At the same time it was all in good fun. No problems with Patrick Reed at all. He's been immense this week.'

The victor was just as magnanimous, in keeping with the accepted sporting spirit that has invariably been a hallmark of the game throughout its history. 'Whether it's the European side, captains, vice captains or US side, it's a big Ryder Cup family. We want everyone to play well. We want to beat them at their best, they want to beat us at our best,' Reed said.

Times have changed.

Now it is January 2023. Instead of the lush, tree-lined fairways of Minnesota we are in the desert of Dubai. Reed is a pariah. Has been for months. He is banned from America's PGA Tour. Now his best option to complete a 72-hole tournament is on Europe's DP World Tour, and that opportunity might soon disappear as well. And although he is currently allowed to play their events, he is no longer welcome.

McIlroy is now officially the best player in the world; the face of the golfing establishment. He is also pissed off to find he is sharing the same hotel as the man who beat him at that 2016 Ryder Cup; the same golfer who two years later downed him in the final round of the Masters, the one major McIlroy has yet to win.

But the antipathy has nothing to do with those results. Indeed, McIlroy was a gracious loser on both occasions. But now the golfing world had shifted on its axis.

Before this seismic change and notwithstanding the passions of the Ryder Cup, professional golf was regarded as one of the most peaceful of professional sports; the garden of Eden in sporting heaven. Players were portrayed as respectful, honest, rule-abiding athletes playing a convivial game in the nicest places. A sponsor's dream with uncharacteristic unsavoury shenanigans invariably brushed from sight. Tours prefer not to publish fines and punishments, unless absolutely necessary.

This blueprint allowed professional golf to develop into a product that was the envy of many other sports. Elite players make fortunes and rarely would a pro bad-mouth another because that would be a breach of their gentlemanly code. It could even lead to official disciplinary action. Tour bosses tried to avoid, at all costs, controversy among their members for fear of deterring sponsors attracted by golf's clean-cut reputation.

However, in early 2023, when Patrick Reed wandered on to the range at the start of the week of the Dubai Desert Classic, golf was a sport rocked by uncivil war. And Reed was a central figure in many of its battles. The game was suddenly questioning the certainties that had underpinned a history of seemingly relentless development and progress.

Skirmishes were breaking out all over; lawyers on both sides of the Atlantic racking up expensive hours to potentially decide golf's future. The sport had been plunged into a bitter and divisive place, far away from the comparative idyll it had occupied for so many years. Symptomatic of this new and troubled environment was how the mutual respect once shared between McIlroy and Reed now lay in tatters.

The US star was the last person McIlroy wanted to see when he arrived in the UAE for the Dubai Desert Classic. Christmas for the world's best golfer had been disturbed when he was served with a subpoena from the American player's flamboyant lawyer, Larry Klayman. He was fighting a case against the PGA Tour that did not involve Reed. But McIlroy, who had been served because of his position on the American tour's board, knew the strong link between the two men. He certainly did not want to make small talk with Reed when they first came across each other in Dubai.

McIlroy is a stubborn character and he blanked his US rival's approach to shake hands on the practice range. Ignoring the American, he instead continued making adjustments to his shot-monitoring device. Reed, who had just shared a handshake with his rival's caddie, Harry Diamond, was unimpressed. The 2018 Masters champion turned, but only after he had tossed a branded tee mockingly in McIlroy's direction. Then he nonchalantly strolled away.

It may seem a trivial incident. The tiny wooden peg golfers use to elevate their golf ball for tee shots is not exactly a hand grenade, but this sort of petulance from both sides has been rarely so conspicuous. This incident happened on a range full of cameras and phones and involved the two highest-profile players in the tournament.

Unsurprisingly, the moment was spotted and equally inevitably the story went viral. Ensuing media coverage set the tone for what proved an explosive and captivating start to the most fractious and significant year in the modern history of golf.

Build-ups to golf tournaments do not usually stir bad blood among the competitors. Then again, it does not usually rain in the Dubai desert either. That night, the weather mirrored the stormy atmosphere prevailing in the locker room. For hour after hour, lightning fractiously illuminated the Middle Eastern skies and loud thunder cracks echoed across the emirate as rain hammered down. The course flooded, as did surrounding roads.

The big question surrounded whether this $9m tournament would spill into a fifth day or be cut to 54 holes – which was a divisive duration in this testy era. Television wanted the event to finish on the Sunday to satisfy its schedules and create the better spectacle. 'They want the bigger weekend crowds for the finale,' said an insider. Tour officials preferred to emphasise the legitimacy of the tournament by playing it over a full four rounds.

DP World Tour boss Keith Pelley, pushing for 72 holes, checked that his biggest playing asset – Rory McIlroy – was happy with the plan. He called him on the Friday afternoon. 'Of course, why wouldn't we play four rounds?' the world number one replied. 'Seventy-two hole golf is championship golf and that's the way it should be.'

So Saturday, normally when the third circuit of a four-round tournament is staged, was the day the tournament reached its halfway stage. Neither McIlroy nor Reed was at their best. Each golfer knocked it round in 2-under-par 70s, meaning that both had the same overall score of 8-under-par.

There was an enticing chance of them being paired together for the third round. If tournament golf were showbiz they certainly would have been put in the same group. If that had been the case, they would have had to shake hands or risk an even greater escalation of their row. I asked McIlroy what he thought of that prospect. 'All I'm thinking about is getting on the range to sort out my game,' he tersely replied.

Golf is not a sport for matchmakers; rules and protocols take precedence. Leaders go out last, but when scores are level, tee times are worked out by the order in which scorecards from the previous round were signed and submitted. For those on the same score, the distinguishing rule states that the earlier player gets the later tee time the next day.

Halfway through the 2023 Dubai Desert Classic the leaderboard was jam-packed and several players were on the same 8-under-par score. It turned out that the sequencing did not work the way most observers and, certainly TV directors, would have wanted. Reed and McIlroy were kept apart for the third round and would play in consecutive groups.

This arrangement was clearly to McIlroy's liking. He stormed around the par-72 layout in 65 blows, having opened up with four straight birdies. The only blemish came at the last, where he struck a horrible second shot into the water in front of the green. It led to a bogey six and did a massive favour to the chasing pack, including Reed.

The Northern Irish star took a three-stroke lead into the final round but knew his advantage could and should have been more commanding. 'I don't think I've ever won in my first start of the year,' McIlroy told reporters. 'Tomorrow is a nice opportunity to try to do something that I've never done before.'

For Reed, no stranger to rules controversies throughout his career, that third round turned 'tee-gate' into 'tree-gate' because of what happened on the 17th hole of his 3-under-par 69. This penultimate hole on the Majlis course is a drivable par-4 that swings from left to right. For decent hitters, there is a short cut to the green, but it means risking a potential tangle with tall palm trees that guard the front-right route to the putting surface.

This is what happened to Reed's drive. His ball did not emerge from the top of one of the palms after careering into the leaves without coming close to hitting the ground. Under the rules of golf, a player has to identify their ball if it becomes unplayable. This provides an option of an adjacent drop with a penalty of one stroke. But, if the ball cannot be confirmed, then the golfer must return to where they played the previous shot and hit again along with a penalty stroke. So if Reed could irrefutably establish the location of his ball, he would play his third shot from close to the green. If not, he would be heading back to hit again from the teeing ground. It was, therefore, in his interests to identify his ball when he arrived on the scene.

The American was assisted by chief referee Kevin Feeney and, with no prospect of scaling the trunk of the tall palm, both peered upwards through binoculars. 'If it had been anyone else, it's a non-issue, right?' McIlroy would later say. But because it was Reed and because it started to look like a significant error had been made, it became yet more headline news.

Reed confirmed he could see his Titleist Pro V1 ball and received the more favourable drop. But evidence emerged suggesting player and referee had been, if not barking, seeking up the wrong tree. Television coverage indicated Reed's shot hitting a different palm to the one where he had been looking. Golf Channel analyst Brandel Chamblee, whom Reed had already begun libel action against for coverage of previous rules controversies (the case was later dismissed), tweeted: 'I've seen many a player guess wrong at the place their ball entered a penalty area (and they almost always get the benefit of doubt) but I can't say I've ever seen a player find their ball in a tree that video clearly shows it didn't fly into.'

After his round, Reed seemed bemused to be asked about the incident. As he departed the brief huddle with reporters, he said to the *Telegraph*'s James Corrigan: 'I would have gone back to the tee if I wasn't 100 per cent sure.'

'I got lucky that we were able to look through the binoculars and you have to make sure it's your ball and how I mark my golf balls is I always put an arrow on the end of my line, because on the Pro V1, with the arrow on the end, I stop before it so you can see the arrow. And then you could definitely see and identify the line with the arrow on the end, and the rules official, luckily, was there to reconfirm and check it to make sure it was mine as well.'

The DP World Tour later issued a statement that said that two on-course referees and several marshals had identified a specific tree in which Reed's ball had become lodged. 'Using binoculars, the chief referee was satisfied that a ball with those markings was lodged in the tree. The player subsequently took an unplayable penalty (Rule 19-2c) at that point directly below the ball on the ground. To clarify, the player was not asked to specify the tree but to identify his distinctive ball markings to confirm it was his ball.'

Ironically, the biggest defence of Reed eventually came from McIlroy: 'I felt it was fine,' he told reporters. 'Kev Feeney is a really experienced referee and he's not going to do anything wrong.' He added: 'Because of certain things in the past, people brought some stuff up, which is maybe unfair in some ways.'

McIlroy's magnanimity came the following day. It was a magic Monday that justified the decision to extend the tournament into a fifth day. His lead was three strokes when he teed off in glorious conditions. The two-time champion's stated aim for the week was to atone for the previous year when he had blown his chances of a hat-trick of Dubai titles by finding that water on the last hole. A birdie on the closing par-5 would have given him victory, but instead his Ryder Cup teammate Viktor Hovland had profited.

This time it was his ultimate Ryder Cup rival, too often his nemesis, who ensured the drama built to a sensational crescendo. Reed had been living rent-free in McIlroy's head from the moment his lawyer served him legal papers a month earlier. This presence grew further with that tossed tee. The fallout dogged both players for seven days. This was the next Monday and Reed still loomed very large in McIlroy's conscience. But during a thrilling final round it was purely because of the American's brilliance as a golfer.

Reed ate into the leaderboard deficit in magnificent style, while McIlroy struggled to summon his superlative form of the previous day. At the par-5 10th, the US star came within an inch of holing for an albatross two and tapped in for a sensational eagle. Midway through the back nine, Reed – in the group ahead of McIlroy – drew level. The two central characters of this volatile and controversial week – one that typified the prevailing febrile world of golf – were now heading down the closing stretch vying for a prestigious title.

Photographer Matthew Harris looked across and said: 'Do you remember Hazeltine?'

'Oh yes,' I replied. It was impossible to ignore their competitive history.

McIlroy, meanwhile, was wishing he had told Pelley to settle for a 54-hole tournament because, if he had, he would have already been on his way home with the trophy. 'In the middle of the back nine, I'm like, maybe I should have said three rounds,' he admitted.

Instead, he was stuck in a dog-fight that went all the way to the final hole.

McIlroy has a chequered history with the famous 18th at the Emirates Club. It was the place where he nervously secured his first tour victory in 2009, when he beat England's Justin Rose by a single stroke. He had cruised to victory on that hole in 2015, but in 2022 messed up badly to let in Hovland. And the previous day McIlroy had done something similar to encourage a chasing pack that, of course, contained Reed – the man he wanted to beat more than any other.

On the final tee, there was a big decision to make. Dare he go for a driver, which would bring into play the water that stretches down the right side of the fairway after it doglegs back towards the iconic clubhouse? Or should he go for a fairway wood that would more likely find the short stuff, but the sort of awkward lie that prompted the dreadful second shot he played a day earlier?

McIlroy chose the driver and eased a tee shot that landed smack in the middle of the fairway. But, on a dangerous angle. It bounced and bounced and ran and ran.

Towards the lake.

It finished inches from drowning. 'I got lucky that my ball didn't go in the water off the tee shot,' he revealed. 'It's such an awkward tee shot for me. Driver is too much and 3-wood is not quite enough.'

It was a massive break, but he was still left with a treacherous lie. Circumstances had made up his mind not to go for the green in two and from 100 yards out he then wedged his third shot to 20 feet beyond the flag. It left a makable putt to win, but no more than that. As he strode around the pond to access the green, the tension was palpable. It was nowhere near as vibrant and loud as had been the case during that Ryder Cup defeat at Hazeltine in 2016, but just as intense.

McIlroy and Reed were locked together at 18-under-par and the American could do no more. He was now signing his scorecard in the recorders' area underneath the sponsors' pavilion at the back of the green.

These were two great adversaries of their era and it was even spicier because their rivalry encompassed a divided sport. Here we had the establishment against the upstart. The model pupil versus the bad boy of the classroom; good versus evil in some people's minds. It was not quite that, but you knew where those who thought so were coming from because it was a battle that embodied remarkable levels of rancour prevailing at the time.

Not that McIlroy was thinking of the wider ramifications. 'I held a putt at Bay Hill a few years ago to win . . . downhill left-to-right,' McIlroy told me. 'That popped into my head as I was reading it, so I had some pretty good memories to draw on.' All he yearned for was his ball to disappear in the same way as it had done in 2018 at that Orlando tournament.

The politics of golf could take a back seat at this moment.

If he made the putt he would be a champion; a miss would mean a playoff and both players having to look each other in the eye for the first time during that long week and a bit. 'I so wanted sudden death,' admitted a senior European Tour Productions television boss, before hurriedly adding: 'A McIlroy win in a playoff would have been perfect!'

The player wanted it done and dusted. There and then – on this 18th green he knew so, so well. His putt tram-lined down his prescribed route. Nerve and accuracy were in perfect harmony. His ball unerringly fell into the middle of the hole.

Just as animated as he had been during his epic Ryder Cup defeat to Reed, McIlroy roared with delight and relief, uppercutting the air with an aggressively clenched fist. It was clear this win meant more than most, perhaps the most satisfying of his career outside his four major victories to date.

'Was there added incentive because of who was up there? Absolutely,' he admitted.

'I think mentally today was probably one of the toughest rounds I've ever had to play. It would be really easy to let your emotions get in the way and I just had to really concentrate on focusing on myself. Forget who was up there on the leaderboard, and I did that really, really well.'

When Reed won their Ryder Cup match he had three letters emblazoned on his cap: 'U', 'S' and 'A'. This time he also had three different letters provocatively on display: 'L', 'I' and 'V'. This is why he had become a pariah. LIV is the name of the breakaway golf tour that has shaken the game to its foundations.

It is financed by Saudi Arabia, in many people's estimation an axis of evil. Others see the Kingdom's involvement as nothing different from the sort of business dealings it is involved in all over the world. Their Public Investment Fund (PIF) had given millions of dollars to Reed and several other big-name players to play a brand-new circuit. Their tournaments are played over 54 (Roman numerals L-I-V) rather than the usual 72 holes.

This new tour seeks to break what they see as a PGA Tour monopoly, which is why the establishment was going through a period of unprecedented upheaval. Like Reed, the upstart league is bold and brash. It seeks to modernise the royal and ancient game; its tagline is 'Golf but louder'.

McIlroy is not a fan. Anything but. 'What it's done to the world of men's professional golf is rip it apart,' says the player who became LIV's most vocal critic when he spoke to reporters.

So by the time these two players clashed in the Dubai desert, they were no longer respectful rivals; they were enemies. Reed one of LIV's expensively assembled recruits, McIlroy as the most prominent figure on the side of the established tours; the lead voice of the status quo. Further afield, long-standing friendships on both sides of the divide had fallen casualty, as had a number of great PGA and European Tour careers.

And here in the desert, we had a row over a tossed tee – branded with a logo of Reed's LIV team, the 4Aces. It escalated because of the unprecedented tumult affecting men's professional golf. It fuelled a bitter but thrilling golf contest while providing a snapshot of a sport at war; one that was repeatedly generating exceptional dramas, both on and off the course.

INTRODUCTION

'Is there anything more quintessentially Global North than golf?' It was a rhetorical question put to me by Professor Simon Chadwick – a renowned expert in the geopolitics of sport. By 'Global North' he was referring to traditional powerhouse nations such as the United States, Britain and other leading European countries as well as Australia and New Zealand. But he was also noting that the world is now tilting 'Global South', with power and influence resting more frequently in countries such as China, India, the Middle East and especially the Kingdom that has done so much to rock the game, Saudi Arabia. For this place, a revered chunk of quintessential 'Global North' is a very attractive prospect.

Golf has traditionally enjoyed a reputation for being one of the most calm and peaceful sports. It is played at a pedestrian pace in largely quiet, tranquil sporting idylls. Players usually compete individually, but they are united by a collective recognition of its distinguishing traits. Golfers share the challenges of trying to conquer a course and capricious forces of nature that seek to disrupt the path of their little white ball while they aim to knock it into a small hole in the fewest possible shots. There is mutual respect, despite the apparent futility of this task.

Golfers tend to band together and convivially share stories and sympathies generated by this maddening pursuit. It is usually all done in a spirit of honesty and integrity, at whatever level it is played.

It has so many attractions despite being somewhat exclusive. Golf carries qualities a country such as Saudi Arabia finds irresistible. The sport tends to follow money and money follows it. The Saudis have more disposable cash than most other nations put together. Why not spend it on something that can help tilt the world's axis in their favour?

At the very top of the game, professional golfers compete for vast sums: figures that yield rewards for a week's competition that would dwarf most people's aspirations for an annual income. This has been the case for most of the professional game's history. These players possess special talents that deserve special remuneration. They can beat courses and the weather and each other in thrilling fashion. Of the many champions the game has produced, Arnold Palmer and Jack Nicklaus were among the most glamorous and well-rewarded sportsmen when they came to prominence in the 1950s, 60s and 70s.

These two titans of the golfing world inspired the setting up of America's PGA Tour, the world's most lucrative golf circuit. It later spawned Tiger Woods, someone who became arguably the greatest sports star on the planet when he hit the height of his powers at the turn of the century.

All year long the tour chases the sun, providing tournaments sponsored by backers with deep pockets and a desire to mix it with the best players in the world. This circuit became the only place to be for the best players. They could compete for millions of dollars, putting them among the richest of athletes while being treated royally. It was and remains an ultra-competitive environment, but with plenty of home comforts: luxury courtesy cars, plush hotels, their every need catered for in a way that was the envy of many other sports.

Europe has a similar set-up with what is now known as the DP World Tour. It does not quite command the same level of grandeur and riches as its US rival. Knock a star off the standard of hotel, a nought or two off prize purses and squeeze into a minibus to be transferred to and from courses from time to time. Yes, the European Tour has famed camaraderie, a high standard of play and it still produces a string of stars, but the PGA Tour was unrivalled.

From its inception in 1968, when Palmer and Nicklaus led the breakaway from the PGA of America, this was a men's professional tour that reigned supreme. Europe could not keep up. It did not have the resources and was shackled by geographical and currency issues that encumber trading across borders. But it still prospered. The European Tour took golf across its continent, into Africa and Asia (Saudi Arabia included) and offers a healthy, adventurous, cosmopolitan living to its members.

And sitting above the tours, the majors continue to grow. These championships remain the career-defining benchmark. Four weeks that constitute the pinnacle of the game. The glamorous Masters at Augusta, the historic Open staged on the UK coastline, the arduous test of the US Open and America's PGA Championship, which struggles for identity but is still a supremely coveted title.

Blue-chip sponsors, television companies and new media enterprises are all attracted to golf. But so too were businesses who believed that the professional game could be bigger, better and worth more money. They did not believe it was fulfilling its potential and came up with plans that started to catch the eye of leading players, administrators and ultimately Saudi Arabia and its gargantuan Public Investment Fund.

The Saudis could see endless benefits to deepening their relationship with golf. Business opportunities could achieve potentially significant returns on massive investment, with tourism providing an additional dividend for a country trying to wean itself off oil profits. Not to mention wanting to improve its tarnished image to the rest of the world. And the Saudis did not seem to care whether this upset the way that golf used to be.

And so they financed a rival league, one that could modernise the game, make it louder and fitter for 21st-century society. It sought the very best players – global superstars, who would be paid enough to sacrifice the traditional riches of the game. This process, which accelerated during the 2020/21 Covid lockdowns and came into being the following year, sparked internal conflict in the sport, the like of which has never before been witnessed in the previously comfortable, easy-going game of golf.

It became a story of opportunity and greed involving eye-watering sums of money. It is about a sovereign country using golf as the vehicle to bolster a battered image and fuel its future. It involves stubborn establishment resolve and a dramatic and unexpected capitulation. One that stunned the entire sporting world, leaving golf mired in yet more controversy and scrutinised like never before. It has pitted golfer against golfer – not only on the lush, luxurious fairways of the elite game but in courtrooms, lawyers' offices and political corridors of power. It is a tale that dominated the 2023 golf season day by day at the majors where it invariably became the main topic of conversation. Yet, it has no apparent conclusion. Golf has been caught in a battle over billions, existential division and identity.

This has been deemed the period of the 'golf wars' and while there are no parallels with the true horrors and misery of armed warfare, within the context of this peculiar and much-loved sport there is a huge struggle being fought on several fronts to secure its future identity and direction.

Having followed the professional game for 21 years as the BBC golf correspondent, this is my account of how the arrival of the Saudi-funded LIV tour and its recruitment of some of the game's most famous names has affected the sport I love. This book charts each development in this ongoing saga as the different factions fight for control of the game. I travel to LIV events and witness how they are trying to modernise the sport. I talk to key figures and players on all sides of the many arguments, Donald Trump included. And I provide contemporaneous, day-by-day observations and thoughts from the most significant weeks on the golf calendar: the four majors as well as the sport's biggest and most transcendent event, the Ryder Cup, where Europe and the United States do battle to win a precious pot of gold.

Does the torrential influx of Saudi cash and other new revenue streams corrupt the future health of what has become a fractured sport? How will it heal? Can the Ryder Cup survive and thrive in this money-dominated era? Can this magical sport win through and emerge unscathed from the many conflicts that rage in the fight for its future?

As someone suggested to me a year or so ago: 'There's a book in that.'

1

LIV ORIGINS

'I thought, the only sport that hasn't evolved in a time when sport was genuinely starting to evolve was golf.'

Andrew Gardiner

An English businessman watched television and then started to write. Just as he had done as a young lad, he lay on his front with a notepad on the floor in front of him. Elbows splayed, pen in hand, the words started to flow. Inspired, he filled page after page. Ideas surged in a torrent. Ironically, what prompted him was boredom. He was sports mad; a golfing geek. He loved the game, adored it, yet his scribblings would ultimately lead to the sport tearing itself apart.

Andrew Gardiner is one of three former corporate finance lawyers who built the Development Capital Group in the late 1990s. He had picked up his notepad and pen while watching a nondescript golf event that had singularly failed to capture his imagination. This was at a time in the mid-2000s when Europe fielded Ryder Cup teams capable of trouncing the United States by record margins, while America boasted the two biggest names in the game: Tiger Woods and Phil Mickelson. Indeed, Woods was arguably the biggest superstar of world sport at the time. His remarkable prowess bolstered the PGA Tour, emboldening further an outfit that never lacked confidence, a sense of superiority and, some would say, arrogance.

But the game was set in its ways. Tournaments, from majors to mundane, were all played over four rounds of 18 holes with cuts at halfway. Start on a Thursday finish on a Sunday. Make it to the weekend and you are paid. Go home early empty-handed. Brutal competition. Unjust in some golfers' eyes, Mickelson's included. Players could put on a show for two days and receive no reward if their golf was not good enough to make the final two rounds. However, if you played very well, you were paid very well. For pros, playing better golf solves most problems. Those who do not, fall by the wayside.

It was a meritocracy that could be cruel but remained attractive through its competitive integrity. The pyramid was set and those who scaled the pointy end had the comfort of an extremely well-endowed back pocket. Sponsors were in plentiful supply; television companies were attracted by the sport's wholesome image, its reputation for fair play and honesty. Golf was the envy of many other sports that struggled to attract such riches. It saw little need to alter a seemingly successful blueprint. There was no apparent imperative to radically reinvent, repackage or innovate. Pro golf had a winning formula, or so it thought.

Others were less convinced and Andrew Gardiner was one of them. Yes, he loved the majors. He was enthralled by annual jousts for the Claret Jug at The Open, Masters' green jackets at Augusta and US Open trophies on the toughest golf courses in America. The Ryder Cup brought a boisterous biennial crescendo that put it alongside the Olympics and football's World Cup as a global sporting spectacle. And the process to qualify for the European and American teams brought a narrative that helped sustain the week-in, week-out diet of tour golf on both sides of the Atlantic.

But was that enough? Gardiner did not think so. There had to be something better. Something that could take men's professional golf to a higher, more impactful and lucrative level.

'I'd spent some time getting to know the European Tour,' he told me. Gardiner accepted an invitation to the 2006 Ryder Cup at the K Club in Ireland, where Europe earned a second successive record win by 18½ to 9½ points. He also visited the Masters at Augusta. 'At that time I was thinking, my God, this is me, a fan of the sport, a sport I have always loved and here I am, with real access,' he said.

Gardiner might have been awestruck by the events and the company he was keeping, but delving into business models he was less impressed. In his opinion, golf was not fulfilling its potential. Without innovation, it would wither. At best stagnate. He believed it needed a proper global circuit. He suggested this concept to the then European Tour hierarchy, only to receive a message that it could never happen. 'It is very hard to come together with an organisation, the PGA Tour, that we've been fighting for 40 years,' he was told.

One European Tour boss put it this way to him: 'They hate us and we hate them. Yes, the cake that would be created would be very valuable. We would have to put in our ingredients and the PGA Tour would have to put in theirs. Their ingredients are bigger than ours so it would then come down to how we would divide the cake. And we'd get crumbs.'

Gardiner insists that he saw a bigger picture. 'Golf was boring, if it wasn't Tiger no one was interested,' he stated. 'I thought, if they're not going to do anything about the future of golf then somebody else has to. Genuinely, I was watching golf on TV, and I was watching a bit that was particularly uninspiring. And I just started to write. I do remember lying on the floor, which is a habit I've had since I was a kid, with the TV on in front of me. And I just started to write and I carried on for days and days because I had this kernel of an idea.'

Gardiner had noted the way that other sports had adapted and innovated since the turn of the century, while pro golf was stuck in its comfortable ways. 'If you could start again, what would you create?' he said. 'I'm a fan of multiple sports. The changes that had occurred in Formula One motor racing and football, rugby, snooker and darts. I knew all that. I thought, the only sport that hasn't evolved in a time when sport was genuinely starting to evolve was golf. Golf has to do this otherwise its relevance will diminish and its fan base will not renew sufficiently to be strong in 20 years' time.'

The precedent for Gardiner's scribblings had been set by Bernie Ecclestone's takeover of motor racing and the revolutionary impact of successive Concorde Agreements that transformed the sport. Formula One became increasingly lucrative, especially for Ecclestone, as it and he exploited television and marketing deals, tinkered with formats and sought to maximise F1's potential. 'I saw so many parallels between the two sports, and Formula One had been transformed,' Gardiner said. 'Ecclestone wrestled control away from the governing FIA. It was done while still making the FIA look like the pre-eminent body in the sport, but actually it became driven by cash and by the teams.'

Formula One had a calendar, a format and it was easy for fans to follow. Crucially, every driver turned up for every race. Spectators and, more importantly, television viewers knew who they would be watching at each and every race. The same could not be said for golf beyond the majors, where all leading players would be involved. The rest of the circuit would be dependent on the whim of the golfer or their sponsor or the need to bolster earnings to retain playing privileges or qualify for the Ryder Cup. It was a mish-mash with little focus. Gardiner saw it as a mess, a significant impediment to the sport being able to fulfil its potential.

Why could conservative, pedestrian golf not do something similar to the flash speedsters of motor racing? He estimates he hand-wrote 110 pages of ideas to revolutionise this sleepy game at its highest level.

And, in 2022, those ideas – top golfers turning up to every tournament, playing in teams aimed at becoming valuable franchises on a global circuit – did, in fact, come to fruition. Gardiner's vision is the one eventually adopted by LIV Golf, the Saudi Arabia-funded entity that has also brought unprecedented turmoil, disruption, rancour, bitterness and uncertainty to the game.

And it all started with Gardiner. 'I set off on a meandering path which for the first few years was me having nothing more than occasional conversations with people in the sport,' he told me. 'I kept waiting for someone to say, you've missed something crucial here. I spent two years waiting for someone, who I thought would know more than me, to say you're wasting your time.'

No one did and so Gardiner embarked on a project that very nearly came off but was halted at or by buffers – depending on which way you want to interpret the metaphor. Certainly, the traditional old guard coalesced to continually reject his proposals. The PGA and European tours were not interested in doing business with him, despite his claims that his plans could yield billions of dollars for the sport and its leading players. Others saw the merit of his ideas and ultimately pounced on them.

Back in 2014, the professional game was struggling. Viewing figures for the biggest events were diminishing, Tiger Woods was no longer the transcendent draw that he had been prior to damaging revelations five years earlier about his private life, which heralded an epic fall from grace. Nike were no longer interested in making golf equipment, Adidas were selling off their TaylorMade club and ball business. The future seemed bleak.

Gardiner's initial idea was to build a golf league around the leading manufacturers. He recalls a conversation with the boss of one of the top companies. 'We sat in a nice hotel somewhere in Surrey and he asked me why do I think golf needs this? He said, "Golf's cyclical." I knew I was sitting opposite the president of a company losing money for the first time in its history. He said, "It'll come back," and I said to him. "OK, it only took the game 200 years to produce Tiger Woods, if you're prepared to wait another 200 years, good luck to you." Let no one be fooled the dramatic increase in the popularity of the sport in the 1990s was down to one bloke. The president burst out laughing when I said that and then said. "OK, you've got me, let's have a proper conversation."'

It was all about gaining the trust of these executives, as Gardiner sought to sell his idea to companies who were already paying millions of dollars to players for using their clubs and wearing their clothes. So it was not such a leap for them to start competing on the manufacturers' behalf – in a similar way to Lewis Hamilton driving for the Mercedes F1 team.

Convinced that he could lure big-money investors, Gardiner convened a top-secret meeting in December 2015 that brought together deadly rival companies from the golf industry. The aim was to sell a concept that would work for those firms as well as the PGA Tour. 'We managed to gather senior executives from all the major brands in golf into a house – an extraordinary property in La Jolla, San Diego,' Gardiner revealed. 'This house was literally jaw dropping. It was on the edge of a cliff, huge. Some extraordinarily famous people had stayed there and it happened to be owned by a shareholder of ours at the time.

'They all came up through the gates and the meeting we had was extraordinary. Because it was about how we do this. I can tell you, the document we had envisaged cooperation with the PGA Tour. Always at its core, it was never about a schism. It was about using the commercial importance of that group of funders of the sport, to gently explain why this was a change that they wanted to see happen.'

Ultimately, the distrust between companies that were such arch competitors made the idea untenable. But earlier meetings with one of the biggest firms in the sports market yielded another idea. What if the teams belonged to leading players? How about Team Tiger Woods? Or Team Rory McIlroy? The Northern Irishman had raced to four majors with his victories at the 2014 Open Championship and the US PGA. Like Woods, he was an out-and-out superstar. 'So that model changed from the manufacturer model to a player-owned model where each player would effectively joint venture with a super-wealthy individual,' Gardiner said.

He was convinced the concept could attract billionaire investment in the way that NFL teams do because there would be a scarcity factor with a strictly limited number of teams, only 12. And they would have the best players in the world.

Gardiner travelled the golfing world selling the idea. 'I spent these few years waiting for someone to turn the music off and it just kept on growing,' he said. 'Even people within the sport could see the need, see the sense and see the dollar signs and the value creation of doing something through a commercial entity as opposed to a members' organisation.'

The structures of the leading golf circuits are restrictive in a business sense. Ultimately, the tours are answerable only to their members, a fact acknowledged by the chief executive of the DP World Tour (previously known as the European

Tour), Keith Pelley. He told me: 'We, and the PGA Tour are both unique organisations because we are responsible for, and have to cater to, the needs of all 400-plus of our members, not just a few.' They are hamstrung. How do you ditch the majority of your members in favour of a chosen few to effectively form an exclusive super league?

Pelley was fully aware of the moves being attempted by Gardiner and his colleagues at the World Golf Group when he took charge of the Wentworth-based organisation in August 2015. He was a leading executive the like of which the game of professional golf had never seen before. Bold, brash and bright. Brim-full of ideas to try to modernise the sport, he left his role as president of Rogers Media in his native Canada to take the job. During his five-year tenure at the North American company, Pelley negotiated a contract worth $5.5b with the National Hockey League.

The European Tour's new boss came into a sport where players were about to be approached to join a lucrative new set-up. Gardiner and his right-hand man Richard Marsh came up with more and more detailed plans for what would be branded the Premier Golf League (PGL). They had backing from the influential Raine Group, a vast wealth company with strong credentials in sports investment. One of their partners, Colin Neville, who boasts an enviable track record in high-level sporting deals, was on board. 'We went from needing 200 million working capital, which was the launch costs of the league, to requiring a billion,' Gardiner revealed. 'There were very few places you could go to get a billion dollars for something of this nature. We had a deal with Raine who became 25 per cent shareholders of World Golf Group which was the parent company of Premier Golf League Ltd.'.

PGL was covertly and confidently courting senior golfing figures, on and off the course. 'The players thought it all sounded great and there were some who were desperately keen on the idea from the start. Some cared about the future of the game, some couldn't have given two shits,' Gardiner told me. 'They wanted to know how we were going to pay the purses. We were talking $10m a week at the time.

'That led us to talk to broadcasters in the US. And they were like, "We really like this. We need it, golf needs it." The gist was, "we're scrapping over 40-odd events a year with only 16 or so that make money. And quite frankly we are sick of losing money on golf. So something needs to change and this is as good a model as we've ever seen."'

But golf is a disparate sport at every level. It is founded in the individual and that ethos runs throughout. Getting different agents to work together proved almost impossible. 'I sat down with the agent of a very, very well-known player who did say basically stop fucking around, just raise a billion. If you do, you get this done,' Gardiner said.

Pelley had been in talks with Gardiner since 2018 but everything was being kept secret. It is reasonable to guess that the European Tour boss would not have wanted to upset the rival PGA Tour because they could potentially make life difficult for his members in events such as the World Golf Championship (WGC) tournaments. There was also the enduring imperative of protecting the interests of all his members.

The Premier Golf League was officially incorporated on 14 November 2019. By then, they knew their formula: 18 separate 54-hole, shotgun-start events – where players tee off simultaneously on every tee across the course – with no cuts and the same top stars turning up for each event. There would be 48 players, separated into 12 teams that could become lucrative franchises.

Sound familiar?

The tournaments would run from January to September. Colin Neville was managing director among seven named individuals according to Companies House. They worked towards launching their league in January 2023 and continued to travel the golfing world seeking to recruit players and convince the sport that this was the best way forwards.

PGL held discussions with Golf Saudi. Money from the Kingdom's $700b Public Investment Fund could make all the difference. It was a potential win–win situation for both parties because this was also a key time for Saudi Arabia and its leader, Crown Prince Mohammed bin Salman (MBS), who had a new vision for his country's future. 'The world is pivoting from Global North to Global South,' Simon Chadwick, professor of Sport and Geopolitical Economy at the SKEMA Business School in Paris, told me. 'Britain, Europe, the United States, Australia and New Zealand are Global North and the likes of

Saudi Arabia, China and Qatar are the Global South. With that pivot comes a change in the balance of economic and political power globally.'

Saudi Arabia is seeking to alter the way it is perceived, to soften an image damaged by constant questions over its record on human rights as well as the 2018 murder and dismemberment of *Washington Post* journalist Jamal Khashoggi. A CIA investigation concluded that the killing was state sponsored at the behest of MBS. It is also moving towards an oil-free future. Its PIF, first set up in 1971, is there to invest in a project aimed at bringing 'Saudi Vision 2030' to fruition. This would mean this strictly Muslim country diversifying economically, socially and culturally.

Golf is seen as a vehicle to drive these ends. This process is also regarded as 'sport washing' by organisations such as Amnesty International and Human Rights Watch, who seek to highlight the horrors they see in the Saudi regime. 'Sport washing is a very good term because it gets people talking about very important issues,' Professor Chadwick said. 'But we do need to get past that it is somehow just Saudi Arabia and the Arab nations that are doing this, because I don't think that is true.' He added that throughout history, regimes – the United Kingdom included – have sought to use sport to burnish their reputations.

'Look at the British empire and the way it deployed sport in the early 20th century [when] there were 107,000 South African prisoners in British concentration camps in South Africa. Of those 107,000, 28,000 died. At the same time, I've got a newspaper clipping talking about the British government sending rugby and cricket teams to South Africa to delight and excite local audiences. With the benefit of hindsight and using contemporary language, that was sport washing.'

History is littered with such examples, Chadwick argues, and he can see why Saudi Arabia has entered the golf market. 'Base camp for any country seeking to garner image and reputational benefits through a presence in elite professional sport is changing perceptions and attitudes,' he said. So the Saudis were interested in investing in a new concept that could shake up the conventional world of golf. 'Is there anything more quintessentially Global North than golf?' Chadwick wondered.

Saudi money would further strengthen the PGL's position and in early 2020 they held a meeting at the Riviera Country Club in Los Angeles with the top 20 players in the world all represented. 'That went very well,' Gardiner said. But America's main golf tour was spooked. 'The PGA Tour was starting to rattle its sabres, in fact, more like wield their sabres.'

The PGA Tour's commissioner, Jay Monahan, wrote to their policy board referring to the potential insurgents as 'private equity' golf, warning players they faced bans if they were to defect. 'I was stood in a Middle East airport lounge with a player when Monahan's memo popped up on his phone and he showed it to me,' Gardiner revealed. 'My blood went cold and boiling at the same time because it was pretty aggressive and referred to us as private equity golf about 20 times. This was clearly a tactic devised by their PR guys to draw down on the private equity stuff. It said that we [the PGA Tour] are going to do a deal with the European Tour which will stop the European Tour from working with us [PGL].'

Throughout, PGL had been courting the European Tour, for whom staging a home Ryder Cup every four years is the key source of revenue and their biggest asset. The PGA Tour has always rued not owning a piece of the Ryder Cup pie. But as the world headed into Covid lockdown in March 2020, the European Tour was particularly vulnerable. It needed to take a £30m bank loan (subsequently repaid) and the PGA Tour regarded the Wentworth-based circuit as a 'distressed asset'.

Pelley acknowledged that this was a tough period. 'Like all companies around the world, Covid forced us to look at our business differently,' he said. 'In the pandemic, revenue streams stopped and we needed to adapt.' Both he and Monahan had taken calls from Raine Capital on behalf of PGL in March 2020 and an offer was made to the European Tour. Pelley told the PGA Tour boss that his board would make a closer examination.

There is no doubt the European Tour was looking at alternative methods to secure its future. The two main options were doing a deal with the PGA Tour or jumping into bed with PGL, who were offering $100m. That was seen as a loan that would ultimately need to be paid back. There were also questions over how quickly PGL's investors would need to see a return.

The alternative idea of some form of amalgamation with the main US tour first occurred at meetings held around the 2016 Ryder Cup at Hazeltine. Perhaps it could lead to a world tour? It was an idea that certainly appealed to Monahan when he took over from Tim Finchem as commissioner the following year. There were a number of follow-up meetings at various locations on both sides of the Atlantic, with no resolution, in the early days of Monahan's reign.

Covid, though, changed things. 'As it has been reported through leaked documents, the PGA Tour were interested in consolidating or merging with us in 2020,' Pelley told me. 'In order to do that we would have needed 75 per cent of the membership to vote in favour and we felt at that time, with so much uncertainty in the game in addition to the global uncertainty caused by the pandemic, that it wasn't feasible to attract that level of support.'

Regarding Gardiner's operation, Pelley and his senior colleagues were sceptical. 'We evaluated the PGL forensically,' Pelley said. 'We came to the conclusion, for a number of reasons, it was not the direction that we, as an executive team, or the board wanted to pursue. At the time, they had no contracts with any top players and we questioned the viability of their overall business plan.'

From July to November 2020 there was no contact between Pelley and Monahan as the European Tour evaluated their position. This involved senior executives including Ryder Cup director Guy Kinnings as well as board members such as former Ryder Cup stars Paul McGinley, Thomas Bjørn and David Howell.

There was also a Saudi opportunity potentially brewing. The Kingdom was brought into men's professional golf by the European Tour with the Saudi International tournament that was first played in early 2019. The UK-based tour had no qualms about associating with the Kingdom despite its record on human rights. And there was now a relationship to potentially further exploit. The tour proposed a $500m sponsorship/investment deal that would include elevated status for the Saudi tournament and naming rights for the secondary Challenge Tour. It was reported that this proposal did not fit with the PIF's vision. They countered with an idea that they would cough up the money in return for the European Tour's commercial rights, but again this did not come to fruition.

Things came to a head in the autumn of 2020. The European Tour did not want to consolidate or merge with the PGA Tour, who simultaneously did not want their rivals to do any deal that would legitimise PGL. Pelley said PGL had put forward a 'compelling offer' but a more preferable option was a 'strategic alliance' with the US circuit.

The European Tour had bought back their television production company from the International Management Group (IMG) a couple of years earlier for $300m. By November 2020, it was valued at $560m. The European Tour offered 15 per cent of the TV company to the PGA Tour, in return for a closer working relationship between the two rival circuits. Monahan joined the European Tour board and the deal was later increased to a 40 per cent stake in the production company.

Both tours needed to strengthen their alliance due to the dramatic changes in world golf that were at that stage only in a period of covert gestation. When the initial deal was struck, the American side had never been more dominant, but the European Tour were getting more than mere crumbs. As they continued to recover from the impact of the pandemic, the alliance was announced on 27 November 2020.

This was a hammer-blow to PGL because the pathway into the golf establishment had been blocked. The strategic alliance forbade the European Tour from doing any kind of merger deal with another professional tour. But this did not deter Saudi Arabia and the golf-mad governor of the PIF, Yasir Al-Rumayyan. 'After our decision to strike the strategic alliance with the PGA Tour and not pursue relations with the PGL, the PIF informed us that they were removing Raine Capital who were running the PGL,' Pelley explained. 'And they were going to build a team to launch a similar product on their own.'

A highly detailed study of the golfing landscape and why the PGL had not come to fruition was commissioned by the Saudis, who were increasingly keen to dramatically expand their golfing footprint domestically and internationally.

After weeks of feverish and thorough analysis, the Saudis concluded it was viable to launch their own new entity. Their plan was called 'Project Wedge' and the idea was to spawn 'Super League Golf' (SLG). They were ready to pour billions of dollars into the game and sought to partner with the golf establishment – the majors and the strategically aligned main tours on both sides of the Atlantic.

It was reported in several outlets that in April 2021 SLG wrote to Monahan to open a dialogue but the letter drew no response.

Officials from SLG set up camp at Jack Nicklaus' Bear's Club in Palm Beach, Florida, a base for many of the world's top players. They were on a recruitment drive to try to lure the biggest names in the sport. They had the deepest pockets imaginable and no imperative for a rapid return on investment, which was a more advantageous financial position than the PGL could ever hold. On 4 May 2021, James Corrigan broke the news in the *Telegraph* that the world number one, Dustin Johnson, was the subject of a multi-million-dollar approach. Other potential names included Britain's 2016 Olympic champion, Justin Rose.

At the time, Corrigan was in Charlotte for the Wells Fargo Championship at Quail Hollow. 'It suddenly became very real because of the Saudis,' the *Telegraph* correspondent told me. 'Before there was always the question mark over where PGL would get the money, but suddenly you could see this was serious because they'd got the dosh. There were rumours about different people going. I remember being in a curry house in Charlotte and I was on the next table to a leading player and he started chatting about another player who was supposed to be going. And he said, "How much money does he fucking need?" It's hilarious that he was one of those who went and the player he was talking about didn't go.'

This was the first in a long series of Corrigan scoops as the *Telegraph* led the way with revelations about how the new league might look and which players would be involved. 'It was trying to sort out the fact from the fiction,' Corrigan said. 'Indeed, some of the fiction turned out to be fact. There were loads of golfers supposedly about to go that didn't. It was quite unnerving because you're not really sure whether you are correct or not.

'Obviously agents wouldn't go on the record but there were people in the background briefing and helping. It was great, though, because you were on the front page all the time. Massive hits, massive interest, more so than we'd ever seen in golf apart from with Tiger probably. It was all cloak and dagger stuff. You'd hear a whisper and then you'd try to stand it up. Some of it was nonsense.'

SLG still wanted to work in conjunction with the PGA Tour and I understand that they sought to persuade Pelley to set up a meeting with Monahan. But the boss of the biggest tour in the world clearly did not take kindly to insurgents invading his territory seeking to recruit his tour's biggest assets.

The Saudi-led plans also became known to senior figures at DP World, the Dubai-based multinational logistics company that, at that time, was close to announcing a lucrative title sponsorship agreement with the European Tour. It is understood that the announcement of the deal needed to be postponed at very short notice in late June 2021. DP World insisted the European Tour sit down with representatives from Saudi Arabia. This led to a hastily arranged gathering in Malta, the only feasible country with sufficiently relaxed rules regarding Covid to make the meeting possible.

Officials from the European Tour, DP World and SLG met for two days. *Bunkered* magazine's website saw minutes from the meeting that said: 'Over ten years, the overall financial injection into the European Tour could reach $1billion' if a deal could be done.

But because of the strategic alliance with the PGA Tour, the European circuit could only do a sponsorship agreement. They could not partner with the Saudis beyond that. That condition was a confidential term of the alliance. Insiders say the Saudis presented the same concept as PGL had been proposing. So the estimate of a billion dollars was dependent on the eventual valuation of equity in the team format being proposed. European Tour bosses were not convinced.

A few days later, on 9 July, there was a further high-level meeting at the Grove golf resort near London, which was attended by Al-Rumayyan, Pelley and R&A chief executive, Martin Slumbers. But no deal could be done. 'It was not an offer,' Pelley insisted to me. 'It was a presentation that was not to be disclosed to anybody. Despite that, we reviewed the presentation with our board in September 2021 and it was quickly dismissed.'

SLG were undeterred, but the failure and hostile backlash towards an attempt to launch a European football 'Super-League' around the same time prompted a rethink on their branding. So in June 2021, they formally became LIV Golf Investments – L-I-V being Roman numerals for 54, the number of holes their radical new tournaments would be played over.

The Saudis knew what they wanted from their involvement and Simon Chadwick is convinced they are already gaining a dividend. 'People are beginning to conceive of Saudi Arabia in very different ways,' the professor told me. 'Already the narrative about Saudi Arabia is shifting away from something that is very negative and instead what we are talking about is a government with a vision and a genuine strategy that is trying to achieve tangible outcomes.'

But to get to that position, the entire project – founded on Andrew Gardiner's scribblings all those years earlier – has needed to navigate tempestuous seas. Unwanted by the golf establishment, LIV have been arch disruptors. They have stirred the golfing waters like never before. They have been confident and calculating. Their players have been branded mercenary rebels while others regard them as pioneers. They fractured a seemingly settled sport and no one knows how it will eventually heal.

But to get to this disruptive position, they needed a leader. Someone with golfing gravitas but who could also be a pain in the ass to the establishment. Someone unafraid of deviating from the party line in a sport dominated by convention. They knew exactly who they wanted. And they got him.

2

GREG NORMAN: BORN TO CONQUER

'This is the biggest decision of my life.'

Greg Norman

On 9 February 1955, Toini Norman played a round of golf. A day later, she gave birth to a double major champion. Toini was the daughter of a Finnish carpenter who had settled in the Australian outback mining town of Mount Isa. She was married to Mervin, an electrical engineer who moved their young family to Townsville on the Queensland coastline and then to the northern suburbs of the state capital, Brisbane.

Their blond-haired son, Gregory, was tall, fit and athletic. He liked to play rugby and cricket and he loved to surf. As a 15-year-old, he caddied for his golf-obsessed mother and figured that he could probably be half decent at that sport as well. This was how one of the sport's most dominant figures first came into the game. He subsequently dedicated himself to it after nearly drowning during a misguided teenage surfing mission, following heavy storms that had generated dangerous swells on the Queensland coast. Exhausted after swimming to safety, Greg realised he was lucky to be alive and that there must be a different pursuit to provide the rushes that had become a staple of his life.

Golf proved to be that outlet. The adrenaline came from his swashbuckling performances on the course, which in turn gave him a platform to become one of the most influential and ultimately disruptive figures the game has ever known.

Inheriting his mother's talent for the game, the young Greg's handicap tumbled from 27 to scratch in less than two years. He was a natural and was also driven by a phenomenal competitive instinct. Two years younger, Mike Clayton was another promising Aussie golfer. 'I first saw Greg play when I was 16 in the Australian interstate junior series,' Clayton told me. 'They were the biggest events. The six states had teams of eight players and we'd play a matchplay series at Easter time. I was the worst player for Victoria and he was the best for Queensland.'

Keen to improve, Clayton made a point of watching Greg Norman very closely. 'You could see he was an incredible player,' Clayton added. 'He was strikingly good to watch; he always was.'

Norman had modelled himself on the greatest golfer in the history of the men's game, Jack Nicklaus, who won a record 18 major titles. 'He grew up, as most of us did, reading Nicklaus' book *Golf My Way* [Simon & Schuster, 2005],' Clayton revealed. 'He was the guy to copy and emulate and everyone did. Greg had that big wide backswing, reverse C'ing and driving his legs and hitting the ball high and smashing it. And he was talented enough to play that way.'

But Norman still needed to serve an apprenticeship as an assistant pro before he could strive for the big time. He initially worked at the Beverley Park club in New South Wales and then became Charlie Earp's assistant at Royal Queensland, where he earned AU$38 a week. 'He spent a year in Sydney and then a year in Queensland,' Clayton told me. 'And he got a national invitation to play on the Australian tour at the end of 1976.

'I was watching his scores. No one had heard of him at all really but if you were in the inner circle you knew who he was. Then he played well for three, four, five weeks and then he went to Adelaide and blew them all away at the West Lakes. He had a 10-shot lead after three days. It was then that everybody knew who Greg Norman was.'

He won AU$7,000 and said he felt like he was the richest guy in the world. 'I had enough money to buy airline tickets and go to Japan and Europe. And I had confidence in my ability to play,' Norman said in a news conference at the time.

The following year, Norman joined the European Tour and quickly became a winner by claiming the Martini International title at Blairgowrie in Scotland. Equally swiftly, he was making an impression off the course. 'He'd got a manager called James Marshall and James gave him a Rolls-Royce to drive around in,' recalled Andrew 'Chubby' Chandler to me. Chandler was a playing contemporary of Norman's on the European Tour and went on to become a manager of multiple major champions. 'He was always outspoken; he was always abrasive. He was always confident in his own ability and confident in his own opinion,' Chandler added.

Norman became a serial winner around the world and an international superstar. He won nine European Tour titles before landing his first PGA Tour success at the 1984 Kemper Open. By then, he was already the darling of the press tent. 'Never would you miss a Greg Norman press conference,' stated former *Times* golf correspondent Mitchell Platts, who went on to lead the European Tour's media operation through the 1990s and 2000s.

'He was always different,' Clayton recalled. 'He was always prickly; he was great for the press. Greg understood better than the players do now that the press needed a story. He would always give them a story; he was brilliant whether it was a stupid story or not. Whether it was an argument with a greenskeeper or whatever, he would always find the way to write the headline.'

Golf already had its 'Golden Bear' (Jack Nicklaus) and reporters quickly dubbed Norman 'The Great White Shark' when he finished fourth on his Masters debut in 1981. He landed his first major five years later when he won The Open at Turnberry by five strokes. A month on, he finished second at the PGA Championship, the third of eight runner-up cheques from majors. Three of those came agonisingly at Augusta in the Masters, including 1986 – the season when his share of 12th at the US Open was the only time he finished outside the top two in the quartet of competitions that mean most. This was the year when he first went to number one in the world. He spent 331 weeks as top dog, a record beaten only by Tiger Woods.

Extraordinarily, he enjoyed only one other major success when he brilliantly won the 1993 Open at Royal St George's with a closing 64 on the windswept Sandwich links. When he was inducted into the World Golf Hall of Fame in 2001, Norman recalled that victory when he held off the likes of Sir Nick Faldo, Bernhard Langer and Fred Couples. 'Everyone was firing at you, coming hard,' Norman said. 'The thing that is most powerful in my mind is a statement I made to myself going to the 10th tee with a one-shot lead. I said, "Do what Larry Bird has always said: I want the ball with two seconds left, one point behind." I wanted the ball in my hands.'

It is astonishing to think that a man of his talents failed to win any of the grand slam tournaments staged in America. 'I think of how great he played,' Davis Love III, a tour contemporary, once said, 'And if he got a few breaks, how incredible his record would have been.'

Former *Times* correspondent Platts contended: 'Greg Norman should have won double digits in majors. Think about how many he came close to winning – those would take him to 10 alone. His ability deserved to win 10 majors, without a doubt in my book. What a wonderful game he had.'

Norman under-achieved at the highest level. 'For non-golfers in Australia, he's the guy who choked away the majors,' Mike Clayton said. 'Greg used to lose those tournaments all the time which is an incredibly superficial and unfair analysis on Greg Norman's career because he was a tremendous player.'

He was more than a golfer, though. Norman had an entrepreneurial spirit and an inbuilt sense of injustice. He hated the control that the PGA Tour wielded over its players. 'I think because he was a non-American playing the PGA Tour he always had a beef about the fact that the PGA Tour was just an American organisation,' Chandler explained. Norman saw a world beyond the USA. He was a global superstar and he believed that was how it should be for all of the world's best golfers.

Norman's views tallied with a sports businessman, John Montgomery, who worked for event management firm Executive Sports International. In early

1994, Montgomery told Norman he wanted to set up a world tour that would include the top 30 or 40 players on the planet. They would play all over the globe and break America's dominance of the calendar. 'You had no other choice,' Norman later told podcaster Steven Levitt. 'That was the only place you could go. So when you came to join the PGA Tour, you had to sign the rules and regulations book. You had to sign your life away. . . . If you didn't sign it, you couldn't play.'

Norman was the first player to be approached about the new idea to break the PGA Tour stranglehold and he loved it. He recognised the international nature of the leading players; England's Nick Faldo, Spain's Severiano Ballesteros, South Africa's Ernie Els, Ian Woosnam from Wales, Colin Montgomerie of Scotland and Zimbabwe's Nick Price were at the vanguard of the men's game.

Norman and Montgomery worked swiftly and with great enthusiasm. They wanted the 'World Tour' up and running with 8 to 12 tournaments by 1995. 'There was no question in my mind golf was going global,' Norman wrote in his autobiography, *The Way of the Shark* (Ebury Press, 2006).

They calculated that they could offer prize money of $3m per event. Of that, $600,000 would go to the winner and last place would guarantee $30,000. At the time, PGA Tour winners were picking up around $60,000 so the figures represented a massive leap. And it was guaranteed money. Play in all the events and the minimum return would be nearly $300,000. Norman deeply resented that PGA Tour players had to stump up for their own expenses and would depart events empty-handed if they missed the cut. 'He was very adamant that the players should be paid a lump sum every week to tee it up whether they made the cut or not,' recalled a former tour executive to me. 'He felt that the players and not the PGA Tour promoted the game and it was them who should be given the money.'

Norman proposed a $1m bonus for the new tour's most successful player. He wanted the golfers to have equity in the project and set about trying to convince his peers to come on board. Once Norman had the players, Montgomery could attract sponsors.

Television coverage was another key component. Established US networks such as NBC, CBS and ABC were unlikely to be interested because they already had PGA Tour deals, but Norman had contacts with Rupert Murdoch's Fox network. After an initial meeting in Los Angeles, Norman and Montgomery negotiated a six-year deal with a four-year option worth $113m.

It was all systems go and the World Tour was officially incorporated. 'Greg was more interested in how much money he and Murdoch could make out of creating golf tournaments outside America,' Clayton observed. 'I suspect Greg was doing it because financially it was something worth having a stake in and Murdoch was in it because he could see that there was a lot of money to be made out of televising it.'

Word spread and the PGA Tour's new commissioner, Tim Finchem, was spooked. He had only been in the job a matter of months and the tour boss saw the proposed circuit as an existential threat. Finchem was a lawyer and had served as a White House advisor in the Jimmy Carter administration. 'You had all Finchem's political nouse against Norman's entrepreneurship,' a former tour official told me. 'Finchem certainly did not like what was going on. He could see here's this guy offering all these players all this money.'

That summer, Finchem rallied the established tours, circling the golf carts into a protective ring. He then announced plans for a new global matchplay tournament. By September 1994, a new federation of PGA Tours was agreed with a strategy to internationalise the game. Finchem also set up a task force to investigate the proposed World Tour and in October, representatives of both sides met at PGA Tour headquarters in Florida.

Norman and Montgomery then called a news conference for Thursday 17 November 1994 at Norman's own tournament, the Shark Shootout at Sherwood Country Club in Thousand Oaks, California. Ahead of it, Finchem urged Norman to abandon plans for the new project. On the Tuesday of that week, he issued a statement saying that he had learned that the World Tour was about to be announced and that it was being underwritten by Fox Sports. The commissioner said it would have 'a negative impact on existing events.' Players, meanwhile, were being urged by the tour not to sign up to the new circuit and it was clear that releases to allow them to play what were regarded as conflicting events would not be entertained by Finchem and his management team.

The establishment was rallying and Ken Schofield, the boss of the European Tour, issued a statement the next day in support of Finchem's position. Like his

American counterpart, he feared dilution of the quality of fields at existing tournaments. A crucial and decisive player meeting was held that evening at Sherwood. Finchem made a personal address, but his star witness was Arnold Palmer – historically golf's most charismatic figure and then still very influential. 'Palmer was scathing with his comments,' recalled a former tour official.

Norman was furious. He was convinced Palmer had heard only one side of the story. 'By what he said, I felt sure that either Finchem or IMG [which represented Palmer] had spoken with Arnold ahead of time,' Norman noted in his autobiography. Norman was frustrated that he never had the opportunity to personally outline his plans to Palmer and the subsequent criticism from one of the game's greats was one of the most disappointing moments of his life.

Palmer's intervention was fatal for the proposed circuit. Finchem seized the moment and soon after, introduced the concept of limited field WGC events.

Outraged, Norman felt that the tour had effectively stolen his idea. In 1995, he confronted Finchem. 'I had two meetings with him, one at Doral and one in my office after Doral,' Norman told reporters in 1996. 'He told me, "Greg, I'll keep you in the loop." That's the last communication I had with him.' Norman was not updated and had further harsh words with Finchem when his plans for the WGCs became public the following year. 'I asked him, "How long have you known about this?"' said Norman. 'He said, "About a month." I said, "Fuck you." Believe me, I'm hot about this one. I told him, "You've lost me."'

Even though the WGCs, which started in 1999, rarely captured the public's imagination and despite the fact that they became very American-centric, they did convince leading players to stick with the status quo. The best golfers now had a handful of tournaments where there would be big prize funds, no cuts and therefore guaranteed money. The way to a professional golfer's heart is usually via their wallet. The commissioner knew that. 'The World Tour was sunk by Tim Finchem when he created the World Golf Championships,' Mike Clayton told me. 'Which were kind of a joke because you'd think the clue is in the name and they might have gone round the world a bit.'

Finchem had also secured the backing of the golf establishment, other tours and sponsors to fight off the threat he felt Norman and his plans posed. 'Greg was never ever going to forgive Finchem or the PGA Tour for what happened. And that went on and on,' recalled a former tour executive.

Nevertheless, Norman remained a figure of great substance in the game. His failure to convert a six-stroke 54-hole lead into a Masters green jacket in 1996, in a strange way, added to his celebrity as a golfer and he went close again at Augusta in 1999, when he finished third.

Norman's international golf course design business was burgeoning and his commercial interests continued to diversify. He remained a fascinating talker, forever quotable. The first pre-tournament press conference I attended as the BBC's golf correspondent was at the 2003 Heineken Classic at Royal Melbourne and Norman held court. I cannot recall the substance of what he discussed, but I will never forget thinking that if all golf news conferences were like this then I had made a significant career upgrade after five years of covering tennis. Of course, it inevitably proved downhill after that Norman tour de force.

At the age of 53, the charismatic Queenslander made an improbable run at the 2008 Open at Royal Birkdale and finished in a share of third place behind the successful defending champion, Pádraig Harrington. Norman was battling back problems but for most of that week he genuinely believed he could lift the Claret Jug for a third time. Thereafter, he played only two more majors, missing the cut at Augusta the following April and then at Turnberry in the 2009 Open that was nearly won by a 59-year-old Tom Watson.

Norman was ready to dedicate himself to business full time. He had a clothing line, property empire and golf course design projects. He became a successful wine manufacturer, and dabbled in restaurants and meat production, eyewear and wakeboarding complexes. It was a hefty and diverse portfolio that gave him a substantial background in commerce. And he was still a major-winning golfer who maintained a grudge against the establishment. By this time, he had fallen out with the St Andrews-based R&A, staying away from The Open for a decade because of a dispute that centred around his ambassadorship for watch manufacturer Omega. And he still had not forgiven the PGA Tour for scuppering his world tour project of the 1990s.

By his mid-60s, Greg Norman still had golfing gravitas, but also plenty of business acumen and an undimmed motivation to redefine the sport he had been born to play. There was no better candidate to front a new international golf league, especially if it was to be financed by a bottomless pit of money.

On 29 October 2021, he was announced as the CEO of the newly formed company LIV Golf Investments. He was all in, stepping away from the Greg Norman Company and its dozen divisions. Norman had absolute belief in the new enterprise and it afforded an opportunity to avenge the crushing disappointment of his failure to launch his world tour idea in 1994.

'This is the biggest decision of my life,' Norman told ESPN. 'That's how much I believe in the people who have been behind this to get it to a point . . . where we will be live and have the first ball in the air in the [spring] of next year.'

He hit the ground running and his appointment marked the first steps towards golf's unprecedented civil war.

3
A SERIOUS BUSINESS

'That type of greed is, to me, beyond obnoxious.'

Phil Mickelson

Greg Norman and his entourage swept through the BBC newsroom in London's new Broadcasting House. His smile was wide and as bright as the brilliant-white shirt he wore beneath a grey sleeveless jacket. As he entered our radio studio, he turned to his accompanying PR executive, Jane MacNeille, and asked: 'Can we tell him the good news?'

'Yes, it's all confirmed,' she smiled, looking up from her phone. 'You're the first to hear this,' she added, grinning in my direction, and it was a stunning revelation. 'We've been given an extra $2b of funding.' This was the morning of Tuesday 10 May 2022.

We had become accustomed to astronomical sums of money being associated with men's professional golf but, even so, this was a staggering sum. Especially for a project that had yet to see a ball struck and was facing considerable institutional opposition. But, it also demonstrated a breathtaking level of progress from the initial launch of LIV Golf Investments barely six months earlier. Extraordinarily, it was now clear that there was resilience to the project that had been widely deemed 'dead in the water' only weeks before. Saudi Arabia were extremely serious about making it work.

Norman had insisted the previous October that 'this is only the beginning'. Now those words were starting to carry substance. The previous autumn, his first act as CEO was to announce 10 new events to be staged on the Asian Tour for the next 10 years. This was seen as a key move because it gave LIV a degree of legitimacy within the professional golfing firmament, but the investment alarmed existing tours, who were hostile to the move.

It was a $200m commitment and in a release sent from their West Palm Beach office, LIV claimed it was 'one of the single biggest investments in the history of professional golf.' Significantly, they were promising tournaments not just in Asia, but also in the Middle East and Europe – traditional heartlands of the Wentworth-based European Tour. Plans were announced to hold an Asian Tour event at the Centurion Club in Hertfordshire (or 'London', as they preferred to say). This was sabre rattling, a pitch for territory. It was an aggressive, daring move; the first advance in the golf wars. Tanks parked on European greens.

'LIV Golf Investments has secured a major capital commitment that will be used to create additive new opportunities across worldwide professional golf,' Norman stated in the release. 'We will be a cooperative and respectful supporter of the game at every level, and today's announcement alongside the Asian Tour is the first example of that.'

The rest of the golfing world gave a collective and sarcastic 'Yeah, that'll be right' sceptical shrug to such seemingly conciliatory language.

'I have been a staunch supporter and believer in playing and developing golf in Asia for more than four decades,' Norman continued. 'The Asian Tour is a sleeping giant.'

It was classic corporate speak that actually translated to 'Watch out golf, we are coming after you.' A 10-year deal had also been agreed to switch the big-money Saudi International competition to the Asian Tour. This move confirmed the breakdown in relations between Golf Saudi and Keith Pelley's European circuit.

The Asian Tour initially suffered heavy criticism for accepting funding from Saudi Arabia's PIF and for infringing on territory occupied by the more established European Tour. 'We've been vilified as bad boys in the press,' admitted Cho Minn Thant, the Asian Tour's youthful chief executive in a news conference ahead of the Saudi event in early February 2022. 'And I really think it's unjustified. . . . I don't see us working with LIV Golf Investments or any other promoter, any other sponsor throughout the course of the season as a bad thing.'

While there was considerable scepticism over LIV's arrival, there was also a recognition that their association with the Asian Tour gave the upstarts a genuine and much-needed foothold within the golf firmament. From the establishment there was distaste at the source of their Saudi funding, but it was clear LIV had wider ambitions to shake up professional golf like never before. But most observers were dubious that they were capable of making such an impact.

Nevertheless, LIV as an entity was up and running. It had offices in the USA and the UK. Executives were being appointed and player recruitment for a bigger project was starting to happen. The latter aspect had always been the great stumbling block. Norman possessed first-hand experience of the difficulties of tempting players with his original world tour idea in 1994. The reality was that the PGA Tour always offered an environment that leading golfers found hard to imagine being bettered.

The same issue confounded those who had recently tried to set up the Premier Golf League. But, crucially, that idea did generate enough noise to put players on alert. A drip, drip effect left some top golfers with the notion that a world outside the PGA and European tours might be viable. As a result, an increasingly febrile atmosphere prevailed at top tournaments. The words 'Saudi' and 'Arabia' and 'Super' and 'League' were increasingly common combinations in the lexicon of locker-room conversations.

Both Pelley and PGA Tour commissioner Jay Monahan were worried. They hinted that they would not give conflicting event releases for that February 2022 edition of the Saudi International. They knew their players were targets and regarded the tournament as a potential LIV recruitment centre. But there was nothing that either boss could do. Reluctantly, they allowed their players to compete in the Jeddah competition.

'We're not in this for a fight,' Norman insisted in a pre-tournament news conference. 'It's disappointing to be honest, personally disappointing, to see some of the attacks that have been taking place unwarrantedly. If you pre-judge anybody without knowing the facts, then shame on you. . . . Are you scared of something? What is LIV Golf Investments doing that you are scared of?'

The Saudi field included the likes of Bryson DeChambeau, Phil Mickelson, Sergio García, Shane Lowry, Graeme McDowell, Henrik Stenson and defending champion Dustin Johnson (DJ) – all of them major winning stars. Losing control of players such as these was what was scary for the established tours. Unprecedentedly scary.

Prize money at the Saudi International was up from $3.5m to $5m, but this week was about more than a golf tournament. It was regarded as a pivotal moment in the evolution of the LIV project. Ominously for the status quo, Norman told reporters: 'Absolutely there are going to be things announced in the future.'

It was an open secret that a golf 'super league' was in the offing. Several players were forced to address the issue in pre-tournament interview sessions. Phil Mickelson fuelled speculation by saying: 'Pretty much every player that is in the top 100 . . . in the World Ranking has been contacted at some point.' European Ryder Cup star Lee Westwood made clear he was interested and had been approached when he said: 'I've signed an NDA.' He added that he thought the sport was currently stuck in its ways with an over-reliance on 72-hole strokeplay format. 'I think golf does need [something] different,' he said.

Mickelson had been relatively diplomatic in his Saudi news conference. This was the first week of February 2022 and he politely pointed out that the perceived threat of an arriving breakaway tour had already kick-started PGA Tour moves to better remunerate their top stars. 'I'm appreciative of the fact that there is competition,' said the reigning US PGA champion and oldest winner of a major title.

'That leverage has allowed for a much better environment on the PGA Tour, meaning we would not have an incentive programme like the PIP [Player Impact Program, introduced to further reward the most successful golfers for the their influence both on and off the course] for the top players without this type of competition. We would not have the increase in the FedEx Cup money. We would not have the increase in The Players Championship prize fund to $20m this year if it wasn't for this threat.'

But that week, the six-times major champion also sat down for an interview with *Golf Digest*'s experienced reporter, John Huggan, a trusted confidant. Theirs was an agenda-setting conversation. 'I was just happy to be getting a one-on-one interview with Phil Mickelson,' Huggan said. 'He obviously had an agenda. I asked him one question and off he went. I sat there for the next 35 minutes and listened. I didn't say very much.'

The interview gave a much deeper insight into Mickelson's antipathy towards the tour, even though it was the circuit where he had made such a considerable name. The player railed against what he felt was the PGA Tour's little-known policy to restrict access to their members' media footage.

'For me personally, it's not enough that they are sitting on hundreds of millions of digital moments. They also have access to my shots, access I do not have. They also charge companies to use shots I have hit.' Mickelson added: 'That type of greed is, to me, beyond obnoxious.'

Huggan recalled: 'The obnoxious greed line was obviously going to be the headline. I gave him the chance to back off, saying, "Do you really want to say that?" And he did. He said, "Yes, that's fine," but he regretted it later. He actually thanked me for kind of trying to save him. He said, "I was an idiot that day."'

But LIV knew they were pushing at an open door with their approach to Mickelson, a player who enduringly had been the next biggest golf star in the world after Tiger Woods. He had been talking to them for some time.

Around this time in early 2022, LIV suddenly seemed to gain real momentum. Rumours abounded about players who were likely to take Saudi riches and sign for their super league concept. Jay Monahan threatened to ban from the PGA Tour anyone who defected, while Norman insisted it would be impossible to impose such a punishment. Along with Mickelson, Dustin Johnson and Bryson DeChambeau were top of the list of probable defectors. Lee Westwood and Ian Poulter were likely to sign up as well. Westwood had referred to it as a 'no brainer'.

Mickelson was the prime candidate but, unknown to Norman and his Saudi backers, two months earlier the greatest left-hander golf has ever known had taken part in a fateful conversation with writer Alan Shipnuck. It was a phone chat that suddenly threatened to derail the entire project. The author was applying the finishing touches to his book on the American star, *Phil: The Rip-Roaring (And Unauthorized!) Biography of Golf's Most Colourful Superstar* (Simon & Schuster, 2022), when Mickelson called him out of the blue. Shipnuck was on a car journey with his family and his daughter was driving.

Mickelson knew the book was being written and that Shipnuck had conducted scores of interviews about him. The golfer did not say his comments were off the record, but it is hard to think that he was expecting them to be published. 'There are three things I believe about that conversation,' John Huggan told me. 'I believe Alan a hundred per cent when he says that Phil did not say this is off the record. However, given what Phil did say I have to believe also that Phil thought he was off the record. There is nobody in their right mind who would say what he said for the record. And I also believe, more sadly, that Alan knew that Phil thought it was off the record because he had to think that. And it is a very grey area. To me he is getting by on a technicality. I'm not sure it is something many journalists would have done.'

Furthermore, Huggan is convinced the interviewee felt the same. 'Phil absolutely thinks that. I know he does because I direct messaged him saying exactly what I've just said to you. All he said I was "One hundred per cent correct."'

Shipnuck insists Mickelson had no reason to think he would not be quoted from their conversation. He says that he had approached Mickelson three times for an interview for his book before the player eventually called him. 'At that point anything he tells me is going straight in the book, unless we agree otherwise,' Shipnuck told Lawrence Donegan during the McKellar Golf podcast on 25 October 2023. 'He never asked to go off the record, I never consented to it. . . . I don't think it is my role to be a life guard and pull Phil back from the edge of the pool. If he wants to jump in the deep end, I'm going to let him. He knows what he is doing. He initiated the conversation and he had things he wanted to tell me.'

The writer is a sharp journalist and believed he had garnered legitimate quotes. Not only that, but they were also dynamite. As explosive as anything any golfer has ever uttered. With the prospect of a Saudi-funded super league growing ever more likely, Shipnuck knew this was the optimal moment. On 17 February 2022, the writer used his *Fire Pit Collective* website to reveal that the golfer had been involved in recruiting players for the PIF-funded project. And he had been doing it despite firmly believing the project was nothing more than 'sport washing' for a brutally repressive Saudi regime. Most significantly, Mickelson was quoted saying: 'They're scary motherfuckers to get involved with.' And to Shipnuck, he justified his involvement with the Saudis because it afforded a 'once in a lifetime opportunity' to alter the way the PGA Tour goes about its business.

The LIV project was devastated; blown asunder by Mickelson's apparent double-dealing, never mind his vitriol towards the Saudi backers of the breakaway. Three days after the comments had been publicly aired, Johnson and DeChambeau issued statements. DJ had previously described the proposed super league as 'a really good concept'. But now his tune had altered. 'Over the past several months, there has been a great deal of speculation about an alternative tour; much of which seems to have included me and my future in professional golf,' Johnson, then the number six player in the world, said in the missive issued through the PGA Tour. 'I am grateful for the opportunity to play the best tour in the world and for all it has provided me and my family. While there will always be areas where our Tour can improve and evolve, I am thankful for our leadership and the many sponsors who make the PGA Tour golf's premier tour.'

Later that Sunday 20 February 2022, DeChambeau, who a fortnight earlier had withdrawn from the Saudi International through injury, issued his own statement. The 2020 US Open champion, who was ranked 12th in the world, said: 'While there has been a lot of speculation surrounding my support for another tour, I want to make it very clear that as long as the best players in the world are playing the PGA Tour, so will I.'

These two former US Open winners (Johnson was also the 2020 Masters champion) had joined the likes of Rory McIlroy, Jon Rahm, Jordan Spieth, Brooks Koepka and Justin Thomas in pledging allegiance to the status quo. Rahm, the reigning US Open champion, summed up the mood when he said in a press conference: 'There has been a lot of talk and speculation on the Saudi League. It's just not something I believe is the best for me and my future in golf.'

Koepka said: 'It's been pretty clear for a long time now that I'm with the PGA Tour, it's where I'm staying. I'm very happy. I think they do things the right way, people I want to do business with. I'm happy to be here and I don't really talk about it with many other players.'

Thomas stated: 'The reason I play golf is to create a legacy and win as many times as I can on the PGA Tour.' And the biggest voice of all, Tiger Woods, also came down emphatically on the side of the establishment. 'I'm supporting the PGA Tour, that's where my legacy is,' he said. 'I've been fortunate enough to have won 82 events on this tour and 15 major championships and been a part of the World Golf Championships, the start of them and the end of them. So I have an allegiance to the PGA Tour.'

So it was little surprise that at that February's Genesis Invitational event in Los Angeles, where Johnson missed the cut, McIlroy insisted the threat of a breakaway league had disappeared. 'Who's left? Who's left to go? I mean, there's no one. It's dead in the water in my opinion. I just can't think of any reason why anyone would go.'

During a press conference at the Genesis, McIlroy went on to describe Mickelson's comments to Shipnuck as: 'Selfish, egotistical, ignorant.' He added: 'It was just very surprising and disappointing. Sad. I'm sure he's sitting at home sort of rethinking his position and where he goes from here.'

Mickelson's reputation as a clean-cut, family-oriented, big-hearted all-American hero was in bits. The following Tuesday, he issued a statement posted on social media. 'I used words I sincerely regret that do not reflect my true feelings or intentions,' Mickelson said. 'It was reckless, I offended people, and I am deeply sorry for my choice of words.'

He also said: 'There is the problem of off record comments being shared out of context and without my consent, but . . . I'm beyond disappointed and will make every effort to self-reflect and learn from this.' Tellingly he also hinted at deeper problems in his private life. 'I have often failed myself and others too,' he admitted. 'The past 10 years I have felt the pressure and stress slowly affecting me at a deeper level. I know I have not been my best and desperately need some time away to prioritise the ones I love most and work on being the man I want to be.'

These were extraordinary words from one of the most confident, assured and articulate athletes American sport has ever known. It amounted to an epic downfall, not quite on the scale of that suffered in 2009 by his great rival Woods, but in a similar ballpark. Like Woods after his multiple infidelities were made public, Mickelson disappeared from public view.

Norman was left shattered. His project appeared ruined before it had properly taken its first breaths. The PGA Tour's resolute stance and threat of life bans seemed to have had the desired effect. Commissioner Jay Monahan's position was never stronger and Norman was on the ropes, a laughing stock in many of golf's corridors of power.

Typically, though, he came out fighting.

On 24 February, the Australian issued an open letter to Monahan. It began with the words: 'Surely you jest.' He added: 'For decades, I have fought for the rights of players to enjoy a career in which they are rewarded fully and properly for their efforts. They are one-in-a-million athletes. Yet for decades, the Tour has put its own financial ambitions ahead of the players, and every player on the Tour knows it. The Tour is the Players Tour not your administration's Tour. Why do you call the Crown Jewel in all tournaments outside the Majors "The Players Championship" and not "The Administration's Championship"?'

Norman then attacked Monahan's strong-arm tactics, questioning their legality. 'When you try to bluff and intimidate players by bullying and threatening them, you are guilty of going too far, being unfair, and you are likely in violation of the law,' he wrote.

By this time it was known that Norman was planning fourteen 54-hole tournaments with $20m purses, but there had been no official launch. After all, there were no players signed. The Saudi-funded commissioner, though, was insistent that his schedule could sit alongside a PGA Tour calendar, with both co-existing. 'What is wrong with that?' Norman's letter said.

And he threatened antitrust legal action if Monahan imposed bans. 'When you threaten to end players' careers and when you engage in unfair labour practices with your web of player restrictions, you demonstrate exactly why players are open minded about joining a league that treats players well, respects them, and compensates them according to their true worth.'

Norman concluded this extraordinary missive with a familiar refrain. 'Commissioner – this is just the beginning. It is certainly not the end.' The letter was regarded as a laughing stock, a last, flailing attempt at credibility for a failing enterprise. It was not the first or the last time that Norman and his Saudi-funded project were underestimated.

LIV Golf Investments was a vital plank in Saudi Arabia's plans. The Kingdom was invested in every respect and Yasir Al-Rumayyan, the governor of its PIF – which was financing the project – was still all in. He is calm, analytical and clever. He loves golf. His Excellency (H.E. as he is known) was a vital figure.

The LIV project did look in trouble, as McIlroy claimed with his 'dead in the water' observation. But if it was on 'life support', it still found a way to keep breathing and many observers believe that was solely down to the composure of H.E. The PIF governor addressed his LIV workforce with a stirring speech and kept the project on track. LIV doubled down and Norman insisted – not for the last time – that 'We're not going anywhere.'

The following month, Norman was in a position strong enough to announce an eight-tournament schedule that would have 48 players competing, no cuts and $25m purses. The Asian Tour event scheduled at Centurion would now be replaced by LIV's inaugural tournament. There would be 10 more events in 2023 before a full 14-tournament league the following year.

A fifth of the prize pot would go towards a team event and $4m would go to the overall winner. They were staggering sums. Norman contended: 'Players will see those prizes being paid out and will want to be part of it.' His recruitment strategy was clear, but in the late winter and early spring of 2022 there remained considerable antipathy among the world's best players. Their commitment to the status quo in the wake of the Mickelson revelations still seemed unwavering. Or was it?

4

HOSTILITIES

'. . . can't wait to leave this Tour . . . A couple more weeks and
I don't have to deal with you anymore.'

Sergio García

Phil Mickelson was skiing when the world's best gathered for the first men's major, the Masters. It was the only time he had been absent from Augusta since 1994 when, ironically, he could not play because he was recovering from a broken leg – an injury sustained in a skiing accident.

Nevertheless, in April 2022, talk of the upstart project he had so spectacularly derailed dominated the Augusta clubhouse chatter while Scottie Scheffler was landing his first green jacket and maiden major title. There was widespread scepticism that Norman could muster a meaningful cast list despite the riches that would be on offer at his new tournaments.

The LIV commissioner made it known that he would look to attract top amateurs to his fields, which was seen as a sign that he was struggling to find

48 players. Norman couched it differently, claiming it was all part of his overall 'grow the game' strategy, by allowing potential stars of the future new experiences.

In mid-April, it was reported that half a dozen DP World Tour players were seeking permission to play LIV's opening tournament, but time was ticking by. The first LIV Golf Invitational Series event was slated for 9–11 June 2022. Any professional seeking an official release from the PGA Tour to compete had to give 45 days' notice. In this case, the deadline was 25 April with the tour then having until 10 May to notify the player as to whether they would be given permission.

LIV needed big names, but the first pro to be associated with the project was far from the elite echelons. Robert Garrigus, a 44-year-old veteran with one tournament victory achieved more than a decade earlier, was the first to apply for a conflicting event waiver. There was widespread derision. 'If he is the best they can get then there's nothing for us to worry about,' remarked a leading PGA Tour player to me as he prepared for May's PGA Championship at Southern Hills in Tulsa, Oklahoma.

Mickelson was again absent for that major, one where he should have been competing as defending champion. Twelve months earlier, he had rewritten the record books at Kiawah Island, becoming the oldest winner of one of the big four titles. Then he was golf's ultimate hero, all smiles, thumbs up – an autograph hunter's dream. Now he was in silent exile while lurid rumours of excessive gambling and matters surrounding his private life swirled around the internet. 'Sad,' commented Rory McIlroy at the PGA news conference. 'This should be a celebration, right? He won a major championship at 50 years old. It was possibly his last big, big moment in the game of golf. I think he should be here this week and celebrating what a monumental achievement he achieved last year.'

But the rumour-mill was turning more positive for LIV. They were getting traction again. Confirmation came in early May when the PGA Tour went to TPC Potomac for the Wells Fargo Championship. Sergio García became embroiled in a rules row during the first round. He had been put on the clock, in effect told to hurry up, while looking for his ball in thick grass on the par-5 10th hole. Television microphones picked up comments from the irate Spaniard, Europe's record points scorer in the Ryder Cup. 'I can't wait to leave this Tour,' García told the rules official. 'I can't wait to get out of here. . . . A couple more weeks and I don't have to deal with you anymore,' ranted the then world number 47.

Almost simultaneously, Westwood and fellow Englishman Richard Bland confirmed their intention to play the LIV event at Centurion. Westwood denied it was something that he had needed to think about long and hard. 'No, it's an opportunity to play in a big tournament,' he told Sky Sports during the British Masters. 'Hence some of the best players in the world [want to play] in England. I love playing in England in front of home fans. Any time there is an opportunity like that I feel like I should take it.' As an independent contractor, Westwood reasoned that he was entitled to do what was best for his career. He pointed to the fact that the established circuits had never previously objected to him playing in Saudi Arabia.

But the tours took a hard-line approach. This was different. Saudi Arabia had become out of bounds and signing up for tournaments financed by the Kingdom's PIF would not be tolerated. The opening event in England was the same week as the RBC Canadian Open, a tournament backed by one of the PGA Tour's biggest sponsors.

Commissioner Jay Monahan sent a memo to his players on 11 May 2022. 'As a membership organisation, we believe this decision is in the best interest of the PGA Tour and its players,' it said. 'We have notified those who have applied that their request has been declined in accordance with the PGA Tour Tournament Regulations . . . As such, tour members are not authorised to participate in the Saudi Golf League's London event under our regulations.' Monahan clearly was not engaging with LIV branding but he was very keen to draw attention to the links with Saudi Arabia.

The commissioner received immediate backing from the world's best player. 'Playing in something that could be a rival series to the PGA Tour, being a member of our tour, it's definitely not something we want our membership to do,' said Masters champion Scottie Scheffler ahead of the Byron Nelson Classic. 'It's going to harm the tournament that we have opposite. . . . I'm sure that's why they did not release the players.'

Norman was furious. There had been a feeling that the PGA Tour would not object until the LIV series moved to one of its four scheduled stops in the USA. But it was now clear that Monahan was standing shoulder to shoulder with his strategic alliance partners in Europe. The Centurion event was in direct competition to the DP World Tour's Scandinavian Mixed event. It was a threat. Permission was refused on both sides of the Atlantic, other than to members ineligible for the tournaments on their schedules that week.

'Sadly, the PGA Tour seems intent on denying professional golfers their right to play golf, unless it's exclusively in a PGA Tour tournament,' Norman said in a statement. 'This is particularly disappointing in light of the Tour's non-profit status, where its mission is purportedly "to promote the common interests of professional tournament golfers". Instead, the Tour is intent on perpetuating its illegal monopoly of what should be a free and open market. The Tour's action is anti-golfer, anti-fan, and anti-competitive. But no matter what obstacles the PGA Tour puts in our way, we will not be stopped.'

This was Norman laying the groundwork for ensuing and expensive legal battles and he knew his pockets were deeper than those of the opposition to fund litigation. He had momentum, but observers still did not know how many players of the highest calibre he could recruit. But the Shark was circling, and it was little wonder he had been smiling when he entered our BBC radio studio a day earlier on 10 May.

This was his first stop on a supposed charm offensive that would put LIV on the sporting map, sell tickets for its inaugural event and change the golfing landscape for ever. And Norman now had extra billions in his back pocket to make it happen. 'We've just got approval to launch our schedule into 2023, '24 and '25. We've got $2b to back that up so we have additional funds in place,' the 67-year-old told me. 'And just because we are talking about '23, '24 and '25, we're looking way beyond that too. We are looking at decades.'

Norman stated that he had five of the world's top 50 and nine of the leading 100 players in the world lined up to play his opening tournament. By now it was expected that European Ryder Cup heroes Ian Poulter and Martin Kaymer were also on board. 'Of course we have had to pivot because there have been some obstacles thrown in our way with a couple of the institutions – the PGA Tour and DP World Tour – but we have pivoted brilliantly,' the commissioner of the breakaway circuit boasted.

My BBC interviewee had Trumpian chutzpah. He spoke with confidence and charm and relied on corporate vernacular to explain shaking up the game. 'Remember, no tour in this world owns golf,' he stated. 'There's been a monopoly in place for 53 years. Players have to go play the PGA Tour, that's it, plain and simple. All we are trying to do is give the players another opportunity to go and play. Obviously they [the PGA Tour] are partnering up with the European Tour and that sends a signal that they are trying to tighten up their monopoly situation. The players are starting to understand some of the [tours'] by-laws might be a little bit less stringent or less penal than what the tour are saying. You'll be banned for life? You cannot ban players for life, they are independent contractors.'

To illustrate the absurdity of the tours trying to prevent their golfers from playing his tournaments, Norman tried to tell me that it would be wrong for the BBC to prevent me from broadcasting for another organisation while I remained in their employ.

'Not if it is a rival broadcaster,' I countered. He seemed momentarily flummoxed.

'Well it depends on your contract,' he said.

Norman also claimed a television deal had been struck, but under pressure admitted it was an agreement to screen his tournaments on YouTube. He also sought to justify his association with Saudi Arabia, a regime so heavily criticised for its record on human rights. 'They're investing in and they want to get their money out,' he said. 'Golf is one of those few opportunities to exist in the world of sport that had virgin space sitting there untapped.' He added: 'I'm very, very proud of the fact that when I go to Saudi Arabia I see these kids and these girls playing the game of golf . . . and the way the game is growing in that country is phenomenal. To me that's what it's all about.'

'Grow the game' – the buzz phrase behind which all golf administrators hide. To me it felt phoney from Norman. There were billions of other reasons behind this project. If the idea was to grow participation in the Kingdom it would be worth knowing the base line from which they were starting.

'So how many golfers are there in Saudi Arabia?' I asked.

'I don't know . . . I can find that number for you but it keeps growing every year.'

It seemed about the only question for which he did not have a prepared answer, but a day later we found out there were others.

Having done the rounds with Britain's broadcast media on Tuesday 10 May, the following day proved 'wobbly Wednesday' for the LIV boss. A gathering with a selection of newspaper and website writers was supposed to be a 'fireside chat' in the clubhouse at the Centurion Club near Hemel Hempstead – which, for marketing purposes, was deemed by LIV to be in London. The opening tournament was due to be held there a month later.

'That phrase "fireside chat" is obviously not super confrontational,' noted *Mirror* sports writer Neil McLeman to me. 'I think they were quite unaware of the hostility of the press and I think the British press is generally more confrontational than from a lot of other countries. And certainly on the issue of Saudi Arabia.'

Sitting in a beige suede jacket and navy blue shirt, Norman held a microphone in his left hand as he tried to continue the charm offensive he had begun the previous day. But the reporters wanted his views on sport washing and Saudi Arabia and specifically the 2018 murder and dismemberment of *Washington Post* journalist Jamal Khashoggi. It was regarded as a state-sponsored crime. US intelligence agencies had concluded the killing was approved by Mohammed bin Salman – something the Crown Prince denies.

McLeman was among journalists who pressed Norman on this and his questioning prompted an extraordinary reply. 'This whole thing about Saudi Arabia and Khashoggi and human rights, talk about it, but also talk about the good that the country is doing in changing its culture,' Norman said. 'Look, we've all made mistakes and you just want to learn by those mistakes and how you can correct them going forward.'

The room was stunned at such a crass response from someone who the day before had told me he was most proud of his skills in 'diplomacy'. McLeman said: 'The Khashoggi issue is a bigger deal for journalists, it certainly is for me.' He described Norman's 'we all make mistakes' response as 'a jaw dropping moment'. The *Mirror* man immediately hit back. 'I said to him, "What are you saying? Cutting up a murdered journalist is just a mistake?"'

McLeman and the other newspaper reporters present had their headline and Norman's quotes became back page fodder across tabloid and broadsheet publications. 'From a PR perspective, you must be thinking "Oh my God, this isn't what we planned",' the reporter added.

Like the publication of Mickelson's reckless remarks to Alan Shipnuck, this was another significant setback, another moment to fuel unprecedented controversy. It provided ammunition for the enemy and made it harder to tempt players from those opposing ranks to defect to Norman's brave new world. But it was not a fatal blow, as was proved in the tumultuous months that followed.

5
LIV GOES LIVE

'Have you ever had to apologise for being a
member of the PGA Tour?'

Jay Monahan

Pulling into the grassy field that served as a main car park, this felt like the big time. In the distance stood rows of white tents, a substantial grandstand and pristine flags. They were emblazoned with the letters 'LIV' – Roman numerals for the figure – that meant so much to the new upstart tour. The driving range and practice putting green were what you would see at a normal tour event. Up the slope from the putting area lay an impressive spectator tented village. There was a huge stage area, and merchandising stalls and refreshment sellers were busily setting up for what they hoped would be a lucrative few days.

Ten weeks earlier, this had been just a pipe dream. Back then, LIV was 'dead in the water'. Now it was very much alive and kicking. It had money – we already knew that – but now there was a venue, players and a tournament to be played. The transformation of the Centurion Club in such a short space of time was a remarkable achievement.

Greg Norman had finally delivered his baby, a rival to a monopolistic monster, as he saw it. His was a brand-new force in golf, one that was about to take first teetering steps. We were at the start of an extraordinary week in the history of professional golf in a peaceful portion of the British countryside. Regardless of the rural setting, the events of this week in early June 2022 reverberated across the golfing globe, generating vast coverage.

A week earlier, LIV had announced their field for the 54-hole tournament. Among the headliners was former world number one Dustin Johnson, the same player who had pledged his allegiance to the PGA Tour earlier in the year. Since then, Norman had persisted with his approaches to the former Masters and US Open champion, each time increasing the offered signing fee. Reportedly, it reached $125m. That was enough for DJ to turn his back on the establishment.

'Dustin has been contemplating the opportunity off-and-on for the past couple of years,' the 37-year-old's agent, David Winkle, said in a statement. 'Ultimately, he decided it was in his and his family's best interest to pursue it. Dustin has never had any issue with the PGA Tour and is grateful for all it has given him, but in the end, felt this was too compelling to pass up.'

Johnson later said of his decision to join LIV: 'I think it's great for the game of golf. That's why I'm here.' He had been due to play that week in the Canadian Open, backed by RBC, who were one of his main sponsors. That deal swiftly disappeared.

Instead, he would be teeing it up alongside the likes of former Open champion Louis Oosthuizen and his fellow South African, Branden Grace, as well as Lee Westwood, Ian Poulter, Sergio García, Kevin Na and Martin Kaymer. 'To be honest, you did not know what you were going to get at the beginning of the year,' Kaymer, another former world number one, told me at the end of LIV's first season. 'On reflection it was the right decision for me.'

Norman, meanwhile, proclaimed: 'Free agency has finally come to golf. This is an opportunity to start a movement that will change the course of history . . . the desire shown by the players to participate in LIV Golf demonstrates their emphatic belief in our model and confidence in what we're building for the future.'

Days later, his cast list for the opening tournament was supplemented by the arrival of Phil Mickelson, forgiven by his Saudi Arabian paymasters for those unguarded comments that came so close to ending the LIV project before it had started. Mickelson said his time away from the game had been 'humbling' and told social media followers: '. . . this new path is a fresh start, one that is exciting for me at this stage of my career and is clearly transformative, not just for myself, but ideally for the game and my peers. I also love the progressive format and I think it will be exciting for fans.

'Just as importantly, it will provide balance, allowing me to focus on a healthier approach to life on and off the course. I am incredibly grateful for what this game and the PGA Tour has given me. I would like to think that I have given back as well but now I'm excited about this new opportunity. I'm thrilled to begin with LIV Golf and I appreciate everyone involved.'

While this was a triumphant time for an organisation that had pulled this tournament together in just nine frantic weeks, it was still an awkward one from a public relations perspective. The British and American media were not about to let go of the notion that the entire project was nothing more than Saudi Arabian sport washing. LIV knew this and recruited Ari Fleischer, press secretary to President George W. Bush, to shape their media strategy.

The previous month, Norman had talked himself into trouble with his ham-fisted 'we all make mistakes' and despite such a high-powered media adviser watching on, it was now time for Graeme McDowell to fall into the same trap. The articulate 2010 US Open champion appeared for a news conference alongside Johnson, Oosthuizen and teenage Thai amateur Ratchanon ('TK') Chantananuwat.

Johnson initially stunned reporters with the revelation that he had quit the PGA Tour. No one does that, or at least they did not until LIV came along, and he was following the example of Kevin Na, who had done the same thing a few days earlier. 'Obviously at this time it's hard to speak on what the consequences will be,' Johnson admitted. And if that meant, as seemed likely at the time, losing eligibility to play for America in the Ryder Cup, so be it. 'I'm doing what's best for my family,' he stated.

Of the quartet answering questions at LIV's first news conference, McDowell was the only figure renowned for oratory skills. 'I wish I had just sat there and said nothing,' the 43-year-old later told me. But this loquacious golfer from Portrush, Northern Ireland – always one of golf's most respected ambassadors – could not help himself. How did he reconcile his decision to join LIV with Saudi Arabia's human rights record? 'This has been incredibly polarising,' he began in his unique hybrid Irish/American accent. 'Take the Khashoggi situation; we all agree that's reprehensible. Nobody is going to argue that fact. But we are golfers.'

McDowell continued to say that he felt golf as a force for good, before adding: 'We are not politicians. I know you guys hate that expression, but we are really not, unfortunately. We are professional golfers. If Saudi Arabia wanted to use the game of golf as a way for them to get to where they want to be and they have the resources to accelerate that experience, I think we are proud to help them on that journey, using the game of golf and the abilities that we have to help grow the sport and take them to where they want to be.'

A more succinct interpretation was that he was proud to be a vehicle for sport washing. His comments made for stinging headlines throughout the UK and USA and set the agenda for the week.

The following day, Westwood and Poulter appeared alongside younger English pros Sam Horsfield and Laurie Canter. It was the two older players who attracted most of the questions. 'That was another occasion where they seemed taken aback that Saudi Arabia was such a hot topic,' recalled the *Mirror*'s Neil McLeman.

The reporter felt there were two key issues – Saudi influence and the fantastic sums that were flowing into players' pockets during a cost of living squeeze adversely affecting so many households across the UK. McLeman also felt the players had been heavily briefed and were effectively parroting scripted answers. 'A good question is one where whatever the answer, it will yield a story,' said the experienced newspaperman.

He had this in mind and wanted to take the players off-script when he addressed the two Ryder Cup heroes sitting at the head of the media centre. 'Is there anywhere in the world that you wouldn't play? If Vladimir Putin had a tournament, would you play there?' McLeman asked.

'That's speculation, I'm not even going to comment on speculation,' Poulter replied.

'In a generality, is there anywhere you wouldn't play on a moral basis? If the money was right, is there anywhere you wouldn't play?'

'I don't need to answer that question,' Poulter said after pausing for a sip of water.

'Sorry?'

'I don't need to answer that question.'

'Lee, do you want to answer it? Would you have played in apartheid South Africa, for example?'

'You're just asking us to answer a hypothetical question which we can't answer a question on that.'

McLeman's statement that they were actually moral questions also went unanswered. It was an excruciating, highly charged exchange that was then played out on news outlets across the world. Two Ryder Cup heroes skewered and unable to provide answers.

'Next question?' Fleischer swiftly intervened.

We also heard from Mickelson, who was the player most reporters wanted to quiz given his near five-month exile. When he entered the room, his gaunt, slimline figure and unfamiliar facial hair were immediately striking. So was his apparent contrition and reluctance to engage. This was a side of Mickelson we had never seen. He was always the smartest guy in the room, the man with all the answers.

'I've made, said and done a lot of things that I regret,' he admitted. 'And I'm sorry for that and for the hurt that it's caused a lot of people. I don't condone human rights violations at all . . . nobody here does, throughout the world. I'm certainly aware of what has happened with Jamal Khashoggi, and I think it's terrible. I've also seen the good that the game of golf has done throughout history, and I believe that LIV Golf is going to do a lot of good for the game as well.'

Mickelson refused to talk about his relationship with the PGA Tour or whether he was serving a ban. He occasionally lost focus or simply flat-batted questions. He described his time away as 'awesome' and did acknowledge difficulties he had faced in his life with gambling. These had been alleged in Alan Shipnuck's biography and in a brief 're-entry' interview with *Sports Illustrated* ahead of this appearance in England, Mickelson admitted to having been 'reckless' in the past. It was later claimed by his former business associate Billy Walters that Mickelson has bet in excess of $1b in his career.

'I've been handling it for many years now,' Mickelson admitted in the June 2022 news conference. 'You're talking about something that was almost a decade ago, and look, me and my family have been financially secure for I can't remember how long, but it was certainly going to be threatened if I didn't address this, and I did. I've had hundreds of hours' therapy and I've worked tirelessly for many years, and I feel really good about where I'm at. And yeah, I'm proud of the work I've done. So I've addressed the issue, and will continue to do so the rest of my life.'

And he did little to dispute reports that he was being paid $200m to play for LIV. 'I feel that contract agreements should be private,' he said. 'Doesn't seem to be the case but it should be.' In all, Mickelson handled 34 questions. The other three players at the top table – Chase Koepka, Justin Harding and TK Chantananuwat – were required to give precisely one answer each once the news conference was thrown open to the floor.

Earlier, the Associated Press reporter Rob Harris had been escorted out of a news conference by security. The reporter was denied a question by the moderator when Na, Talor Gooch, James Piot and Sihwan Kim were at their microphones. Harris claimed the session had been cut short from the half hour allotted. The implication was that the organisers were trying to dodge his awkward questions. Such incidents rarely, if ever, happen in the sleepy world of professional golf, or at least they never used to. Harris was allowed to return after heated arguments.

But an even more contentious incident occurred while Mickelson was speaking and it involved his nemesis, Shipnuck. The American writer claimed he had been thrown out of the media centre. He tweeted: 'Well, a couple of neckless security dudes just physically removed me from Phil Mickelson's press conference, saying they were acting on orders from their boss, whom they refused to name. (Greg Norman? MBS? Al Capone?) Never a dull moment here.'

The biographer then sent a text message to Norman. 'Are you aware I just got muscled out of Phil's press conference by a couple of your goons? Luckily for you guys I kept my cool and deescalated the situation. Please call me to discuss.'

'Did not hear. Thanks for letting me know,' Norman replied.

'That's funny because:' Shipnuck returned, attaching a photo showing his confrontation and someone in the background shiftily looking on. That person was Greg Norman.

Throughout all of this I was reporting for what felt like every BBC outlet imaginable, some of which I had not even known existed despite having spent more than three decades on the staff. Radio, television, online; everyone wanted a piece of this story. It had everything: money, morality, greed, international relations and innovation. A grand old sport was being shaken to its foundations and editors who would never ordinarily give golf the time of day were suddenly interested.

To be fair, the intrigue waned once the talking largely stopped and 48 golfers – rebels or pioneers, depending on your point of view – began playing. Then it was just golf. And for those three days, not very exciting golf either. In fact, quite boring. South Africa's Charl Schwartzel eased to a very convincing win. There was little jeopardy as he made himself $4m richer for three rounds of golf. Schwartzel's all South African 'Stingers GC' won the team element, meaning significant cheques also went to Hennie du Plessis, Branden Grace and Louis Oosthuizen. In truth, the action was only pepped by a drip feed of interviews with new and significant LIV recruits: Bryson DeChambeau, Patrick Reed and Pat Perez.

'It's refreshing to see team golf again. It takes me back to college and Ryder Cup days,' Reed told LIV's streamed coverage. 'You're not just playing for yourself – you're playing for your team over there and that camaraderie. I'm excited about seeing more golf. You're not just seeing coverage from featured groups – you're seeing it from everywhere.'

Crowd numbers were reasonable and enthusiastic but many were there on freebies. Tickets had either come from the Centurion Club, distributed via their members, or fans had used discount codes pumped out on players' social media channels. There was a younger dynamic, many of those attending arrived late and they were not there for the golf but rather performing acts in the evening, including Craig David. 'There were decent crowds and it was a different demographic,' observed former manager and promoter Andrew 'Chubby' Chandler to me. 'It was the 20- to 40-year-olds, in their jeans, caps turned backwards; "I'm here for a few pints and to see my idols."' He added: 'It showed me that golf is changing.'

We had certainly never seen a prize presentation quite like the one on the final evening that celebrated Schwartzel's victory. With Greg Norman watching on, the PIF governor, Yasir Al-Rumayyan, was in triumphant mood. He proclaimed that 54, LIV's number, was 'the perfect score in golf', reasoning that this amounted to 18 birdies on a par-72 course. He then stated that he would award $54m to any LIV player who shoots a round of 54. That would be four strokes fewer than the record score for a single round on the PGA Tour.

Extraordinarily, for some of the LIV stars, such a sum of money was comparatively small beer. Nevertheless, the entire ceremony celebrated largesse. It was all about the money. There was very little about sporting glory.

This was the new era for men's professional golf.

On the other side of the Atlantic, PGA Tour commissioner Jay Monahan was predictably less impressed. He had announced indefinite bans for those who defected and told TV viewers at the Canadian Open that these rebel players had merely signed for a 'series of exhibition matches'. The normally mild-mannered administrator was scathing. He contended that those players 'would have to be living under a rock' not to know they would face heavy criticism for accepting Saudi Arabian riches. He fatefully added: 'I would ask any player that has left, or any player that would ever consider leaving, "Have you ever had to apologise for being a member of the PGA Tour?"'

As for the golf in Toronto, it was rather more raucous than at the Hemel Hempstead course where it was supposed to be 'Golf but louder'. A certain Rory McIlroy fired a closing 62 to edge out Justin Thomas and Tony Finau and defend his Canadian Open title. 'This is a day I'll remember for a long, long time,' McIlroy said in a TV interview. 'Twenty-one PGA Tour wins, one more than somebody else.'

Greg Norman won 20 events on the US tour. Touché.

McIlroy was not just motivated by his hatred of LIV; it was also personal with Norman. The Northern Irish star thought they were on reasonable terms and had exchanged cordial texts earlier in 2022, only for Norman to then claim in a *Washington Post* interview that McIlroy had been brainwashed by the PGA Tour. As revealed in the *Irish Independent*, the four-times major winner promptly vowed 'to make it my business now to be as much of a pain in his arse as possible.' So this was a sweet victory on the eve of the US Open.

With the PGA Tour suspending players who switched to LIV, the DP World Tour swiftly announced a one-tournament ban and £100,000 fines for the 16 players who had defected from them. This added to the tension gripping the game.

At the BMW International in Munich, Sergio García was involved in a tempestuous locker-room outburst. In response to news of the punishments, the Spaniard yelled at fellow players: 'This tour is shit, you're all fucked, you should have taken the Saudi money.' Scottish star Bob MacIntyre was said to be one of those present and later in the week tweeted: 'Amazing how fast you can lose respect for someone that you've looked up to all your life.'

Men's golf was on twin tracks in this new and unfamiliarly fractious world. It seemed those lines could only now come together at the four majors. But there was one exception. The JP McManus Pro-Am attracts the most astonishing list of players to the Irish businessman's Adare Manor course near Limerick. From Tiger Woods down, no one says no to JP for this charity event, which is usually held every five years.

So, less than a month after LIV's launch in England, several of their players – now two tournaments into their virgin schedule – joined tour loyalists, Woods included, at this two-day event on the course that will stage the 2027 Ryder Cup.

Professional golf was in turmoil. Meetings were being held throughout what should have been a celebratory gathering. Woods was in talks with Rory McIlroy, among others, trying to thrash out ideas on how to counter the existential threat posed by the PIF-funded upstarts. Indeed, they worked so closely, both players contracted Covid just a week before The Open Championship.

Even more virulent were endless rumours of other players, including European Ryder Cup captain Henrik Stenson, being about to switch to Greg Norman's circuit. After his first round, the normally affable Swede politely turned down my request for an interview. That had never happened before and his refusal fuelled a feeling that his head was being turned. This despite the forthcoming honour of leading Europe's attempt to regain that precious trophy in Rome.

Those golfers who had already signed for Saudi riches endured a torrid few weeks of criticism. They were seen as greedy mercenaries who were ruining their sport. They were Saudi shills on the make and they were doing it with scant regard for the rest of the game.

The criticism had followed them to LIV's second event at Pumpkin Ridge Golf Club in Portland, Oregon where Branden Grace landed the $4m jackpot and Dustin Johnson's 4Aces line-up, which included Talor Gooch, Patrick Reed and Pat Perez, secured team spoils.

'Saudi Arabia is trying to sportswash their reputation,' claimed Sean Passananti, whose father died in the 9/11 attacks carried out by al Qaeda terrorists, at a protest ahead of LIV's second event. Even though Saudi Arabia's government has always denied involvement, 15 of the attackers were Saudi nationals. 'Instead of admitting their support and funding of al Qaeda, they are trying through the honourable game of golf to buy legitimacy.'

Headlines across the world continued to condemn LIV golfers. Meanwhile, tour loyalists shrugged, acknowledging that the rebels had made a lucrative choice but that they would now not be welcomed back into the traditional fold.

Ian Poulter, Spaniard Adrián Otaegui and South Africa's Justin Harding appealed against the DP World Tour ban that prevented them from competing in the upcoming Scottish Open. The initial hearing was on Monday 4 July while Poulter played at Adare Manor. He had arrived on a private charter from Oregon that had been laid on for the LIV players. The Scottish Open was three days away and the following week was the 150th Open Championship at St Andrews. This was peak season for British golf.

Poulter and I spoke after his first round in Ireland and while we conversed, he repeatedly glanced at his phone because the verdict was imminent. 'I've been a member of the European Tour for 24 years,' he said. 'I've played 389 tournaments, seven Ryder Cups and I've been vice captain for one of those. I've played more than my minimum requirement every single year and with all that in mind I've never given up my membership once, even when I went to the PGA Tour to play. . . . I feel offended that I'm being suspended from playing.'

Poulter believed there was space in the calendar to play on multiple tours and did not see why LIV should be regarded as different from any of the other circuits around the world. 'Have I ever been denied a release before, for any event anywhere in the world?' he said, eyes widening in tandem with outstretched arms that formed an exasperated shrug. 'Is it any different? That's my question,' the 46-year-old Englishman added as the pitch of his voice rose.

He outlined a vision where he would like to still play DP World Tour events in a slimmed-down schedule that would also include the LIV Tour, allowing him more time with his family. 'Yes the purses are huge, there's no getting away from that. So to provide for Luke, Amy, Lily and Josh [his children] and their kids is something that I'm actually proud of and I'm proud of the option to play [LIV] because I think the product is really good as well. You guys might not think that, but I do.'

He continued: 'If you're offered an opportunity to play golf and have more time to yourself and with your family and earn more money then, if you don't take it, I think you've made a mistake.' He went on to say that no one has any right to cap how much people should earn. 'I keep being asked, "Aren't you rich enough?" No one tells Elon Musk or Jeff Bezos that they've earned too much and that they should stop going to work and trying to make more money.' Poulter then walked off, checking his emails once more.

It had been an impassioned plea from someone who was convinced he was still a European Tour loyalist. Wentworth HQ did not see it that way and nor did a legendary figure of European golf who heard an edited version of Poulter's comments on BBC Radio 5Live that evening. His text to me made clear his disdain for someone who had been a Ryder Cup teammate on several occasions. It went on to say: 'Shocking to think he believes in suing the Tour is a good idea. . Have your cake. . eat it. . and sue the Baker!! Say he wins. . I wouldn't want to be him in the Locker Room. .'

But Poulter, Otaegui and Harding did win a stay on their bans. The news came through on the Monday evening. Upon learning the verdict, the veteran player who had been texting me described the outcome as 'shocking'.

Arbitration body Sport Resolutions' verdict was pending a full hearing. It meant LIV rebels were, temporarily at least, free to play on the DP World Tour. The case was heard by His Honour Phillip Sycamore CBE. This retired Circuit Judge ruled in favour of the appellants on procedural grounds, finding that European Tour boss Keith Pelley was not able to act impartially. 'There was no process by which the Chief Executive came at all close to replicating the guidelines for a disciplinary hearing,' Judge Sycamore concluded. 'It was unfortunate that he was on record as having made strong adverse public statements on LIV, and clearly as Chief Executive he had a vested interest in promoting the interests of the Respondent [the DP World Tour] over the interests of LIV.'

This heralded perhaps one of the most fractious periods in the golf wars. LIV players were competing in Scotland, an event jointly sanctioned by the PGA Tour, but they were far from welcome. Harding took full advantage of being allowed to play with an opening 65. He was clearly not put off by the legal proceedings. 'I'm pleased to have been able to come here and play,' he told me after his round. The South African said the crowds had been very generous but admitted: 'There are times when it is a little bit uncomfortable when you are walking around, but at the same time each to our own. We've got to look after ourselves really.'

Harding failed to capitalise on his strong start and eventually finished 66th in a tournament won by American Xander Schauffele. Poulter posted rounds of 78 and 72 to comfortably miss the cut while Otaegui played all four rounds in 3-over-par to finish tied for 42nd.

The bandwagon then made the short journey north of the Firth of Forth to the home of golf, St Andrews, for the 150th Open. It was a historic occasion and a thrilling championship that momentarily deflected attention from the rancour and indignation gripping the game. But, the sport was still embarking on an uncharted, controversial and tortuous journey towards a highly uncertain future.

6
BIG GUNS AND BIG MONEY

'I just won the British Open, and you're asking about that?'

Cameron Smith

It is a long and winding road from Delaware to PGA Tour headquarters at Ponte Vedra Beach in north Florida. Wilmington, in the small mid-Atlantic state, is where a significant and potentially awkward bend was rounded by the PGA Tour thanks to an orchestrated intervention from golf's two biggest stars.

By mid-summer in 2022, Tiger Woods and Rory McIlroy had seen enough. In Ireland, they had acquired Covid but more importantly a collective belief that it was time to stall the LIV march. It had been accelerating and was heading to an inevitable high with the signing of a newly crowned Open champion.

In August, Cameron Smith's imminent defection to the tour, run by his fellow Australian Greg Norman, was an open secret. He had done nothing to dispel the rumours while answering the Press Association's Phil Casey on the July evening of the Aussie's Open triumph at St Andrews. 'I had spoken to one of the LIV players off the record,' Casey told me. 'I was actually working on a line I'd heard about Henrik Stenson joining LIV. But while we were talking about potential moves the subject came up of an all-Australian team that would include Cameron Smith.'

'Come the Sunday night of The Open, Smith was the champion,' Casey added. 'No one particularly wants to ask anything controversial at the winner's press conference. I certainly wasn't keen to be that person, but I didn't know if anyone else was going to ask it.'

So at a packed champion's news conference, usually an unequivocally joyous and celebratory occasion, the atmosphere took an uncharacteristically tense turn, despite Casey's diplomatic phrasing of his question.

'Cam, apologies for having to bring this up in these circumstances,' the experienced and well-respected reporter said. 'But your name continues to be mentioned and has been mentioned to me this week about LIV golf. What's your position? Are you interested? Is there any truth to suggestions that you might be signing?'

'I just won the British Open, and you're asking about that?' the champion replied, nonplussed. 'I think that's pretty not that good.'

'I appreciate that, but the question is still there. Are you interested at all? Is there any truth in that?'

'I don't know, mate. My team around me worries about all that stuff. I'm here to win golf tournaments.'

Casey later told me: 'If I was way off beam he could have said that it was rubbish, but he didn't.' It was clear Smith was going. That 'no comment' was nigh on confirmatory. 'Our role is not to be cheerleaders,' Casey added. 'Everybody likes good stories of people winning and it was a great story the way that he did it. But if people don't ask questions to get news then you're not going to find out stuff until it is announced.'

For traditional golf fans, Smith's non-committal reaction to the LIV question probably soured the evening. It had been a day to celebrate golf in all its majesty, a momentous final round in the oldest and most prestigious golf tournament in the world. Smith beat McIlroy into third place to land his first major title with a sparkling closing 64. It was a fitting way to seal the title at a landmark 150th Open.

And it was a stinging defeat for the Northern Irishman, who had not won one of the big four titles since his fourth major success at the 2014 PGA Championship. He had gone into the last round at the iconic Old Course sharing the lead with Ryder Cup teammate Viktor Hovland. They were 16-under-par, four strokes clear of halfway leader Smith and American up-and-comer Cameron Young, who eventually took the runner-up spoils.

There is no such thing as a script in sport, which is one of its intrinsic attractions. But, then again, it had seemed a perfect narrative for McIlroy to triumph at the home of golf, a place where he had missed, through a freak football injury, the chance to defend his lone Open success seven years earlier. This defeat was surely an even bigger blow because he had lost to someone ready to jump to LIV. McIlroy and Smith spoke in the days that followed The Open. It was said to have been an 'awkward' conversation.

Smith was going, but not until the completion of the PGA Tour season the following month at the Tour Championship in Atlanta. His brilliant victory at St Andrews left the then 28-year-old well-positioned to potentially land the tour's season-ending $18m FedEx Cup jackpot. So it was worth staying with the status quo – for now.

As it turned out, Smith faded to finish 20th in the season-long standings and banked a mere $640,000. His golf lacked the authority of his glorious performance at The Open and indeed the quality of his March victory at the prestigious Players Championship. Perhaps his impending defection weighed heavy, perhaps he was spent. Either way, with the PGA Tour season complete, he was soon depositing a reported $116m for signing his LIV contract. He admitted in a Sky Sports interview that he was 'ready to cop some heat'.

When Smith's signing was announced, Mike Clayton believed the talented Queenslander was limiting his chances of adding to his major tally. 'Cam Smith is the most bizarre signing they have got,' the former tour player told me. 'When Adam Scott and Geoff Ogilvy won their majors you would have sworn they were more than one major guys. I think Cam is a one major guy if you go to LIV

because you are forsaking your competitiveness for money. You are not going to
be as sharp playing that tour as you are playing the PGA Tour. Maybe he decided
"maybe I'm a one major guy, I'll take $100m and I'll ride off into the sun with it
and I'll play LIV." But I think he had a shot at being a two or three major guy. I
think if you sign with LIV you probably pass that up but only history will tell us
if that view is right or not.'

Before Smith's exit came confirmation that Stenson had also been lured by
LIV's lucrative offer. It left Europe without a Ryder Cup captain and Luke
Donald, initially overlooked, took on the role. 'I've signed a contract as Henrik
did and I'm giving them my word,' the Englishman told me. 'That's all I can do
and I promise you I will be seeing this through until the end. I've not been
approached by LIV to play on their tour but I have this amazing opportunity to
be this Ryder Cup captain.'

Smith's departure was a hammer-blow to the PGA Tour. Their Tour
Championship is the culmination of a short series of playoff tournaments that
began with the FedEx St Jude Championship at TPC Southwind in mid-August,
before moving to the BMW Championship at Wilmington Country Club in
Delaware the following week. And this is where Woods and McIlroy staged their
intervention. They knew Smith was leaving and rumours circulated that a
number of other players would follow suit. It was now vital to come up with
plans to stem the flow.

Woods had played The Open but was still feeling the legacy of his
devastating February 2021 car crash that nearly cost him his right leg. He
hobbled around the Old Course and missed the halfway cut. It seemed clear
he was no longer a competitive golfer. Indeed, the 15-times major champion
was nowhere near eligibility for the closing tournaments of the 2022 PGA
Tour campaign. Fields whittle down progressively through the playoffs to
leave the season's leading 30 golfers, who contest the Tour Championship at
East Lake, Atlanta.

Woods might easily have been on vacation or looking after business interests
far away from the game. McIlroy had no such option and was in the thick of the
battle for the playoff spoils. But both were prioritising trying to salvage the future
of their beleaguered circuit.

'I know what the PGA Tour stands for,' Woods, a record-equalling 82-time winner, had told reporters at St Andrews. He sees the tour's future existence as the pre-eminent circuit as a measurable gateway to much of his extraordinary legacy. Future champions should be able to compare their feats with his and we can be pretty certain few will get close. 'The players who have chosen to go to LIV and to play there, I disagree with it,' he said. 'I think that what they've done is turned their back on what has allowed them to get to this position.

'What is the incentive to go out there and earn it in the dirt?' he added. And he speculated that the younger LIV recruits might be sacrificing all that is glorious in the game. 'Some of these players may not ever get a chance to play in major championships. That is a possibility.'

For much of his career, Woods has fought shy of revealing his deepest-held opinions to reporters. Usually, he avoids controversy wherever possible, rarely adding fuel to whatever fire might be raging at the time. Not on this occasion. These were powerful words. And for all his usual reticence, they came from the man universally regarded as possessing the strongest voice. 'He is the hero that we've all looked up to,' said McIlroy, who had a Woods poster on his boyhood bedroom wall, to reporters before the BMW Championship. 'His voice carries further than anyone else's in the game of golf. His role is navigating us to a place where we all think we should be.'

But it was clear that even Woods' words could not always match the power of massive money. Especially when the game was split and mired in uncivil war. 'It's definitely fractured,' admitted Olympic champion Xander Schauffele. And Smith, golf's hottest property, was joining fellow box office major winners such as Phil Mickelson, Brooks Koepka and Bryson DeChambeau by signing for the Saudi Arabia-funded upstart circuit. Koepka's defection immediately after June's US Open had been another savage blow to the PGA Tour.

McIlroy and Woods are tight. They are close neighbours and even closer friends and business partners. Sensing the need to flex muscles of player power, the Northern Irishman called a meeting of the biggest names competing in Wilmington for the afternoon of Tuesday 16 August. Woods was his star witness. 'I think it shows how much he cares about the players that are coming through and are going to be the next generation,' McIlroy said.

Woods flew from his Florida home by private jet. Justin Thomas, the PGA Tour player closest to Woods, said at the BMW Championship press conference: 'It probably was just not something that he felt was appropriate to do over Zoom. . . . I think it shows how passionate he is about golf and wanting to improve it.'

The record holder for time spent as world number one was accompanied by former Ryder Cup teammate Rickie Fowler. He was still one of golf's most popular figures despite a downturn in form that rendered him ineligible for that week's BMW Championship. Woods wore a checked casual shirt and dark jeans as he emerged from the jet after it landed at Atlantic Aviation's private airport at New Castle, Delaware. He then drove Fowler in a SUV nearly 10 miles north on the Interstate 95 (I95) to the Hotel du Pont in downtown Wilmington. They arrived for what appeared to be one of the most important gatherings of the golf wars era.

Woods' presence and influence was highly significant. 'I think it's pretty apparent that whenever we all get in the room, there's an alpha in there, and it's not me,' McIlroy deadpanned. Thomas went further, saying: 'I think if someone like him is passionate about it, no offence to all of us, but that's really all that matters.'

With a PGA Tour Player Advisory Council meeting planned for the next day, the timing was vital. Commissioner Jay Monahan had held a Q&A session with players the previous week in Memphis and was scheduled to field another barrage of questions. Woods and McIlroy felt he should be armed with a plan and they had an idea. 'We're moving into a different era,' McIlroy observed. 'And we just have to think about things a little differently.'

The plan was simple – the best players playing each other more frequently and for bigger money. They needed the leading stars on side, hence calling this Tuesday meeting to set the ball rolling. It was accurately portrayed by *Golf Digest* as the evening that 'Rory and Tiger took the PGA Tour's fight with LIV Golf into their own hands.'

It was the meeting where the notion of 'elevated' events gathered greater emphasis from the initial plan to stage just eight such tournaments. 'The important thing is the players got together and decided this is the direction we want to go,' said veteran tour loyalist and former US Ryder Cup captain Davis Love III. 'We understand the game and we understand access and . . . a little bit we understand marketing. And we have to do what Tiger and Rory and the big guns want to do.'

The meeting lasted three and a half hours. There were around 20 golfers present, including the tour's biggest stars, the likes of Jordan Spieth, PGA champion Thomas and US Open winner Matt Fitzpatrick. Up-and-coming Chilean star Joaquin Niemann was present as the players thrashed out a plan of how to counter the LIV threat. Also in the room was businessman Colin Neville, a partner at the Raine Group who had been an influential figure in the ultimately failed bid to launch the Premier Golf League.

Those involved in Delaware remained tight-lipped afterwards. 'I think I'd be pretty unhappy if I saw one of those guys from last night just blabbering to you guys what we talked about,' said Schauffele. 'You probably wouldn't get invited back to the next meeting.'

Even the usually loquacious McIlroy was reticent but did divulge: 'All the top players on this tour are in agreement and alignment of where we should go going forward. And that was awesome.'

They discussed a plan to have a series of tournaments that could involve as few as 50 players, but they would be the top stars and they would be competing for at least $15m. Most of the 12 tournaments would be worth $20m and the prize fund for the tour's flagship Players Championship would grow to $25m. There was an urgency that this should be nailed down fast. Golf does not usually move so quickly.

Monahan can be eloquent but is a reluctant public speaker. The commissioner limits detailed contact with the media to his tour's biggest weeks – The Players in March and the Tour Championship in late summer. Seven days after the Delaware meeting he was in Atlanta for the season finale and as a result of the previous week's meeting he had news to impart at a press conference. He called it 'a remarkable moment' and spoke of partnering 'with our players' before confirming that another four events would be elevated to an average prize fund of $20m. They would be on a par with the eight that had been announced in June.

But to Monahan, the biggest news was the seemingly unequivocal support from those leading stars who had met in Wilmington. 'It's the headline,' he stated. 'Our top players are making a commitment to play in all 12 elevated events, as well as The Players Championship, the Masters Tournament, the PGA Championship, the US Open, and The Open Championship.

'They will also add at least three more PGA Tour events to their schedules. Our top players are firmly behind the tour, helping us deliver an unmatched product to our fans, who will be all but guaranteed to see the best players competing against each other in 20 events or more throughout the season.' The tub-thumping tour boss called it an 'extraordinary and unprecedented commitment.'

Monahan added that the tour's controversial Player Impact Program would double with the top 20 most impactful stars splitting $100m. To be eligible for a share of the spoils, players would be allowed to miss only one of the tournaments that would be termed 'designated' events. Eventually they were given the moniker 'signature'. The commissioner also announced that every fully exempt player on the tour would be guaranteed to earn at least $500,000, regardless of their season performances.

Where was all this money coming from? Monahan admitted the tour would be raiding its reserves but insisted it was generating more money than ever and that existing sponsors were on board to stump up bigger financial commitments. But it was a punt. No one could be sure this was an affordable package, especially with legal fees mounting.

The commissioner was taking the status quo down a very similar trail to the one blazed by LIV. Limited fields, guaranteed money and dipping into vast financial reserves. Furthermore, the backing of the top stars was not as universal as Monahan had claimed. Smith was already a lost cause, but Niemann, who was involved in the Delaware discussions, soon joined The Open champion in signing for LIV.

Other top players were not enamoured with being compelled to commit to so many tournaments. Jon Rahm, a Spaniard who feels obliged to play European events, forebodingly wondered how he could cram everything into an already crowded schedule. 'I hope, maybe between some of the Europeans that play

PGA Tour more full time, we can reach an agreement of maybe figuring out a schedule to where it makes it easier for us,' Rahm said at the BMW Championship press conference.

It emerged that grievances were being aired to McIlroy, now comfortably the prime figure in the locker room. Fascinatingly, they came into the public domain after Netflix's *Full Swing* (2023) documentary eavesdropped at the Tour Championship his conversation with high-ranking tour official Andy Pazder. In the East Lake clubhouse, the cameras show McIlroy relating conversations with players who expressed reservations. He stated what his response to them had been: 'If I'm willing to do this, so should you.' He told Pazder: 'I could say to these guys, no other athletes in the world get to choose when and where they play. We've all just gotten a little soft.'

It was a stance that did not pass the test of time. But the PGA Tour now had a framework to its fightback. The politics did nothing to distract McIlroy, who romped to the $18m jackpot at the Tour Championship. Off the course, with the help of Woods, his impact seemed to have been even greater, although it was not until early the next spring that the bosses at Ponte Vedra Beach were ready to unveil refined schedule plans to their membership. In the meantime, LIV headed to their own Florida destination – or at least one that belonged to a kindred spirit.

7

THE TRUMP CARD

'Do you think Biden could do that?'

America's 45th commander-in-chief

Golf media centres are usually temporary structures, reflective of the nomadic nature of the sport. They are giant white tents with scoreboards and video monitors. The sound of mobile generators powering noisy air conditioning is a familiar accompaniment. But not for LIV's season-ending Team Championship, another bold and brash tournament worth a colossal $50m and regarded vital to the long-term strategy of the start-up circuit.

For this week in October 2022, spent close to Miami's international airport, reporters were housed in the grand Ivanka Trump Ballroom at Trump Doral, the home of the famed Blue Monster course. Beneath glistening chandeliers, reporters shivered in an air-conditioned chill. The system was in keeping with the surrounds: hi-tech, ultra-efficient and silent.

But the environment remained loud.

Noise came from the room's occupants, the majority of whom were LIV employees working for the tour's media channels. Raised voices were needed to be heard over a thumping bassline pumped through loudspeakers. The atmosphere in the room felt significantly younger compared with the usual, where mainly reserved, greying, male, middle-aged reporters are in attendance. It was certainly a stark and youthful contrast to the familiar feel ahead of a pre-tournament press conference.

At the head of the room was a stage in front of prominent black LIV billboards. Eight seats and microphones were in place for the team captains who would be introduced to the media. Just after 9 a.m., they entered the room, led by the then four-times major winner Brooks Koepka. Behind him came fellow team skippers, Ian Poulter, Joaquin Niemann, Kevin Na, Martin Kaymer, Cameron Smith, Phil Mickelson and Bubba Watson. They had won 15 major titles between them.

Each golfer took their seat. Mickelson looked confused as to which one to use until it became clear that the winner of three Masters green jackets should be located centre stage. As they entered, the hubbub died down and, barely noticeable, Greg Norman looked on contentedly. He leaned, inconspicuously, against the white walls of the ballroom, effectively camouflaged by his open-neck white shirt.

For LIV's front man, this was a huge week. An opportunity for the team format – the means identified to pay LIV's way in the long term – to truly take off as a concept. These would be the first steps towards a potential franchise system that could yield big bucks and allow the project to make a return on the massive investment made by Saudi Arabia's PIF.

Norman was bullish with his corporate speak in the build-up, saying in a press release for the event: 'The Invitational Series finale, played at the fan-favorite Blue Monster at Doral, is befitting our game-changing model that delivers an innovative, one-of-a-kind experience for players and fans. I'm looking forward to this monumental event that will harness the beloved traits of team golf and head-to-head rivalries in a historic setting.' The former world number one had also signalled LIV's intent by stating that the event, 'will propel us into a team-focused league from 2023 onward.'

But for this press conference, he was silent, as were the audience of LIV employees and journalists as the captains were introduced. The opening proceedings carried a similar feel to a winning Ryder Cup news conference. On those occasions, the victorious team sits together, full of high jinks, jokes and mickey-taking. The difference here was that a ball had yet to be struck.

In charge of proceedings was Su-Ann Heng, a former top-ranked golfer in her native Singapore and a lead on-course commentator for LIV's streamed coverage. Heng introduced the top table and the teams they represented. The remaining players stood in the wings while she explained a somewhat convoluted format.

Eight teams would play on the Friday for the right to join the top-four seeded line-ups for the weekend action. Determining which teams would play each other was akin to informal schoolyard sport, where line-ups are likely to be assembled by picking the best players first, leaving the weakest to last. In this version, the higher-seeded captains could choose the poorest opposition.

'Let's get this thing kicked off and started,' Heng said. 'We're going to start with Smash GC, Brooks Koepka. Brooks, who did you choose to play the quarter-finals with?'

At this point, Mickelson, looking far more upbeat and cocksure than the haunted figure we had seen at many of the earlier LIV events, interjected with the sense of mischief that characterised so much of his career in the media spotlight.

'Let me just clarify that he doesn't have to pick from the last four, he can pick from all seven teams,' the veteran smiled. 'So if you want a rematch of the '21 PGA, you could pick our team and we could play each other.' The veteran was alluding to the PGA Championship of a year earlier at Kiawah Island, where Mickelson had sensationally pipped Koepka, a former world number one, to become the oldest major champion. 'I'm just clarifying the rules because I don't know if everybody understands,' Mickelson added with deadpan timing.

'I'll continue,' Koepka, dressed in a mint shirt, drawled seemingly non-plussed. 'But if you want to play, we can play . . . you probably don't know this because you've never been number one in the world.'

'That's true,' Mickelson admitted.

'They give you a little trophy. I've got two of those, so I could bring one of them to show you.'

'That's a beautiful green shirt. Do you have a green jacket?' Mickelson countered, reminding his rival of past successes at the Masters.

'I do not, but I will, though, don't worry,' Koepka countered. 'Anyway, we did not choose Phil's team, we chose the Niblicks.'

This was the team captained by Bubba Watson, who was not playing because of injuries that had kept him out of action all season. He sat at the end of the table and looked to his right and joined the theme by saying: 'What? I've got a green jacket, Phil.'

Each knockabout barb generated laughter from the LIV employees in the audience and from fellow pros on the top table. One of the execs from the tour's PR company, Performance54, later suggested there had been a genuine edge, real animosity, but it felt as forced as a prelude to a made-for-TV pro wrestling bout. It felt out of place in a sport such as golf but it was symptomatic of an enterprise where entertainment is the name of the game. Part of the project to revolutionise the sport, trying to strip it of formality.

But it was also noticeable that the touch points of the barbs were the Masters and the US PGA. In other words, the majors remained golf's measuring sticks, even in this knockabout LIV era.

Koepka continued by deliberately mispronouncing Watson's Christian name. 'Booba has been calling me the wrong name all year – Bruce – so I felt like it was a good opportunity to get back at him.'

'I'm not worried,' Watson replied. 'You might have more injuries than me. You are getting older.'

Heng interrupted the joshing and revealed that instead of the crocked Watson, Harold Varner had been nominated to face Koepka, the Smash GC captain. 'Bubba, tell me what you're thinking. You're the first team to get picked. I don't know what they're insinuating here, but tell us what you're thinking?'

'Harold told me he's definitely getting a point against Bruce.'

The levity continued as the line-ups for Friday's action were revealed, and players traded jovial barbs until reporters were invited to ask their questions. Then it turned serious. There was a Jumbo-sized elephant in the room.

That morning, the *Guardian* published an interview with Rory McIlroy, who had claimed a feeling of 'betrayal' that former friends and Ryder Cup teammates had jeopardised their future participation in the biennial match by joining LIV. He was referring to the likes of Ian Poulter, Lee Westwood, Sergio García, Graeme McDowell and, by implication, Henrik Stenson, who lost the European captaincy for joining the breakaway tour. This interview was the latest verbal grenade tossed in LIV's direction by a man on top of the golfing world. McIlroy had returned to the world number one position by retaining the CJ Cup on the PGA Tour the previous weekend.

For a Ryder Cup legend such as Poulter to be accused of betrayal demanded a response from the Englishman. I called for the microphone and asked the question: 'There was an interview with Rory McIlroy that's been published this week in which he described you guys going to LIV, in Ryder Cup terms, as a "betrayal". I need to ask you what your reaction to that was?'

Poulter stared back. 'A betrayal?' he started. 'We can still qualify for the team as far as I'm aware. Unless we've been told we can't qualify, then I'm still ready to play as much as I possibly can and try and make that team.'

'I think the point he was making was the very fact that you may have jeopardised a Ryder Cup future, and likewise for Lee and Henrik and Graeme. I don't know if they'd be prepared to comment?'

'I mean, look, my commitment to the Ryder Cup, I think, goes before me,' Poulter replied. 'I don't think that should ever come into question. I've always wanted to play Ryder Cups and have played with as much passion as anyone else that I've ever seen play a Ryder Cup. You know, I don't know where that comment really has come from, to be honest.'

Westwood indicated he did not want to reply. Stenson said that he had not seen the newspaper article and McDowell said the same. Afterwards, in the corridor outside the ballroom, Poulter made clear his irritation at being asked about McIlroy's comments. He felt it was unfair to have been put in that position and suggested he had 'had enough' of the way he was being treated by the golf media. Poulter has always been one of the most amenable and quotable golfers, indeed he was honoured by the Association of Golf Writers in 2014 with their Arnold Palmer Open Award for his strong relationship with the media. That connection turned sour following his move to LIV.

There were other questions in the news conference that reflected the ongoing battle with the golfing establishment. James Corrigan of the *Telegraph* asked Mickelson: 'Phil, a couple of weeks ago you said you saw LIV trending upwards and PGA Tour trending downwards. I'm not sure if you saw, but Rory McIlroy came out and said that that's just propaganda on your behalf. Can you speak to that?'

'Well, first of all, what a great win he had last week,' Mickelson began diplomatically. 'He played some great golf. I think it was an impressive victory. Maybe I shouldn't have said stuff like that, I don't know, but if I'm just looking at LIV Golf and where we are today to where we were six, seven months ago and people are saying this is dead in the water . . . and here we are today, a force in the game that's not going away, that has players of this calibre that are moving professional golf throughout the world. . . . It's pretty remarkable how far LIV Golf has come in the last six, seven months. I don't think anybody can disagree with that.'

This reply drew applause from the room, the vast majority of those clapping being attached to LIV. The golf media did not join in; our reaction was as cold as the air conditioning. But it was not a snub. Applauding an interviewee in a professional environment is simply not the done thing, regardless of LIV's efforts to change the golfing landscape.

Mickelson was the target for the next question on the McIlroy interview in which the world's best player called for an end to the 'us and them' conflict that had enveloped the sport in 2022. The three-times Masters champion can be a canny operator in interview rooms and adopted full deflection mode.

'You know, I think a lot of Rory,' he replied. 'I really have the utmost respect for him, and I look at what he's done in the game and how he's played this year and his win last week and number one in the world now, and I have a ton of respect for him. We'll have three months off after this event to talk about things like that . . . but this week something is happening that I don't want to deflect focus on.'

LIV wanted attention to centre on their golf that week. There was a tournament to be played, the like of which professional golf had never seen before. And before that, there was the pro-am and that was always going to be all about one man – the host – former US president Donald J. Trump.

America's 45th commander-in-chief had craved acceptance and recognition from golf's hierarchy. One of the reasons he bought the famous Turnberry resort in Ayrshire was to host The Open Championship, the oldest and most prestigious tournament. He was forced to brush aside the notion that his lack of political correctness might lead to the famed course disappearing from The Open rota. He rebranded it Trump Turnberry after his 2014 purchase of the course and hotel, which most recently held the 2009 Open won by Stewart Cink.

When he announced £150m worth of improvements, I suggested his controversial campaigning style for the presidency might result in the R&A looking past Turnberry for courses to stage golf's most historic major. He told me I was a 'bad reporter' adding: 'Maybe one day you will apologise.'

History is not on his side on that one.

Despite course improvements that arguably make it the finest links in Scotland, Trump Turnberry has not come close to holding The Open again. That will remain the case for as long as it stays in his hands. 'We will not return until we are convinced that the focus will be on the championship, the players and the course itself,' said R&A chief executive Martin Slumbers in a statement in early 2021. 'And we do not believe that is achievable in the current circumstances.'

Trump's best chance of holding a men's major was going to be the 2022 US PGA Championship, which was slated for the Trump National Golf Club at Bedminster, New Jersey. However, in the immediate aftermath of the January 6 Capitol riots of 2021, the PGA of America decided it had become inappropriate for their biggest event to be played on a course owned by the country's outgoing president. The championship was switched to Southern Hills Country Club in Tulsa, Oklahoma.

This proved one of several snubs by the golfing establishment. In 2017, Trump fumed when the PGA Tour moved a World Golf Championships tournament from his beloved Doral to – of all places – Mexico, the country at the heart of so much of his disparaging campaign rhetoric. After more than half a century on tour, his Miami resort no longer enjoyed such elevated status and Bedminster being dropped by a major was a further blow.

So it made sense for Trump to jump into bed with LIV, united as they are in opposition to the golf firmament. He also had links with LIV's backers. It was reported that Saudi Arabia's PIF ploughed $2b into a firm controlled by Trump's son-in-law, Jared Kushner, and $1b into a company run by former Trump treasury secretary, Steve Mnuchin.

'I've known these people for a long time in Saudi Arabia and they have been friends of mine,' Trump told reporters, when LIV (rather than the PGA Championship) arrived at Bedminster. This was in July 2022 for what was the third tournament of their inaugural season. 'What they are doing for golf is so great; what they are doing for the players is so great. The salaries are going to go way up . . . nobody ever knew it was going to be a gold rush like this.'

Families of 9/11 relatives picketed the course in protest at Saudi Arabia's involvement in the 2001 attacks. 'Trump is the former head of state,' said Brett Eagleson, founder of 9/11 Justice. 'He's the former most powerful person in the world. You're supposed to have a set of morals.'

Undeterred, Trump arrived for the pre-tournament pro-am at Bedminster fashionably 10 minutes late. Norman was there to greet the former president and his son Eric as they joined Dustin Johnson and Bryson DeChambeau. Golf is normally played with a maximum of four players per group, but this was to be an unorthodox 'five-ball' with Yasir Al-Rumayyan, the governor of PIF and chairman of Newcastle United football club becoming the fifth man in the group.

Kushner and his wife Ivanka watched as Trump, wearing his trademark 'Make America Great Again' (MAGA) cap, teed off. 'I'm glad that's over with,' said the former president with uncharacteristic humility after despatching his opening shot. He then proceeded to drive off in his buggy, forgetting that the PIF governor was still to hit.

Trump's presence in that pro-am did not result in masses descending on the main event the following day. Crowds were relatively sparse, and Mickelson was heckled with 'Do it for the Saudi royal family,' before dumping a tee shot into a green-side bunker on the 16th hole.

In the *Guardian* newspaper, writer Bryan Armen Graham provided an eye-witness account of the underwhelming atmosphere. He wrote: 'Organisers declined to issue official attendance figures, but Friday's session played out before no more than a couple thousand fans despite a largely papered house and $75 grounds passes going for $2 on the secondary market.'

But the script for the tournament itself was deserving of a decent-sized audience. Aside from the host, one man was centre of attention that July week: the deposed European Ryder Cup captain Stenson. His signing was a sensational coup that struck at the very heart of golf's establishment. The Swede played a wide-eyed innocent when he was paraded by his new employers, protesting that he had not left European golf in the lurch. 'I made every arrangement possible to be able to fulfil my captain's duties,' he insisted to the press at a LIV news conference. 'And I've had great help here from LIV to be able to do that. And still, the decision was made that I was to be removed. I'm obviously disappointed over the situation. But it is what it is, and yeah, we move on from there now.'

Stenson moved on in style.

He has the reputation of playing his best golf when he is at his most financially secure. Earlier in his career, when he fell victim to jailed fraudster Allen Stanford, his form fell off a cliff and it was a long way back to the top of the game. Now, his inflated signing-on fee – thought to be around $40m – acted as further balm to his golf. He was brilliant across the three rounds of his LIV debut and despite having fallen to 171st in the world, he claimed the $4m winner's cheque. Stenson beat Johnson and Matthew Wolff by two strokes. He later told reporters in Abu Dhabi: 'In all the circumstances, that was one of the best achievements of my career, behind only winning The Open and The Players Championship. I'm at my best when my back is against the wall.'

LIV could not have asked for a more newsworthy champion. 'It's about looking forward,' Stenson smiled in the immediate aftermath. 'I'm super proud with the focus I managed to have this week.' He added that he felt 'extra motivation' given the backdrop to his recruitment. 'That's been a bit of a theme over the course of my career, I think, when I really want something, I manage to dig a little bit deeper.'

Trump, meanwhile, was living with the idea that wider recognition of his golf properties would now come via LIV. His Doral course sits at a busy junction not far from Miami's international airport, where a frenetic crossroads of six-lane thoroughfares is monitored by traffic lights that demand utmost patience and attention to avoid missing what seem the briefest of green lights.

On the Wednesday two days before the Team Championship, my Uber was directed on to the wide driveway that arcs its way through a scattering of sumptuous villas and swimming pools to the drop-off area for the resort's reception. This is also the clubhouse for the Doral course and there was little sign of anything significant occurring. No one batted an eyelid as I hauled, unhindered, cases of broadcast equipment towards the Ivanka Trump Ballroom.

The following day was pro-am day, which was perhaps not the time to arrive in the ostentatiously white jeep that was the vehicle for my taxi ride. There was now a heavy police presence at the busy intersection. Our car was stopped at the gates, the bemused driver – unaware of the presence of his country's immediate past president – was ordered to open the back of the jeep. A large German shepherd dog leapt aboard and excitedly sniffed around my cases, but none of the broadcast equipment triggered any reaction. We were waved on.

When I reached the practice putting green that morning there was a line of secret service golf buggies. Several pros were honing their skills, while Poulter stood chatting to a British journalist; the player was still sore at being asked about McIlroy's comments of 'betrayal' the previous day.

At 8.55 a.m. came a palpable sense of movement. The buggies started to edge towards the first tee, with Trump leading the way in a pure white shirt, black trousers and distinctive scarlet MAGA cap. He drove slowly, a middle-aged blonde female official from Doral was in the passenger seat. When he arrived at the first tee, Koepka, his playing partner for the front nine, was waiting along with Trump's son Eric and 15-year-old granddaughter Kai – daughter of Donald Jr – and easily the most talented of the amateur golfers in the group.

Music played from nearby speakers. Water could be heard tumbling from adjacent artificial waterfalls, all beneath perfect blue skies. Trump bent low, with widened legs saving his hamstrings, to tee up his ball. He took three gentle practice swings before swiping it down the right side of the fairway. 'Beauty!' called one of a handful of sycophantic onlookers who had made it into this otherwise behind-closed-doors pro-am.

'Do you think Biden could do that?' questioned the 76-year-old who was about to announce a third run at the presidency. Trump answered his own question before anyone else could speak. 'I don't think so!'

A group of reporters followed him down the first, and on the second tee, Riath Al-Samarrai, of the *Daily Mail*, got in first. 'What do you think of LIV, Mr President?'

'It's great,' Trump replied. 'Unlimited money.'

He then marched off in search of his ball and we knew our next best chance of grabbing a word would come towards the end of the front nine when Koepka would be replaced by Sergio García as Trump's professional partner. I waited by the par-5 8th green, holding my BBC-branded recording equipment prominently because few things are more attractive to the former president than a microphone. I might get lucky. He stroked home a short putt for a five on that long 8th hole. It helped that the group could use the best drive of the four players, an even greater assistance because Koepka was smashing typically monstrous tee shots. Nevertheless, Trump was pleased with his putt and made eye contact with me as he strolled to the next tee. 'Another par,' he nodded, as if to say this had been all his own work.

We had to wait until he had completed all 18 holes before he spoke to the media. After the penultimate hole, Trump assured autograph hunters that he would satisfy their demands at the end of the round. I stood close to a knot of these spectators, many of them hoping to have their MAGA hats signed by their hero. But once he finished playing, the lure of my microphone proved a bigger attraction.

Trump breezed past the autograph seekers to join me and a small group of reporters, to whom he delivered his latest verdict on LIV. 'It's big time money and it's unlimited money,' he stated. 'The Saudis have done a good job and they love golf. It is different, we are having a good time.'

He then claimed that the PGA Tour had failed to take advantage of a chance to cash in on Saudi investment. 'The Tour mishandled it so badly,' he said. 'The

Tour, the people at the top, something should happen. They had an advantage of dealing with very good people with unlimited money. Something should have been worked out very easily and the Tour decided to go, as Richard Nixon said, to stonewall it. What the Tour did was bad for golf.'

He was taking the opportunity to talk up the breakaway tour, suggesting that they were on the verge of making significant signings to bolster their line-ups. 'A lot of others are coming over, big names,' Trump said. 'The star system is always very important in sports. You don't have the star system you are not going to be successful and they've got the stars.'

With what was admittedly the softest of softball questions, I asked whether the arrival of LIV signalled a return of big-time golf at Doral, given that a 54-year run as a PGA Tour venue had ended in 2017. 'Well it does,' Trump said, warming to the theme. 'It [Doral] doesn't need it because it is doing so well. It has been a great success from day one. The Tour wants to be here badly. The players are in love with this place, they always have been.'

He was now riffing, but at times it felt from an alternative golfing universe. Next, he was suggesting the R&A were ready to bring back their most prestigious championship to his beloved Turnberry. 'The Open wants to come back,' he said. 'It is rated the number one course in Europe now. We did a big surgery on Turnberry and it has gotten great reviews, even from people who hate me. They want The Open to go back.'

The R&A swiftly reacted by saying there was no change in their position.

Sergio García, Trump's playing partner for the back nine, meanwhile headed for the media centre to deliver a more substantive message. The Spaniard called time on his record-breaking Ryder Cup career. No European player had won more points, but he was not going to play enough tournaments on the DP World Tour to retain membership and seemingly, therefore, eligibility for the 2023 match in Rome. His walkout after just one round of September's BMW PGA Championship was another aggravating factor.

'Obviously I knew some of the things that might happen if I joined here,' García said at the LIV press conference. 'You can see that some of the guys on the other side don't really want me here. I don't want to be a burden to anyone and even less in a Ryder Cup. I'd rather be away from that, as much as it hurts, and make sure Europe has the best chance of winning, than me being there and three or four guys that are going to be upset.'

McIlroy was chief among the objectors. He used to be very close friends with García, who was an inspirational figure to the Northern Irishman in his formative years. They were Ryder Cup partners and McIlroy was a groomsman at the Spaniard's wedding. But LIV initially destroyed their relationship. They shared an angry text exchange in June 2022 around the time of the US Open as their friendship disintegrated, seemingly, irretrievably. When it later became apparent that García's honorary membership of the DP World Tour could make him eligible for the Ryder Cup, McIlroy reiterated his opposition. A terse 'No' was the answer when a Spanish journalist asked McIlroy if García should still be considered for selection for the 2023 match.

'I think it is very sad,' García told the *Telegraph*'s James Corrigan when they walked together at LIV's opening event of the 2023 season in Mexico. 'I think that we've done so many things together and had so many experiences that for him to throw that away just because I decided to go to a different tour, well, it doesn't seem very mature; lacking maturity, really. But Rory's got his own life, and he makes his own choices, the same way that I make mine. I respect his choices, but it seems like he doesn't respect the ones I make.'

This was enough to prompt Europe's most successful golfer to wade into the row. Sir Nick Faldo, who captained García in the 2008 Ryder Cup, tweeted: 'Now this is rich coming from the most immature player I've ever witnessed!' Faldo, six times a major champion and before García Europe's record points scorer, had previously branded the Spanish star 'useless' in the aftermath of Europe's heavy defeat at Valhalla, where he won only half a point.

García, often an exuberant figure on the golf course, appears at home on his new tour. He is able to wear shorts and the informality is to his liking, as is the buzz around the tournaments. In Miami for the climax of LIV's inaugural season it felt more like a pop festival than a golf tournament, especially around the sprawling clubhouse and its vast terrace, which overlooks the course.

Glasses clinked, cigar smoke wafted, the hubbub was loud and the beat of constantly pumped music was even louder. People were there to be seen, many of them wearing adoring MAGA caps. It was very much a social event with a discernibly youthful vibe. In the spectator village, it was possible to acquire a Cameron Smith-style mullet at one of the stalls, and there were chipping and putting games and a huge range of fast food and even greater quantities of drink.

Outside the Doral gates, a more reserved and reflective atmosphere prevailed. Protesters carried banners objecting to LIV's Saudi Arabian backers. Pat McCabe had travelled 90 minutes in rush hour traffic to join a small knot of demonstrators. He held a sign saying: 'TRUMP'S LIES AND LIV GOLFERS' GREED ALLOWS SAUDI GOVERNMENT TO SPORTSWASH AND CRIME.'

'I was actually standing on the sidewalk in front of the sign for Trump National and the police told me that I could not stand on that side of the road,' he told me. 'The Saudi government and its Public Investment Fund has decided to spend billions of dollars in the US to basically make them look like good guys and unfortunately everybody knows about the 9/11 attacks with 15 of the 19 hijackers coming from Saudi. The other reason I am here is for Jamal Khashoggi, the *Washington Post* reporter that was murdered brutally and quite frankly the third reason I am here are their crimes against women that happen every day in the country,' McCabe added.

'And unfortunately Trump is getting money to hold these events at his courses and the golfers are getting paid bonuses to join the tour, most notably Phil Mickelson who is getting $200m. I just saw a woman go by with a shirt that said, "Go Phil". I said "Ma'am don't sell your soul. I know Phil did but you don't have to join him."'

All things considered, it felt almost incongruous that a golf tournament was being played. But the dozen teams spent three days working their way through the convoluted format to build to what became a compelling climax. Appropriately, Dustin Johnson holed the winning putt for the 4Aces to hold off Smith and his Punch GC team. Johnson clenched his right fist, knowing it was now time to party. He had more reason to celebrate than anyone.

Aside from a colossal signing fee, Johnson had proved himself the most successful player in LIV's initial eight-tournament season. As a result of that and his team's success, he netted winnings of $33,637,767. 'It's been amazing,' Johnson said. 'Obviously, the fans are what makes it. This week's been incredible. This whole season has gotten better and better.'

He and his teammates, Patrick Reed, Talor Gooch and Pat Perez, split $16m for winning the team competition. It was little wonder the 47-year-old Perez commented: 'I feel unbelievable.' The veteran was among the least successful players on the LIV roster, yet still banked more than $8m from the seven tournaments he played.

These were the sort of figures that Greg Norman felt would prove irresistible to several more players far higher up golf's pecking order than Perez. As Trump said, 'unlimited money' was a very attractive thing. It had already taken away from the established tours some of the biggest names in the sport. Everyone at LIV was nodding in agreement with the USA's most recent past president when he said that more superstars would be defecting to the upstarts.

'We've had a lot of headwinds,' Norman told viewers of LIV's streamed coverage of the final day of their inaugural season. 'We've weathered all the storms, and we're here. We've got a great crew of people and we've got a great product and we're off and running.'

But how fast and for how long? The pace of LIV's momentum was about to slow.

8

MEETINGS, MONEY AND CHANGE

'LIV have done a phenomenal job. Just listening to the players, what we want, what we need. That's been the cool part of this process.'

Brooks Koepka

Interstate 95 runs from top to bottom of the east coast of the USA. Tiger Woods and Rickie Fowler used the freeway to attend the crucial Delaware meeting in August 2022 and by the following March, the southern section of the I95 was being populated by expensive vehicles carrying PGA Tour stars to Ponte Vedra Beach. For many, it was a relatively short hop from Orlando, where they had played in the Arnold Palmer Invitational (API), the fourth of a dozen events in the 2023 calendar given substantially increased prize funds.

These tournaments became extra lucrative as a result of the arrival of LIV and the subsequent Delaware meeting. It formed the blueprint of the biggest names playing against each other for the largest purses on a more regular basis. January's 2023 opener – the Sentry Tournament of Champions in Hawaii – was worth $15m, with the prize pots swelling to $20m for the WM Phoenix Open in mid-February, the following week's Genesis Invitational in Los Angeles and then the API at Bay Hill in early March.

These colossal prize funds brought the most out of the very best talents on tour. Jon Rahm and Scottie Scheffler built a near duopoly in claiming the largest slices of these gargantuan prize pies. Rahm won the elevated tournaments – or 'designated' as they were now termed – in Hawaii and Los Angeles. Scheffler defended his title in Phoenix and won the $25m Players Championship. It was just what the tour needed. Week in, week out, the hottest players were contesting titles in thrilling fashion. It was the ultimate advertisement for their product at a time when the circuit was under most pressure to deliver.

By contrast, LIV's first two events at Mayakoba in Mexico and Tucson, Arizona produced the opposite. The Mexican opener marked the launch of their 'first official full league season'. The previous year's hastily but impressively arranged eight 'invitational' tournaments were termed 'Beta' events to test the water.

Now it was all systems go despite a troubled winter break in which LIV lost a number of key executives, including managing director Majed Al-Sorour and the acclaimed COO, Atul Khosla. 'We respect A.K. and his personal decision,' said LIV CEO Greg Norman. It took 12 months for LIV to appoint a replacement chief operating officer while PR agency Performance54 took over the day-to-day running of the operation. Lawrence J. Burian, an executive at Madison Square Garden, eventually took on the management role by joining the LIV staff.

But why did Khosla walk away at the end of LIV's inaugural season? There was speculation that there had been a breakdown in relations with Norman. There were rumours of an overspend to the tune of $180m and others wondered whether Khosla had concluded that the upstart tour's lofty ambitions were untenable.

The previous October, Khosla claimed to me that a major television deal was in the pipeline and that a number of leading players were about to sign for LIV. Players were expecting big names. In Miami, Martin Kaymer told me: 'You should see who we have got coming next year.' It was thought that new recruits would include Olympic champion Xander Schauffele and his Ryder and Presidents Cup partner, Patrick Cantlay.

But instead they secured the signatures of a rather less heralded quintet: Chile's Mito Pereira, Sebastián Muñoz of Colombia, New Zealand's Danny Lee, experienced American Brendan Steele and the highest ranked of the five, Belgium's world number 34, Thomas Pieters. 'I'd be pretty disappointed when I'm singing and dancing about Thomas Pieters,' observed former manager Chubby Chandler to me. 'I'd want a bit more than him for my big signing.'

The new recruits offered plenty in geographical reach, especially in a key Latin American market with Pereira and Muñoz, but, as Chandler realised, much less in star power. They also struggled to secure the kind of television deal for which they had hoped. LIV testimony in later court papers suggested they saw their contract with the CW channel – an entertainment platform with no history of golf coverage – as being with a 'secondary network'. They alleged this was because more established golf broadcasters had been unlawfully warned off by PGA Tour broadcast executive Thierry Pascal.

Publicly, the golfing establishment and the upstarts could not have been further apart. Both parties seemed entrenched with neither giving an inch. Rancour remained at every level. But in the background, top secret moves were afoot to try to find common ground. British businessman Roger Devlin was chair of the exclusive and prestigious Sunningdale Golf Club. An Oxford graduate, he was chairman of Persimmon PLC, Britain's largest house builder. He had also served as chairman of the bookmakers William Hill as well as chairing various private equity companies and for seven years until 2019 he was the first senior independent director of the Football Association. In short, he was very well connected.

According to papers released at a future US Senate hearing, on 8 December 2022, Devlin sent an email to the then incoming PGA Tour Board member Jimmy Dunne. The missive stated that PIF governor Yasir Al-Rumayyan and

Amanda Staveley, with whom His Excellency had worked in acquiring the Premier League's Newcastle United Football Club, had invited Devlin to 'help find a solution to the great issues that divide LIV and the PGA.' Top officials at Europe's DP World Tour later told me they were 'fully aware' of the moves being orchestrated by the British businessman.

Devlin explained that Al-Rumayyan had 'great ambitions to support, grow and modernise the sport and is clearly well equipped to fund these goals.' He offered potential ideas, including 'co-sanctioned regular PGA tournaments which could come together designated as an Aramco Series' and a 'Golf Development Fund' which 'would be managed and administered by Saudi Golf in cooperation with the governing bodies.' The following day, Devlin sent a short follow-up to stress that his original email, 'written in good faith in an attempt to move hitherto entrenched positions, is Without Prejudice.'

Dunne, an investment banker, joined the PGA Tour Policy Board in November 2022. He is a member of some of golf's most exclusive clubs – Augusta National, Shinnecock Hills and Pine Valley – and was president at Seminole, the famed Florida layout. He was a founding member of Sandler O'Neill and Partners advising on mergers and acquisitions. He lost 66 employees in the September 11 attacks on the South Tower of the World Trade Center in 2001.

On Monday 12 December, Dunne replied: 'Roger – I would like to have a cup of coffee first – just like to visit with you not to discuss anything specific just like to know you a little before anything else if you are up for that – best Jimmy.'

Devlin replied on the same day, enquiring whether that would be a 'virtual' cappuccino? And pointing out much as he would love to travel to the States, it's quite a long way for a coffee!

Dunne replied: 'So sorry thought you were in Florida.'

Devlin followed up with another email on 3 January 2023:

Jimmy,

Happy New Year!

I hope it will be a more peaceful one in the golfing world.

I do detect that since I first corresponded with you a month ago the Saudi position is hardening, as they are confident LIV will prevail over the long term if only because of their limitless financial resources.

Please let me know if you feel an introductory call would serve any purpose, as we are perfectly happy to fly to Florida for a meeting but only if we are confident there is a basis for discussion?

My diary is better this month than in February when I have a number of immovable commitments.

Roger

Dunne responded swiftly with just five words: 'Probably not at this time.'

Meanwhile, Greg Norman's breakaway tour ploughed on. They started their own platform with their LIV+ app and there was little sign of background rancour when they launched their season in Mexico in late February 2023. It was typically brash, bold, informal. And at times deluded.

A dozen four-man teams were destined to compete over 14 tournaments. Host Arlo White claimed they would be competing for 'The biggest prize in golf history' and that the 12 line-ups were 'battling, all in lockstep.' The footage was centred on the area that LIV most wanted to exploit, a team format expected to attract high-end investment. It was a clear sign that this aspect was seen to be critical to LIV's future. Norman appeared in the booth and said that LIV had 'accelerated this beyond light years,' adding: 'I'm looking forward to 2023 to be exceptional.'

With new recruits on board, White suggested: 'The fields seem a lot deeper to me this year'. It was pure hype with negligible editorial value. The broadcast highlighted team uniforms and commentators announced who they would be pulling for over the coming season. The primary objective of creating a market to sell team colours was clear. 'You don't want to be the team that trails in last place in the merch sales,' stated commentator Jerry Foltz.

But the move to team uniforms brought collateral damage. 4Aces skipper Dustin Johnson's long-term deal with Adidas had been ripped up. 'I was with them for 15 years,' DJ confirmed at a press conference in Mayakoba. 'We had a great relationship. It's still really good. We mutually agreed on parting ways . . .

obviously playing for LIV . . . it was better for both of us to part ways. For me being the captain of the team . . . being able to go out and find a clothing sponsor is more beneficial than waiting another year.'

Meanwhile, on day one of the new season, across the course a Slash guitar riff echoed as a countdown from 10 seconds began. As per the inaugural season, it was a shotgun start. Players spread across the course began their rounds simultaneously on the 18 different tees of the El Camaleón layout – designed, of course, by Greg Norman.

The highest-profile grouping started on the first tee. Galleries stretched down the side of the hole to see Dustin Johnson, the inaugural individual champion, find the fairway. Cam Smith, captain of the renamed 'Ripper' team, found the right rough while local favourite Abraham Ancer made up the threesome. Smith was the only one of the group not wearing shorts.

In the build-up to the tournament, Johnson said something very prescient: 'Golf is golf.' It might not be the most inspired saying, but it perhaps sums up LIV's biggest problem. Because for all their considerable hype, when the shotgun sounds, what follows is just golf. As absorbing as the action can be for enthusiasts, it is still a pedestrian sport with long gaps between shots and relatively few explosive moments. 'It doesn't really matter where you play, where in the world, what tour you're on. It's still golf,' Johnson added.

And so, despite the high-energy build-up, the sporting action almost comes as an anticlimax. While the PGA Tour had stumbled across a winning formula that was getting the very best out of its top stars, LIV struggled. The Mexico tournament was largely a damp squib. Though not for Charles Howell III. The experienced American banked $4m, for what was only the fourth win of his 23-year professional career.

Howell finished 16-under-par and won by four shots from Peter Uihlein. There was no jeopardy and Smith, in a share of fifth place 10 strokes behind, was the only major winner on the LIV roster to make the top 10. Johnson was tied 35th in the 48-man field.

Howell's 'Crushers' team, which included Bryson DeChambeau, Paul Casey and Anirban Lahiri, shared the $3m team prize after winning by nine shots. 'To come off with a crushing start I guess you could say was pretty fun,' said

DeChambeau at the post-tournament press conference, the team skipper who finished 24th in the individual competition. 'You couldn't ask for more as a captain. Very proud of these guys, and this is the reason why I re-signed them.'

The team competition took precedence in post-round discussion. Howell, who had not won since 2018, had to wait until the final question of the victors' news conference to address the most lucrative win of his career, and he was bang on message with his answer. 'The depth of the fields out here really need to be talked about and appreciated because these are 48 world class golfers,' he said. 'Let's not sleep on the fact that the extremely young guys out here can play and win, as well. For me, it's a huge deal. You're fortunate to win anywhere, anytime, but against this field . . . it's awesome.'

Three weeks later, the LIV bandwagon rolled into Tucson and it was a similar story. Again, the big guns failed to fire. Many observers pointed to the long off-season to excuse anaemic performances from LIV's most expensive signings. Smith and Brooks Koepka finished only 2-under-par to share 24th place. Johnson was three strokes better to come 13th, Patrick Reed was 18th, Phil Mickelson 30th and DeChambeau 44th of the 48 starters.

But the tournament did build to an exciting climax, Danny Lee winning a four-man playoff against Carlos Ortiz, Brendan Steele and Louis Oosthuizen. It was Lee's first win in eight years and was most welcome because, until signing for LIV, his career had seemed in terminal decline. 'The best part of my game is probably I'm always confident, and I always believe in my game,' he said at a LIV news conference. 'And even I was falling apart a little bit the last couple years.'

Lee was enticed to join LIV by his captain in the 'Iron Heads' team, Kevin Na. 'It was a life-changing decision,' said the New Zealander, who was 267th in the world when he switched tours. 'I wasn't getting what everybody thinks; like everybody is getting $100m, $50m, $30m. I wasn't in that situation. Kevin just called me: "Hey, do you want to come over and play for my team?"'

With a schedule that included Mayakoba, the Greenbrier – where he had won on the PGA Tour – and Sentosa in Singapore, Lee saw venues he enjoyed playing. 'Then Kevin just told me that he knew I was working hard. He could see that my game is so close to being great, but he told me that this environment of LIV Golf is probably better for me than staying out on the PGA Tour . . .

probably because I tend to play too many weeks in a row. I mean, you can't play great every single round. . . . On a fourth or fifth week in a row when you have a really, really bad first round, sometimes it's really mentally hard to grind it out for that second round to make the cut. But here, you only have 14 events. You've got to make the most of it, and I don't want to let anybody down on my team.'

The Spanish-speaking quartet of Ancer, García, Ortiz and young Spaniard Eugenio Chacarra, who make up the 'Fireballs GC' line-up, took the team spoils by four strokes from Johnson's 4Aces.

On Twitter, Kevin Van Valkenburg, the editorial director of the popular *No Laying Up* podcast, highlighted the lack of star power on LIV leaderboards in their first two tournaments. 'It feels like one thing that would help LIV isn't happening: The "popular" players aren't facing off enough because many of them have been blah,' he tweeted. 'If I was Yasir Al-Rumayyan and I had to justify this venture to MBS [Mohammed bin Salman, Saudi Crown Prince], it would feel easier if Cam Smith and Brooks and Bryson were winning and drawing more fans rather than CH3 and Danny Lee.'

Van Valkenburg noted the way Mickelson had complained about how the big names had been the life support to the lesser lights in his days on the PGA Tour. 'Phil's whole point was that the Tour needed to evolve because the star players were carrying the Brendan Steeles and Danny Lees and Charles Howells of the game. Now Phil has helped create a world where they are kings.' These observations were read by veteran Englishman and LIV loyalist Lee Westwood, who sarcastically posted three emojis crying with laughter.

In the absence of stellar leaderboards, the first two LIV events failed to make much of an impression on the CW Network. Weekend viewing for the Mexico tournament averaged at 286,000 on the industry standard Nielsen ratings. They were an eighth of figures for the PGA Tour. But five days later, LIV put out a press release claiming overall viewing figures of 3.2 million using iSpot, a TV advertising measurement and analytics company. 'iSpot has a broader glimpse of the way viewers view content than simply the panel process,' said chief media officer Will Staeger. 'These numbers take into account not only the Nexstar stations and the combination of CW and Nexstar, but also set top boxes, connected TVs, out of home and video players, so the attempt here is to be comprehensive and thorough.'

But for the Tucson tournament final round, Nielsen figures slipped further to a mere 274,000 CW viewers after averaging 284,000 for Saturday's second round. The *Sports Business Journal* reported that 24 per cent of US households were unable to watch LIV on traditional television because their local CW affiliate station did not carry the golf coverage.

By contrast, PGA Tour members had been parading before the cameras of the mighty NBC, both at Bay Hill and then for the flagship Players Championship at the circuit's headquarters in Ponte Vedra Beach. This was the biggest tournament before April's Masters and the most eagerly anticipated competition of the year so far.

Leave the I95 at Butler Boulevard and when that comes to its end turn right on to the coastal State Road A1A. Then look out for PGA Tour Boulevard – the turning to the right after the Nona Blue restaurant, ironically, owned by LIV recruit Graeme McDowell. The tree-lined boulevard carves through old swampland now populated by expensive housing. Once the gatehouse barrier has been passed, it is a short but slow drive to the competitors' car park. A fleet of official Lexus SUVs occupied most of the spots, but conspicuous by its absence was a space for the defending champion.

Usually, the build-up to The Players centres around whether the previous year's winner can make history and become the first to successfully defend the title. That would certainly have been the case had Cam Smith been able to compete. He would have arrived at the Stadium Course at Sawgrass as the reigning Open champion. But, indefinitely suspended from the PGA Tour, the Aussie, who lives close to the course, was left kicking his heels in the week of the American tour's biggest tournament.

'I grew up my whole childhood watching the event,' Smith told *Golf.com* in a TV interview. 'I would love to get out there. I don't know how it would be received, me getting out there and watching, walking around in the crowd. Might be pretty funny, I would love to do that.'

Smith was not spotted on the premises that week and, reportedly shunned by high-end local golf clubs, chose to play with mates on a nearby nine-hole public course called The Yards instead. It is located five minutes' drive from the Sawgrass gates. Nothing more could illustrate the fractured nature of the men's game than the reigning champion playing in such close proximity, while unable to defend his title. 'Yes, it's awkward,' admitted PGA Tour commissioner Jay Monahan at a news conference. 'But, you know, ultimately that's a decision he made.'

There was still a great sense of anticipation for what lay ahead on the golf course that week, especially with Rahm, Scheffler and McIlroy – the top three in the world – having posted wins already in 2023. For the benefit of TV, they were grouped together for the first two rounds.

Off the course, this was also a crucial week for Monahan. He sought to bring onside his membership following the approval of updated schedule plans from those initially drawn up at the Hotel du Pont in Delaware, a lot further north on the I95. And this involved McIlroy – jokingly referred to as 'the vice comish' in some sections of the media – because he had become the front man for the tour's response to the LIV threat. It was his job to sell now detailed plans that had gone through painstaking refinement before gaining board approval at the previous week's Arnold Palmer Invitational.

Building up to this momentous decision, which involved reducing fields, boosting prize money and getting rid of halfway cuts, McIlroy had a hotline to PGA Tour HQ at Ponte Vedra Beach. Or was it vice versa? Either way, there were countless calls and Zoom meetings involving him along with members of the Player Advisory Council and the tour's senior management.

Then came a seven-hour board meeting in Orlando on the Tuesday before the API. McIlroy was a key figure at that gathering, which ultimately shaped the nature of the PGA Tour calendar for 2024. 'It's extraordinary,' said Monahan when asked to describe the Northern Ireland golfer's commitment. 'Where we were last summer to where we are now is largely a reflection on the amount of time and energy he's put in.' Monahan went on to highlight McIlroy's commitment to understanding concerns of the entire PGA Tour membership rather than just the elite few who first gathered in Delaware.

At The Players Championship, in the March slot that followed the Bay Hill board meeting, it was time to unveil the plans. At 7.30 a.m. on the Tuesday of tournament week, curious players gathered in the clubhouse. McIlroy was the main voice, even though his priority might otherwise have been struggles with a new driver. The biggest tournament outside the four majors was only two days away and he was struggling to find fairways. Others would have foregrounded that issue but, instead, he was the man pitching the PGA Tour's future to its membership.

The likes of Jon Rahm, Justin Thomas and Max Homa skipped the gathering. They were getting ready for The Players. It was a more important meeting for competitors more likely to be affected by the introduction of a string of 'designated' tournaments. They would be among the most valuable on tour, averaging $20m purses but cut to 70–80 players and thereby excluding a significant rear portion of the membership. 'The temperature in the room was nowhere near as hot as I anticipated it to be once the information was laid out,' McIlroy told reporters. He was not referring to the effectiveness of the Sawgrass air-conditioning system.

Refinements from what was discussed back in Wilmington were aimed at mollifying the rump of the tour's membership who would have been concerned at being excluded from the most valuable tournaments. 'The presentation in Delaware was very self-serving for the 20 players in that room,' McIlroy admitted to players in the meeting. 'We were looking at fields of 50 to 60. We were looking at only 10 players dropping out of that top 50 every year, so a retention rate of 80 per cent.'

This had been a red flag to the tour because it would mean not enough churn and limited opportunities for progression. 'The tour were like, look, the typical retention rate for the top 50 has historically been around 60 percent, so let's try to get back to that number,' McIlroy explained. 'So the structure that has been rolled out here is vastly different from the one that we all talked about and the guys saw in Delaware, and I think for the betterment of everyone.'

By far the strongest line in his news conference was an acknowledgement of what LIV had done to the professional landscape. 'The emergence of a competitor to the PGA Tour has benefited everyone that plays elite professional golf,' McIlroy stated.

Monahan did not couch it in such terms but admitted it was a 'challenging environment'. Throughout an hour-long press conference, he never once mentioned LIV by name or the source of their funding. Nevertheless, it was clear the arrival of the upstart league had forced the PGA Tour to think outside the box, hence the radical changes he was outlining. 'There are no sacred cows, we're just trying to get to the best possible outcome, and that is to continue to grow this tour and its pre-eminence,' Monahan said. 'There have been a lot of conversations. There have been a lot of bad ideas that we came up with along the way. But candidly, I think the level of discussion has been really helpful.'

Although the plans were radical, they remained true to the ethos at the heart of professional golf; that playing better golf is always the answer. If you perform well enough, you will be eligible for the most valuable tournaments. If you do not, then you will only be able to compete in regular 'full-field' events that carry less prize money, kudos and ranking points. They also involve halfway cuts that could mean going home empty-handed.

As for the 'designated' tournaments, many onlookers recognised the similarity of limited field, no-cut competitions to the character of LIV tournaments where no one goes home early. 'I've spent the last year reading how good full fields and cuts are!' Westwood, often a vocal LIV recruit, wryly observed on Twitter.

Elsewhere, there was concern for the DP World Tour because the US circuit's plans were totally American-facing. They spelled the end of WGC tournaments, ironically brought in to thwart Greg Norman's 1994 bid to challenge the PGA Tour. Those events had the backing of all the main global tours. There had also been changes to the official golf world rankings, which significantly favoured US tour players. A day after Monahan outlined his plans, a senior management figure from the European Tour told me: 'One thing's for sure, we've got to have a very strong fall season.' The autumn now seemed the only time of year when they might attract star names to their tournaments.

Throughout the LIV era, Westwood sought to highlight how Europe was increasingly marginalised by the PGA Tour, despite their 'Strategic Alliance', which was nominally struck to benefit both circuits. The veteran of 25 European Tour victories tweeted: 'So..Do away with the WGC's. Load the OWGR [Official World Golf Ranking] in your favour. Create 10 limited field events for just PGA Tour members (like WGC's). Add to that 4 majors, Players, FedEx Cup. That's a full schedule for a top player. That's growing the game (sarcastic wink emoji) What Strategic Alliance?'

Among PGA Tour players the response to the changes was mixed. 'There's not going to be any model that makes everybody happy. That's just a stone-cold fact,' Justin Thomas, who ended the season outside the top 70 on the PGA Tour, stated in his Players Championship press conference. 'But . . . when every single one of us signed up to play golf, we knew that the better you played, the better tournaments you were going to be into, and the worse you played, you may not even have a job anymore.' He added: 'I just don't see how it's not better. It's going to push all of us.'

Few players are more dedicated than Britain's Aaron Rai, who won the 2020 Scottish Open on the European Tour before graduating from the secondary Korn Ferry circuit two years later to win full playing rights on the PGA Tour. This is someone who has scaled golf's pyramid, starting on the lowest step of the now defunct PGA EuroPro Tour in 2014. By repeatedly 'playing better golf', he graduated to the extent that he was now a debutant at the 2023 Players Championship and that week he enjoyed a sensational hole in one on the famous 17th hole in his third round.

A thoughtful character, he accepted the proposed changes, even though they could make his tour life harder. 'A lot of thought and deliberation has gone into making these decisions, probably more than I have,' the Wolverhampton-born pro told me. 'I think overall we have to trust that the decisions have been made in the best interests of the tour overall. So from my side, that's part of the PGA Tour moving forwards and that's fine. It's just part of the game now and part of how we are measured as players; how our seasons are measured and whether we get in the biggest events in the future. There is no point in wasting my time in judging what is right or wrong, it's about putting that effort into the game to be the best player I can be.'

Other players were less enthusiastic. Tour veteran Ryan Armour likened those left behind in full-field events to 'mules'. He angrily suggested that these players might be good enough to play pro-ams and carry out public relations duties but no longer of a standard to compete for the tour's biggest prizes. He told *Golf Digest*: 'Say you finished 75th on the points list, just using that as an example. Yes, you had a really good year, but you don't get in any of the designated events. Why wouldn't you take a LIV contract?'

Monahan spoke to BBC Radio the day after those Armour quotes were published. He told me: 'Any time you go through change it is going to be hard and people are going to have a difficult time adapting to it. People are going to be critical of it, but we have spent so much time and energy with our players, including our top players, thinking about our entire membership. And I'm confident that next year what I'm talking about, fans will be responding very favourably towards us.'

The commissioner is as approachable as he is measured. 'I look at every player the same way,' he added. 'They have every ability and every opportunity to be the number one player in the world. And the model that we've moved to continues to give them that opportunity. And it continues to reward those players that perform the best. So the meritocracy is firmly in place.'

Unlike 2023, there would be no compulsory rules tied to the number of designated events played. 'Jay has been very clever,' said a high-ranking European Tour official. 'He's given them freedom. That's a very big word in this when you consider how tied in the LIV players are. Freedom is a key component here.'

Monahan agreed when I put that point to him. 'It absolutely is,' he said. 'That's the nature and the basis of the game. And you're trying to balance freedom with creating an opportunity that the players want, which is to compete against each other more often.'

I interrupted and asked: 'Something not available to those who have signed for another league?'

'It's something that is very important to an organisation that's been around as long as the PGA Tour, now 55 years.'

He did not take the bait.

While some rank-and-file members pushed back on the proposals, the acid test would come in the form of deterring leading stars from defecting to LIV. Initial evidence was encouraging and the PGA Tour would have been further heartened by the first signs of player discord in the breakaway league.

Rumours began to circulate that Brooks Koepka was suffering 'buyer's remorse' and was starting to wonder about ways back into the establishment fold. However, publicly, the four-times major winner told a different story. 'LIV have done a phenomenal job,' he told the *Independent*. 'Just listening to the players, what we want, what we need. That's been the cool part of this process. The transparency. This is our first full season and I'm very pleased with it.'

A players' meeting at their second 2023 event in Tucson suggested the LIV environment was more opaque than transparent. Reports suggested that some of the golfers thought their contracts were for 10 tournaments rather than the 14 in the league schedule. In the inaugural season, team earnings were kept by the players, now the spoils would go into the team's funding as they readied themselves to be put on the open market for investment. According to a report by the *Fire Pit Collective*, a player was heard to say: 'Why are we standing on the podium spraying each other with champagne when we don't get the money?'

LIV's second season showed signs of belt-tightening compared with the lavish approach to their initial campaign. Suddenly, it no longer looked like it was being financed from a bottomless pit of cash. Chartered jets between tournaments were shelved and cuts made to event budgets were apparent all the way down to the standard of media dining, which had been outstanding at the 2022 tournaments.

Nevertheless, the players were still playing for colossal sums. As Kevin Na told the *Fire Pit Collective*'s Alan Shipnuck: 'There is a shit-ton of money out here, and I already got a shit-ton. If you play well, you're gonna win a shit-ton more. I'm not worrying about the details.'

Perhaps a bigger concern was the standard of play. How competitive is shotgun-start, 54-hole, no-cut, guaranteed-money golf? The PGA Tour hit the heights with Scottie Scheffler heading into his Masters title defence, defending his Phoenix crown and winning the $25m Players title. Jon Rahm was on fire until a stomach bug took him out of Sawgrass after the first round and McIlroy's missed cut could be attributed to the distractions of reshaping the tour. He bounced back with a new driver shaft and a return to his trusty Scotty Cameron putter and duly impressed in his run to the semi-finals of the last WGC Matchplay in Austin.

With none of LIV's stars making an impression in the opening two tournaments, the 18 eligible to play the Masters headed to Augusta with very little competition under their belts. Koepka played just 15 rounds to get battle hardened and admitted in a LIV press conference in Orlando that he 'wished there was more front loading to get ready for Augusta.'

Cam Smith completed only 11 competitive rounds in 2023 before embarking on his tilt for a first Masters green jacket. But he attacked the perception that his new tour was a soft touch. 'There's a lot of chatter going around about "these guys don't play real golf anymore" and I think it's BS to be honest,' he said.

Nevertheless, The Open champion conceded that LIV stars needed to give a good account of themselves at the year's first major. 'I think it is important for us to go there and really show a high standard of golf, which we know we're all capable of.'

Another key question surrounded the reception LIV players might receive at the first Masters since breaking away. 'I'm really not sure, to be honest, I hope that it's fine,' Smith said. 'I've had a great career around Augusta, and I hope I haven't pissed anyone off. I guess we'll wait and see, there are a few guys who have a stronger stance on LIV.'

The nearer they got to tee off in the Masters, the more diplomatic most players became. The last thing they needed was outside noise. Their priority was playing their best in one of four landmark weeks of the year. Stoking the flames about the fractured nature of the men's game would not help in that quest.

A more peaceful air seemed to be descending, compared with earlier in the season when LIV's Joaquin Niemann stoked the potential rivalry that came courtesy of his new employers arriving on the golf scene. He told *Golf.com*: 'I think it's going to be more fun knowing that they hate us.'

The first of that quartet of weeks was the Masters. Always eagerly anticipated, the tournament ends eight major-less months on the men's calendar. That period had been among the most rancorous in the history of the game. It was an unprecedented spell that gave a momentous backdrop to the most glamorous tournament in golf. It was an event teeming with potential storylines both on and off the course.

9

MASTERS DIARY

Augusta National Golf Club, Georgia

SATURDAY 1 APRIL 2023

Atlanta airport's International Terminal is mobbed. Storms hit the Eastern Seaboard and bring travel chaos. Flights from Europe are especially busy and tonight there is a 100-yard queue of travel-weary passengers waiting to access a packed immigration hall. After a couple of hours, bags are retrieved. It is time to join another mass of humanity gathered outside. Haphazard and lengthy queues wait increasingly impatiently for taxis and buses. I'm eventually at the head of the one waiting for a bus to the rental car lot. 'Ain't seen nothin' like it sir,' says the airport worker trying to keep order on the pavement. 'It's them storms, man,' before adding knowingly: 'And the Masters is comin'.'

SUNDAY 2 APRIL

Augusta is a pretty unremarkable Georgia city located close to the South Carolina border. It was where the legendary American soul singer James Brown ('I Got You', 'I Feel Good') endured a troubled childhood in abject poverty. It is populated with cramped residences serviced by haphazard and primitive-looking overhead power lines. The outskirts are leafy with idyllic estates of large detached family homes, many of which appear expensively priced on the rental market for Masters week. They offer value for money because the handful of chain hotels in the area charge a prohibitive fortune this particular week.

The city is a two and a half hour drive along the I20 from Atlanta. Exit on Washington Road, which extends to Broad Street, the main drag through the city centre. Before it is reached, though, you pass every fast food joint and chain restaurant imaginable. A dual carriageway of cholesterol and refined sugar.

Numerous ticket touts set up outside Waffle House, McDonald's, KFC or TBonz. Hooters have a sign saying the flamboyant John Daly will be making his annual appearance to flog his personalised merchandise.

Then, at the top of the hill, stands a pristine, white giant water tower with a deep green emblem stating 'Augusta, Georgia'. It is surrounded by trees and a high green fence, beyond which is a place regarded by golf fans as paradise: the Augusta National Golf Club.

Vast parking lots sit where once hundreds of people lived. It is land bought by the club that stages the Masters. Traffic supposedly flows but in reality crawls. The club's footprint grows ever greater. Near the water tower sits the tournament's press building, a relatively new facility built in less than a year. From the outside it resembles a white mansion with slate grey roof. It could have housed the Wilkes family in *Gone with the Wind*. In reality, it offers the most sumptuous working conditions any sports journalist will ever encounter.

It sits at the far end of the competitors' driving range and is a five-minute buggy ride from the first tee. It was our working home for a couple of years, the hub for our BBC Radio Masters commentary. Now, for the second time we are located in Augusta's 'International Content Centre', where all of the world's broadcasters are housed. It is similarly styled and an equally impressive facility, full of studios and offices serviced by scores of broadcast trucks. They are neatly gathered in a Formula One-style paddock outside.

Everything about Augusta is pristine. It might be a cliche but it is true, there is not a blade of grass out of place. What you see on the golf course is reflected in the vast surrounds. The sprawling country house-styled building that is the Content Centre is not even on the Masters site. You have to drive down Washington Road with the famous Magnolia Lane on your right. That is where the forbidding 'Members Only' sign hangs beside imposing green iron gates. They remain open this week, but shut out the rest of the world from this most private club for the rest of the year. In keeping with the colour scheme of the place, the magnolia-lined lane is bordered by kerbs painted Augusta green.

Our working headquarters are further down Washington Road on the opposite side. It takes a winding buggy ride through an underpass for us to access the course. The paths are as brilliant white as the buildings, the roads unblemished and grass borders, surrounded by neatly ordered ochre pine needles, are lush and deeply verdant. It is mown every night to maintain its weed-free sense of perfection.

These buildings are nigh on brand new, but they have a permanence that suggests they have been there for decades. LIV is not the only golfing entity that enjoys an apparently bottomless pit of money.

Traffic is relatively light approaching the course. It is only Sunday and not the Sunday of this trip that matters. Golfing attention is split. The PGA Tour is in San Antonio where Corey Conners is winning. In Orlando, LIV are completing their third event of the year. A certain Brooks Koepka is winning there.

That Miami press conference of last autumn creeps into my mind. 'I'll have one of those one day,' Koepka said to Mickelson when they discussed Masters green jackets. Who knows?

Tiger Woods is on the premises. There's less hype this year because he is not making an unlikely comeback from a shattered right leg, as was the case 12 months ago. He is all smiles. Hits a handful of shots on the range before sauntering with his increasingly familiar limp out on to the course. He is armed only with putter and wedges. Short game prep is the order of the afternoon.

As Koepka completes his win – becoming LIV's first two-time winner – word emerges from Orlando of a bullish feeling among the breakaway tour's 18 stars who will tee it up here at Augusta. In the event of one of them winning next Sunday, Greg Norman reveals plans for the LIV contingent to gather in celebration at the 18th green. He tells James Corrigan, of the *Telegraph*: 'I came within touching distance on a few occasions and I suppose it stands out as the big absence on my CV. That's part of why it would mean so much to see one of our LIV family in the Butler Cabin. I would be the happiest man in the world.'

What a scene it would be. Augusta officials have been given fair warning, but I can't see it happening myself.

MONDAY 3 APRIL

It does not matter how much Augusta National invests into the city's roads system, there is always early morning gridlock on practice days. This one is no exception. The club admit more spectators on these days than those when the tournament is at stake. An insider suggests an attendance of 50,000 fans is whittled down to around 26,000 when the competition begins. The added attraction for spectators on practice days is that they can bring in cameras. Mobile phones are never allowed. This creates a surprisingly refreshing world where people are free from the tyranny of their handheld devices.

Thousands of people swarm across the back nine to watch a gently limping Tiger Woods in the company of a hoodie-wearing Rory McIlroy. Fred Couples and the 20-year-old Korean wonder boy Tom Kim make up the four-ball. The cynic in me says that Rory and Tiger are strategically ingratiating themselves with one of the most exciting young talents in the game, someone with geographical pull that would be very attractive to an upstart rival tour.

It looks like light practice. Most attention is spent on the quirks of the Augusta greens. Woods and McIlroy are relaxed and they gain rapturous ovations as they depart the final green.

The biggest names are called in for press conferences on the Monday and Tuesday of Masters week. The interview room is like a luxurious lecture theatre and each seat has its own microphone. Embedded in our accreditation are chips that inform the moderator – a member of the club's media committee – of who is sitting in which seat. It means they can call you by name if you have raised your hand to ask a question.

I do this when Cam Smith comes in. He is the only LIV player called for interview – it is rumoured Phil Mickelson declined the chance – and Smith's form has been mediocre at best. I wonder how different it is to be preparing having completed only four tournaments – three of them LIV's 54-hole events – so far this year? 'I think before last year's Masters Tournament, I played four times,' he says. 'I played four times this year. I don't think I've necessarily played less before the tournament. I think it's more to do with my preparation before I started up. I feel like I'm tournament-ready.'

He insists there is no animosity from old PGA Tour rivals following his switch to LIV. 'I spent probably an hour out on the range already this afternoon. It was good to see some familiar faces. Lots of laughs and lots of handshakes.'

So what about Greg Norman's claim that the LIV guys have chatted about getting together to form a celebration party if one of their number ends up winning the green jacket? 'There definitely hasn't been a conversation with me,' he admits. 'I definitely got left out of that one!'

It is a commendably honest press conference. Smith admits about LIV: 'The fields aren't as strong' and addresses the issue of wearing LIV branding – a contractual obligation to wear team patches – during the tournament. 'For me personally, I have another set of clothes made up this week without them,' he reveals. 'We haven't really heard much from Augusta National about the logos, and for me personally, I'm really proud of where I'm at and what I'm doing. Unless it's a problem for these guys, I'm going to wear it.'

Elsewhere, Kevin Na stokes the prospect of the rival tours doing battle at the sharp end of the tournament, saying: 'I think the fans and media are making it more interesting. If you have a LIV versus PGA Tour coming down the stretch, it'll be fun.'

The only concern is the weather forecast. It is already damp under foot, there is rain predicted for all four tournament days. McIlroy loves a soft course. Maybe that is why he is so jaunty?

TUESDAY 4 APRIL

More good news for McIlroy and the rest of the golf establishment. News breaks that the DP World Tour have won the arbitration hearing against LIV players. It will be official on Thursday – the first day of the Masters. Timing!

McIlroy is not drawn on the breaking news during a composed and confident news conference. He is not alone. It is striking that LIV and attendant controversies are being parked by players from both sides of the divide. Symbolic of an outbreak of locker-room peace, McIlroy plays nine holes of practice with Koepka, after the American won the LIV event in Orlando. 'He texted me congrats on Sunday,' says the US star to reporters at Augusta. 'Then I asked him if he wanted to play. . . . There's an open line of communication between me and him. I think we're pretty honest in where we are at.'

Koepka also admits: 'I just wanted to play with him, just compare my game. I know he's been playing well.'

Tiger Woods is quizzed on why the Excel Sports agency that represents him and is run by his manager Mark Steinberg does not have any clients playing for LIV. Woods says he has no direct influence on the management company but when asked if he has indirect influence, he says with a knowing smile: 'I have my opinions, yes.'

Woods is among 30 or so Masters winners who gather for the evening's champions dinner in the Augusta clubhouse. Six of them are now LIV players, including Phil Mickelson. As they tuck into Scottie Scheffler's cheeseburger sliders, firecracker shrimp, Texas rib-eye, blackened redfish and warmed chocolate chip cookie, Mickelson is uncharacteristically quiet. Fuzzy Zoeller, the champion on debut in 1979, tells *The Augusta Chronicle* that he 'didn't speak at all' during the dinner.

Mickelson later says to reporters: 'I thought it was really a special night and fun to be a part of.' Other sources tell us that LIV was not a topic around the dining table. That elephant sat in the corner of the room.

Tuesday evening of Masters week for reporters is spent with the DP World Tour, who host a big dinner in the ornate ballroom at the neighbouring Augusta Country Club. We are quickly warned there will be no comment on the reports that they have won the case against LIV players. 'I'm sure we'll have something to say later in the week,' CEO Keith Pelley teases.

There is, though, plenty of LIV chatter among guests. Representatives from other golf bodies are present. The PGA Tour are watching closely Saudi Arabia's ownership of the Premier League's Newcastle United. The Kingdom insists it does not amount to state ownership yet are claiming immunity from discovery in their antitrust case with the tour because of the PIF's sovereign status. This apparent inconsistency is regarded as a valuable anomaly and today a new ruling in the PGA Tour's ongoing antitrust case in California has gone in their favour. Saudi officials are fighting and losing the battle against being subject to discovery. It is a development that seems to be buoying officials from all constituencies of the golf establishment. Inconveniencing the Saudi funders is a key component in their efforts to win the war because PIF representatives will not want to be forced to testify.

Pelley uses his speech to promise lots of change to the European Tour in coming months. He sets a deadline for July's Scottish Open to reveal details.

Elsewhere, Harold Varner III raises eyebrows with an extensive interview in the *Washington Post*. The American has always been clear he moved to LIV for money and not for the often cited reason of trying to increase golf's popularity. 'They're full of shit,' he said of his LIV colleagues. 'They're growing their pockets. I tell them all of the time, all of them, you didn't come here to fucking grow the game.'

The front pages of the *Post*, though, are dominated by one story. Donald Trump pleads not guilty to 34 felonies in a New York courtroom.

WEDNESDAY 5 APRIL

Augusta structure their interview schedule to leave the way clear for their chairman to be the lone voice on the eve of the tournament. Fred Ridley addresses a packed auditorium and explains why Greg Norman has not been invited. 'The primary issue and the driver there is that I want the focus this week to be on the Masters competition,' the chairman tells us.

There are echoes here of the R&A's stance on not holding The Open at Turnberry while Trump owns the Scottish links. Ridley goes on: 'I would also add that, in the last 10 years, Greg Norman has only been here twice, and I believe one of those was as a commentator for Sirius Radio.'

The traditional par-3 contest, on a typically flawless remodelled short course, is won by American Tom Hoge. That means he will not win the Masters. No one has done that double in the same year.

While divisions that have fractured the sport have been played down all week, they are evident in the start sheet for this fun curtain-raiser. LIV players largely grouped themselves together with Sergio García and Bryson DeChambeau in the first pairing. Varner with Talor Gooch and Thomas Pieters and Abraham Ancer plays with Joaquin Niemann and Mito Pereira. Koepka has coalesced with LIV colleagues Jason Kokrak and Patrick Reed and the final trio is also all LIV: Dustin Johnson, Charl Schwartzel and Louis Oosthuizen.

McIlroy, meanwhile, chooses to play with Ryder Cup teammates Shane Lowry and Tommy Fleetwood. There are smiles all round, but the serious stuff is about to start.

THURSDAY 6 APRIL

The email dropped just after 5 a.m.

It is the first morning of the Masters but the golf headlines have been made in London. As expected, Sport Resolutions rule in favour of the DP World Tour rather than the LIV players who appealed against their punishments for playing the opening breakaway events last year.

The European Tour issue a statement, which says:

> The decision follows an arbitration which took place before an independent three-person panel, chaired by His Honour Judge Phillip Sycamore CBE, from February 6-10, 2023. In summary, the Sport Resolutions panel found that:
>
> 1. Keith Pelley, the DP World Tour's Chief Executive, "acted entirely reasonably in refusing releases".
> 2. The relevant regulations are lawful and enforceable. The regulations "cannot be said to go beyond what is necessary and proportionate to the [DP World Tour's] continued operation as a professional golf tour" and the DP World Tour has a legitimate and justifiable interest in protecting the rights of its membership.
> 3. The sanctioned members "committed serious breaches of the Code of Behaviour of the DP World Tour Regulations by playing in [LIV Golf events] despite their release requests having been refused".
> 4. All of the players' challenges therefore failed, their appeals are dismissed in their entirety, and the £100,000 fines originally imposed must now be paid within 30 days.

It is being billed as a big win, but a leading TV executive who has regular dealings with the DP World Tour uses a football analogy to describe the outcome as 'a shot being saved, rather than a goal being scored'. In other words, the final whistle remains a long way away and the game is nowhere near over.

Reflective of golf's stormy backdrop, dawn reveals heavy skies for the ceremonial tee off led by legends Jack Nicklaus, Gary Player and Tom Watson. They hit their shots and make way for the opening twosome, Mike Weir and LIV's Kevin Na, to strike the first shots in anger. Na feels unwell and lasts only nine holes before withdrawing.

If his fellow LIV players who compete on the DP World Tour are feeling sick at the verdict, they are refusing to divulge their feelings. 'Once tournament week starts, especially majors, I don't look at anything, read anything,' claims Patrick Reed to reporters.

Sergio García also states he has not seen the ruling. 'How can I talk about something I don't know?' he says, irritated. 'Obviously I don't look at the news. So I don't know what happened. I'm not going to talk about something without all the information that I need.'

Brooks Koepka very quickly establishes himself as the most likely player to prompt Greg Norman's predicted group celebration come Sunday night (if we finish on time, given the stormy forecast). He fires a scintillating 65 to join Jon Rahm and Viktor Hovland at the top of the first-round leaderboard.

But a row brews with publication of footage that suggests Koepka's caddie Ricky Elliott informed the bagman of playing partner Gary Woodland that they had hit a five iron into the 15th green. This would be in breach of Rule 10.2, which forbids sharing such information to advise a fellow competitor. The Masters committee investigate and find no breach. Former Ryder Cup skipper Paul McGinley tells US TV viewers he finds that 'staggering'.

Koepka typically laconically dismisses the fuss. 'We looked at it when we got back in,' he says. 'GW and Butchie [caddie Brennan Little] had no idea what we were hitting; I know that fact because GW asked me what we hit walking off.' It is OK to ask after the shots are hit.

Koepka looks ominously good, especially having just won in Orlando. Rory McIlroy, by contrast, makes another frustrating start.

Five birdies but a damaging double at seven, three putts at 11 and having picked up shots at 15 and 16 he drops one at 17. He holes a vital par putt at the last to get into the house at level par, seven shots off the pace and in 37th place. Not what he wants.

But he makes history, conducting the first in-round interview at the Masters. He walks the 9th hole with an earbud chatting with the CBS commentary team. Golf is evolving. Maybe because of the pressure of an upstart rival tour. 'I thought it would be a cool thing to do,' McIlroy told reporters in the post-round conference.

Later, on the 14th hole, Max Homa does the same thing. 'I feel like you should do it,' he says. 'That term, grow the game, gets thrown around a lot. At times we don't know what it means, but it does feel like that's a good way to maybe gain some perspective for the fans to enjoy golf a little bit easier. I mean, it's like being on a phone call for 10 minutes. It's not the end of the world. It might be a shade distracting, but I think if it's 5 per cent distracting and it's 95 per cent something positive for golf, I can get past that.'

Phil Mickelson was always one of the most popular figures at Augusta. Now regarded as a LIV ringleader, his reception from the patrons is more muted than in the past. 'I thought it was great. It's been great all week,' he insists. He cards a decent 71 on his return after missing last year's tournament. Asked what was going through his mind as he surveyed the scene on the first tee, he says: 'That I get to play Augusta National in the Masters and this is an awesome day, no matter what I shoot.'

FRIDAY 7 APRIL

A panicked bystander says it sounded like gunfire. People in grandstands overlooking the 15th green gasp. Spectators, patrons as they are known here, start running. That is usually a no-no in these parts. The wind has been whipping across the course, by no means gale force, but enough to bring down three tall, slender pine trees in a domino effect. Branches tangle in neighbouring canopies, slowing their fall sufficiently for the galleries to scatter. It is still amazing no one is hurt. The hooter sounds, play is suspended with 39 players still to complete their second rounds.

They will resume chasing a relentless Brooks Koepka. The LIV star compiled a bogey-free 67 to back up an opening 65. A year ago, he was missing the cut here. He tells me he tried to punch out the back window of his courtesy car, such was the frustration he felt at the time. Now it is defiant, calm satisfaction. He seems back to the player he was when winning four majors in quick succession in 2017, '18 and '19. He has now fully recovered from what he felt might have been a career-threatening knee injury.

'The whole goal is to win the Grand Slam, right,' Koepka says. 'I feel like all the greats have won here and they have all won British Opens as well. I guess it's one more box for me to tick.'

So matter of fact. So confident.

He has taken the Saudi money but has been comparatively lukewarm on LIV and, unlike most of the breakaway players here, he is not wearing team branding or anything that suggests he is a LIV player. We wonder if defecting would have been a more difficult decision to take if he had been as healthy as he is now? 'I think it would have been,' he admits.

Are the Masters committee happy with their decision not to impose a two-shot penalty for potentially illegal advice dispensed to Woodland the previous day? They have looked at further footage. Koepka can be seen stretching out all five fingers on his gloved left hand. Was it another signal to tell his playing partner that he hit a five iron into the 15th green? Koepka is quizzed again by officials. 'I'm taking my glove off,' the leader insisted. 'The last thing I'm going to do is give it [advice] to Gary Woodland, a U.S. Open champ. And the funny part about it, is I think if he would have known we were hitting five, he would have hit six because I don't think Gary is that short.'

It seems that is the end of the matter. LIV supporting social media is affronted that he is being 'victimised' but delighting in how Koepka is dominating the tournament.

There is also glee that McIlroy is toiling terribly. Having been so confident and behaving with such an air of destiny, he is now falling apart. Soon after Koepka finishes, the Northern Irishman signs for a 77. It is a miserable return as those breezes began to swirl. And at 5-over-par the winds are not enough to blow him back into the tournament. Yes, he was runner-up last year but that is two missed cuts in the last three years for the man who is currently number two in the world. He departs without comment. Even his staunchest supporter in the press building admits: 'That is not a good look. He should have spoken.'

SATURDAY 8 APRIL

It is another early start and rain is falling as we get to the course before first light. The tournament is in a race to finish on schedule.

When those trees came down they signalled the end of Friday's play. You would hardly know they ever existed this morning. A typically neat clean-up leaves the affected area near the 17th tee immaculate.

Tiger Woods is in a battle to keep alive a proud record of making it past the halfway cut in every Masters he has played as a pro. It looks in jeopardy when he bogeys the last hole to slip to 3-over-par. Golf's ultimate competitor does not care about the inclement weather taking a toll on his fragile body. 'I hope I get the chance to play this weekend,' he tells reporters. He means later today and tomorrow.

Woods needs help from Justin Thomas or Sungjae Im. If either drop shots on the way home then the cutline will move decisively in Woods' favour. It is cold, wet and windy. Thomas, Woods' best friend on tour – almost a family member – falls to pieces. He slips to 4-over. He is out; Woods is in. Thomas looks near to tears; inconsolable.

Jon Rahm makes a gutsy birdie on 17 as the rain teems down. His bogey at the last is not bad either given the saturating conditions. The Spaniard signs for a 69 that takes him to 10-under-par, two behind Koepka and guaranteeing he will be alongside the American for the third round.

Remarkably, they will also play with the young amateur Sam Bennett, who is a big story from the first two days. He lost his father terribly young due to early onset Alzheimer's. His dad's scrawled final message, 'Don't wait to do something,' is tattooed on the inside of Sam's forearm. I tell BBC listeners he seems to be following his father's message to the letter.

Augusta announce an $18m prize fund, a record for the tournament but $2m short of LIV's individual purses and those of the PGA Tour's designated tournaments. The winner will get $3.24m and Bennett thinks he is in the hunt. His head hits the interview room table in frustration when it is pointed out that he is ineligible for a cent of prize money because of his amateur status.

A dozen of the 18-strong LIV contingent make it to the final two rounds to guarantee a Masters payday. With Na and Oosthuizen as early withdrawals, Sergio García, Bryson DeChambeau, Bubba Watson and Jason Kokrak are the others taking an early bath.

Everyone wants to make the cut, but you could be forgiven for swapping a hot soak for going out again in these conditions. The players are in threesomes for the third round, using the first and 10th tees in a 'U-shaped draw'. It means Woods, who makes the cut 'on the number' at 3-over is in a familiar position of being in the final group. Less customary is that he is starting his round on the back nine rather than the first tee.

Woods toils in increasingly severe conditions. I'm on BBC Radio telling our British listeners that conditions are like a winter's day on Teesside, another colleague suggests the Lake District. We are not doing much for our country's tourist board. Then again, what we are experiencing is not exactly helping Augusta's cause to be regarded as a desired destination. Woods looks worse and worse. He seems in agony. He can hardly walk. It is very sad to see. A great sporting titan is struggling against and losing to a failing body.

At the other end of the leaderboard, Koepka and Rahm are starting to separate themselves from a chasing pack that cannot keep pace in the ever worsening weather. The duel is being billed as the establishment against the upstarts and in more judgemental quarters as good versus evil. It has a similar vibe to McIlroy v Reed in the Dubai desert – that was also a rain-hit tournament.

Here, even Augusta's famed drainage cannot cope. The hooter sounds in mid-afternoon. Another early end and now very little wiggle room to avoid the first Monday finish in 40 years. Seve Ballesteros won in 1983. Tomorrow would have been his 66th birthday. An omen maybe?

His compatriot Rahm will have to make up four shots on Koepka who is 13-under-par, but when they resume their third rounds the American leader will putt first to save par from 11 feet. The Spanish chaser has 9 feet for birdie, a potential two-shot swing from the off lies in wait.

SUNDAY 9 APRIL

A day full of possibilities begins with two inevitabilities. First, Woods pulls out. He was facing 29 agonising holes, starting on a chilly, but thankfully dry, morning. He cites a flare-up of plantar fasciitis in his heavily repaired right foot. 'I'm disappointed to have to WD this morning,' he tells his 6.6 million Twitter followers. We wonder when and if we will ever see him compete again.

The other certainty, well it feels that way, is Koepka misses and Rahm makes. We do get that two-shot swing. Game on, but both toil on the back nine. They each come home in 38 untidy blows for rounds of 73. Koepka maintains a two-stroke lead, but the chasing pack are now harbouring hopes of a final round tilt at the green jacket. Viktor Hovland is only three back, world number four Patrick Cantlay is four behind in fourth – spooky.

It's America versus Europe for the Masters, LIV v PGA Tour too, but golf's politics are taking a back seat for the closing round. This is set to be a classic major with Koepka and Rahm, two big beasts, in the final pairing.

Between rounds, Koepka was asked about letting a four-shot lead slip to just a couple of strokes. He testily stated that it had been two at the start of the third round and that it remains so. He is irritated by the question. Rattled maybe? He needs to reassume the certainty of the first 36 holes but undermines that with a wild pull left off the first tee.

Koepka makes an adventurous par and it is not until the third, where Rahm makes a brilliant birdie, that there is movement on the huge white leaderboards. The advantage that had been four at the start of the day is down to a single shot. Koepka bogeys the treacherous par-3 4th. Now they're level.

Then the American cannot get up and down from the back of six. Another shot gone. Rahm is ahead for the first time since sharing the top of the leaderboard after his first round 65. Then comes a sensational pitch into the par-5 8th for a second birdie and the Spaniard is two clear before both drop shots at the ninth. The European PGA Tour star remains a couple of shots clear.

Cheers echo through the pines, the sun begins to shine and the Masters finally feels like it should. There is spectacular golf, good and bad, all over the place but a glass ceiling seems to prevent the chasing pack from getting beyond 6- or 7-under-par. Hovland and Cantlay are particularly afflicted, but Rahm remains imperious.

The 28-year-old cruises round Amen Corner before picking up another birdie at 13. His tee shot at the next leaks right, as does Koepka's. Then the Spanish star channels his inner Seve, fashioning an inspired approach that takes the back left contours of the undulating 14th green (a piece of St Andrews real estate in deepest Georgia) and nestles next to the flag. A tap-in birdie. Game over. Surely?

Among the chasing pack, who shatters the glass ceiling? Astonishingly, it is Phil Mickelson. On the distant fringes all week, he casts off the indifferent form of his LIV career. The 52-year-old veteran birdies the last two holes for a 65 – his lowest Augusta round since 1996 – and sets the target at 8-under-par. 'Mickelson is not going anywhere right now,' I tell BBC listeners. 'He's going to sit back and see what the young ones can do. He enjoyed that.' He does sit and watch, keeping hungry reporters waiting, maintaining his low profile of the week.

You never know down the stretch at Augusta. 'A lot of good can happen and a lot of bad,' Mickelson later observes. But Rahm already has one arm in the green jacket by the time his only blip occurs. It come on the final tee. He gets lucky. The ghost of Seve nods a wild drive out of the trees and into open space short of the 18th fairway. From there, he makes par for a closing 69. A 'Seve style' four, he says in the Butler Cabin before receiving the jacket.

What a performance. He gave the field a two-stroke lead by four-putting the first hole on Thursday, played in the worst of the weather and won by four. Mickelson ties for second with Koepka, who cards a poor 75. He seemed to run out of steam. LIV, though, have two of the first three spots and with Patrick Reed tied fourth, they have half of the top six placings. Joaquin Niemann makes it four in the top 20.

The Greg Norman-predicted 'Team LIV' celebration on the 18th green becomes a distant memory. Mickelson, meanwhile, plays down perceived rivalry between the tours at this event. 'I wouldn't look at it like that,' he says. 'I'm very appreciative that we're here; that we are able to play in the majors. And I thought it was exciting that this tournament rose above it all to have the best players in the world here and lost all the pettiness; that was great.'

Rahm, though, is the man of the moment. He is back to world number one. The green jacket suits his burly shoulders. On first wearing, he glances at the fit. It is perfect in every regard. 'I got you, I feel good,' as the great Augusta resident James Brown used to sing.

TUESDAY 11 APRIL

Somewhere on the M25.

Atlanta airport was far more civilised for the return journey. Traffic flowed around Augusta too. The jams were gone; life was back to normal. You would never have known that this otherwise largely unremarkable US city had just been centre of the sporting world.

Heathrow was not bad for queues either, but traffic is typically slow for the taxi ride on London's orbital motorway. My phone buzzes with a news alert. 'Rory McIlroy pulls out of this week's RBC Heritage'. It is a designated event; he should be playing. It was his idea to have all the best players in the world competing against each other more frequently. Rahm is there. Defending champion Jordan Spieth, who has said he is exhausted by the new designated schedule, is there too. All of the other big names on the PGA Tour are there. But now, bar one.

Rules state you can only miss a single designated event this year. McIlroy already did that with the Hawaii Tournament of Champions in January, so he is now in breach of his own rules.

It later emerges his absence at Hilton Head will likely cost $3m out of his $12m payout from the previous year's Player Impact Program. There's little sympathy among his peers. 'He knew what the rules were,' says PGA Tour stalwart Joel Dahmen to reporters at the RBC Heritage. 'So, he knew what was coming. He also has so much money, he doesn't care about $3m.'

If ever a quote summed up the dividends being felt by the leading players as a result of the golf wars and the state of play at the top of the men's game, that was surely it.

10
FINES, BANS AND . . . ACCORD

'Maybe we should sit down and talk. . . . They must realise by now that we aren't going away.'

Greg Norman

Back in Augusta it is as though the air has been sucked out of the place. The city swiftly returned to its usual state in the days that follow the Masters. The imposing gates to Magnolia Lane and its verdant kerbs swing closed, the 'Members Only' sign that hangs at the entrance reminds passers-by that this most private golf club will remain exactly that for the next 50 weeks. Indeed, the course shuts for the summer when alterations are carried out in sultry heat too intense for members to enjoy playing golf, even at the famed Augusta National. That opportunity comes again when it reopens as temperatures drop the following autumn. Outside, traffic flows again, the jams disappear and the golfing bandwagon moves on.

Clearly, the majors were now golf's legitimate battleground. The only place where all of the world's best players can gather to take on each other. The words of former Aussie tour player Mike Clayton seemed prescient. 'It's going to be the good guys against the bad guys,' he told me at the start of 2023. 'The game is split but there's going to be this coming-together at the four majors. The day that a LIV guy wins one it's going to be massive. It's inevitable a LIV guy will win a major at some point, you would think.'

For PGA Tour players, the journey to Hilton Head and the RBC Heritage event is relatively short. It was another designated tournament, another $20m up for grabs, more than had been at stake for the previous week's major. LIV golfers, meanwhile, prepared for a much longer and pivotal voyage to Australia.

LIV's recruits departed Augusta with a pep in their step. Their collective performance at the Masters had boosted credibility. *Golf Digest*'s headline was 'Masters 2023: LIV Golf is winning'. Brooks Koepka proved he remained a force in the game and 52-year-old Phil Mickelson sharing second place was an added bonus. No one saw that coming. 'What Phil did on the final day with his 65 was akin to Rory McIlroy's charge to second place in 2022,' a leading player from the DP World Tour told me. 'Except Rory got way more credit for his 64. It was still a backdoor runner-up spot. Phil did it when everyone thought he was finished.'

McIlroy left Augusta after his miserable missed cut without comment. It was a wretched display few expected from a player who had ended the previous year as world number one. 'It sucked,' he finally admitted at a press conference at Quail Hollow in May 2023. 'It's not the performance I obviously thought I was going to put up. Nor was it the performance I wanted. Just incredibly disappointing.' Despite an early exit from The Players Championship, his form going into Augusta was largely encouraging, but now it seemed his prominent role as a golfing politician might be catching up with him.

In the two biggest tournaments of the year so far, McIlroy failed to make it beyond the halfway stage. The Northern Irishman knew missing the Heritage would hit him in the pocket, but for once in this money-laden era of men's professional golf, dollar signs were not everything. As his 34th birthday approached, McIlroy confessed a need to address his 'mental and emotional well-being'. He said golf had 'totally consumed my life for the last 12 months.' His salary sacrifice might have been $3m well spent.

McIlroy did not reappear on tour until the first week of May at the Wells Fargo Championship, a tournament played on one of his favourite courses, Quail Hollow in Charlotte, North Carolina. 'It's been a pretty tumultuous time,' he admitted at a news conference. 'I needed to reassess everything. That's what I'm looking forward to, and maybe not putting so much into it. And understanding there are other parts of my life that are important.'

Reassessments were going on elsewhere. British businessman Roger Devlin had not given up brokering a peace deal in the golf wars. On 14 April, five days after Jon Rahm had won the Masters, he wrote to Jimmy Dunne again on the same 'LIV/PGA STRICTLY PRIVATE AND CONFIDENTIAL and WITHOUT PREJUDICE email thread (released in the Senate hearing papers), revealing that the DP World Tour's boss was keen for a peace deal.

> Jimmy,
> As I'm sure you are aware we have hacked out a very rough proposal through the intermediation of Keith Pelley. This concentrates LIV's schedule largely within the fall season in accordance with Jay's wishes. As a dealmaker you will appreciate timing is everything. I believe we have a window of opportunity to unify the game over the next couple of months, otherwise I fear the Saudis will double down on their investment and golf will be split asunder in perpetuity.
> Let me know if you see any merit in a conversation?
> Roger

It is not clear whether this prompted what followed but very soon after this email was sent Dunne made a big move. He went right to the top of the opposition camp with a WhatsApp exchange with Yasir Al-Rumayyan, released in the Senate Hearing papers:

> Yasir – my name is Jimmy Dunne I am a member of the tour policy board I would like the opportunity for a call and then hopefully a visit best Jimmy.

It was a strikingly casual introduction to a man used to being referred to as 'Your Excellency', but it drew a favourable response:

Sure, would like to get in a call. I'm available now if that works for you.
Best,
Yasir

Dunne later replied:

So sorry was on golf course and board meeting – will call

After a couple of abortive attempts, both men completed a call that lasted approximately 20 minutes. After the conversation, Dunne sent via WhatsApp the message:

Thank you so much for the conversation will be back Jimmy.

These first steps towards a potential peace deal had been taken at 16.22 ET on Tuesday 18 April. Cordial emoji-laden texts followed from both men, with Dunne suggesting that fellow PGA Tour Policy Board member Ed Herlihy should also join future talks that could take place either in America or London.

It was a time when the LIV project was gathering momentum. Their tournament in Adelaide was a massive hit, their biggest success to date. It helped quench an Aussie sporting thirst by bringing world-famous golfers Down Under. 'In Europe and Britain you take it for granted,' Mike Clayton told me. 'You can see these guys at least three or four times a year – you can see them every week in America. We never see them.'

The Adelaide event was a genuine sell-out, a fact the breakaway league was desperate to celebrate. Ironically, they had capitalised on the indirect consequences of the PGA Tour's domination of the golf calendar.

By introducing a schedule over the previous decade that ended in late summer and started again almost a week later, a wrap-around season, the

American circuit had made it impossible for other established tours to prosper. 'The PGA Tour's wrap-around season was terrible for Japan, terrible for Australia,' Clayton said. 'It's not the PGA Tour's job to worry about the rest of the world, but the unintended consequences of the wrap-around tour was that it really hurt the overseas tours because it denied them their time in the sun – November and December.'

Although this was April, LIV arrived in golf-mad territory starved for too many years of top-level competition. Australia also wanted to celebrate having The Open champion in their midst. 'My mission was always to bring an event to Australia,' Greg Norman said to Fox Sports. 'To bring 48 of the best players . . . down to Australia regularly where you could build true value.'

With a nod to the Presidents Cup – the PGA Tour's biennial Ryder Cup-style clash between the USA and the 'Internationals' being staged at Royal Melbourne in 1998, 2011 and 2019 – LIV's CEO upped the rhetoric. 'The PGA Tour come in and raped and pillaged for one tournament – what is it, every 12 years – and they suck it dry and leave,' he said to Fox Sports. 'We are a leader in so many different ways and we are leading so far ahead of the Presidents Cup in delivering to Australia.'

Norman's comments were typically bullish but had more substance than much of his often Trumpian expressions on LIV's potency. They certainly reflected a growing confidence in the LIV set-up. 'Now, even the players are saying "Why don't we play two tournaments?" I know I am getting enquiries from other states and I look forward to unlocking those opportunities,' the LIV CEO added.

Everything said publicly pointed towards a future where LIV would be a permanent fixture in men's golf. 'Somebody came in and offered competition to the PGA Tour and they didn't like it,' Norman told News Corp Australia. 'Somewhere down the line in some way, shape or form, the two parties have got to come to the table.'

Norman's tone was perhaps more conciliatory but without sacrificing confidence in his product. He told the *Telegraph*: 'Maybe we should sit down and talk . . . why shouldn't it be sooner rather than later? They must realise by now that we aren't going away.' He had no idea that, elsewhere, talking had indeed begun.

What ensued at the prestigious Grange Golf Club in Adelaide could not have been more removed from the genteel traditions of the Augusta National a week or so earlier. It was golf 'party-style', where beer flowed copiously and fans offered raucous support. Players including Bryson DeChambeau downed alcohol from their golf shoes on the range – 'doing a shoey' – to the delight of a rowdy, young, male-dominated crowd.

The high point was not Talor Gooch's victory but a final-round hole in one for Chase Koepka, brother of Brooks. It came at the par-3 12th, known as the 'Watering Hole'. The pin was located in a friendly gathering spot to give the best chance of a big moment, showbiz meets competition, and commentator Jerry Foltz even predicted the likelihood of a tee shot disappearing into the cup. It was not the work of a clairvoyant that the announcer was proved correct and Koepka's success was just what a company selling its product on the motto 'Golf but louder' wanted.

Not that the party central 'Watering Hole' was an original premise. The idea of pitching a raucous stadium around a short hole was taken straight out of the PGA Tour's Phoenix Open playbook. Nevertheless, it still provided the biggest moment, to date, in LIV's short history. The shot made global headlines and spectacular social media footage went viral. Chase Koepka's nine iron landed 10 feet from the hole before the ball smoothly moved from right to left and disappeared into the cup. It sparked pandemonium. 'There it is,' roared commentator Arlo White. 'We promised you an ace on 12 and Chase Koepka has delivered!'

The player jumped into the air. Torrents of beer, plastic glasses and cans rained down. Thunderous cheers from the packed crowd echoed across the course. Similar scenes have played out on the 16th at the Phoenix Open, but when they do they tend to draw reproachful reactions and spark clampdowns on spectator behaviour. Here, there was a fundamental difference. These antics were celebrated and encouraged. 'That's one of the great moments in LIV Golf history,' White proclaimed.

Pumping music was cranked up, flames shot into the air from giant screens that flanked the hole. It became impossible to see the green because of the debris that had landed from the stands. 'I smelled like beer the whole entire rest of the day, it was wild. A crazy experience,' Koepka said. Few present seemed to notice the irony of such revelry being funded by Saudi Arabia, where alcohol is outlawed. They were too busy following instructions on big screens proclaiming a spontaneous 'sing along' to celebrate. Strains of Neil Diamond's 'Sweet Caroline' were belted out across the course. 'So Good! So Good! So Good!'

Gooch won his $4m first prize despite a final-round wobble after leading by 10 shots through the first 36 holes. The local press were impressed by the spectacle, reporting 'enjoyment and awe among the Adelaide public'.

After finishing fourth with a closing 66, Smith added to the hype. 'I would go as far as to say this is the best event I have ever played,' he beamed at the LIV press conference in Adelaide. It was quite a statement from someone who won his first major at the 150th Open on the iconic Old Course links of St Andrews.

'I'm probably biased a little bit, being from Australia, but this is what LIV Golf is about,' he continued. 'There's obviously a want in Australia for really high-quality golf and I think the fans here really enjoyed what LIV offers. There's no reason why we can't make it bigger. . . . For Aussies, I think this is the benchmark for not only, I guess, Australian LIV Golf, but kind of world LIV Golf. . . . This is probably the best atmosphere, infrastructure, crowds that we've had. It's pretty cool to call that our own basically.'

English former world number three Paul Casey added: 'Everybody here in Adelaide has had just the best time. They're so starved of world-class golf. I think this is the best field they've ever had assembled in Australia, outside of maybe a Presidents Cup. . . . They've embraced it.'

Another Englishman, DP World Tour player Eddie Pepperell was less impressed, especially with the hype that surrounded Koepka's hole in one. He took to Twitter and cited the Phoenix Open for hosting the original party hole. 'This has been happening at Scottsdale for years now, so not sure how much LIV is really changing things,' the two-times tour winner stated.

This prompted another outbreak of hostilities in the golf wars, as LIV's admittedly inebriated Richard Bland hit back. 'Ed . . . tell me where on DP World there's been a hole like this?' the veteran Englishman tweeted. 'Because in 22yrs of playing the tour I can't think of any. But maybe your 15 minutes on tour you know different.'

Bland had famously won the 2021 British Masters at the Belfry for his one and only European Tour success, a win so romantic it resonated enough to earn him a LIV contract. Pepperell has a waspish sense of humour and a sharp mind. 'Where to start. . . ' he replied. 'Suppose it's simple; in my 15 minutes I won more events than you did in 22 years. What the Tour has done (just to name a few); GolfSixes, Heineken hole at Himmerland, Beat the Pro in Holland. The Tour, which you spent 22 years on did ok for you mate.'

Bland was quick to back down, admitting he had tweeted after downing a few. 'I apologise for what I said,' he tweeted. 'I should know better not to tweet under the influence.' Nevertheless, the spat led to Bland being subjected to a Twitter 'pile-on' that prompted the veteran to deactivate his account. 'I'm sorry that happened,' Pepperell later told me.

Potentially more significant exchanges were taking place on the other side of the world. As LIV wrapped up their first raucously successful trip Down Under, they were oblivious to the fact that the man who was bankrolling them was now in talks with the PGA Tour.

Yasir Al-Rumayyan met with Jimmy Dunne in London on 23–24 April. A deal was on the agenda and they were not alone. PGA Tour Policy Board Chairman Ed Herlihy was at Dunne's side. Herlihy was a partner at Wachtell, Lipton, Rosen & Katz and one of Wall Street's most sought-after counsellors for mergers and acquisitions. Amanda Staveley and her colleague at PCP Capital Partners, Mehrdad Ghodoussi, were also involved, along with Mohannad S. Alblehed and Brian Gillespie of the PIF and global strategic advisor Michael Klein of M. Klein & Company.

Over dinner and the cigars that followed, Al-Rumayyan, Dunne and Herlihy talked golf. It was a get-to-know you encounter, where they were discussing their own swings as much as the set-up of the global game. The next morning, His Excellency partnered Herlihy to victory over Dunne and Gillespie at the ultra-exclusive Beaverbrook Golf Club to the west of London. They parted after lunch and Herlihy had made it clear that it was vital the pro game was unified. The *New York Times* later reported that Al-Rumayyan paused before replying: 'Let's see how that would work.'

In the course of their exchanges over those two unlikely days of accord, Herlihy and Dunne became convinced that Jay Monahan, their commissioner, should meet their Saudi rivals. Staveley sought to maintain the momentum with an email sent on 26 April, as released in the Senate papers.

Gentlemen,

Firstly, many thanks for making the time to meet with us in London. We felt the time spent together was invaluable – and we were particularly encouraged by your guidance and determination to find a solution to the current issues between the PGAT and LIV. Evidently, there's a real opportunity to build something truly remarkable – preferably under one roof.

As we discussed, it will be helpful to have a regular weekly catch up over zoom or the phone to keep updated on various matters. I am connecting the core team over email; understanding confidentiality is critical at this important time. Should you want this list expanded to include others – please let me know.

Separately I will liaise with His Excellency's office and revert back with suggestions for a zoom meeting next week. I enclose the electronic version of Monday's presentation for your files.

Looking forward to moving this project forward.

Thanks

Amanda

This quest for a win–win solution was happening in complete secrecy. To the outside world, the continuing differences between LIV and the golf establishment remained evident, especially with the breakaway circuit in such bullish mood. They were perhaps summed up best by three-times PGA Tour winner Pat Perez, who has become an outspoken LIV player and advocate. He responded to a question on how Monahan would be feeling about LIV's success in Australia, by saying: 'We don't give a damn how he feels. We know how he feels about us, so it's mutual.' In some media outlets this quote was attributed to Dustin Johnson, and LIV PR Jane MacNeille took to Twitter to clarify: 'Hey! It was actually Pat that said that, not DJ. They reported it incorrectly.' Curiously, Perez's comments did not make it into the official press conference transcript.

Other developments were occurring in the USA, where American Ryder Cup captain Zach Johnson seemed to hint that Brooks Koepka and Johnson might still be eligible for September's match. This was a surprise. It was thought that their PGA Tour suspensions would nullify their memberships of the PGA of America, which is a prerequisite for Ryder Cup eligibility. However, the two players had quit the tour before they could be suspended and had paid their PGA subscriptions. The US skipper said at the Zurich Classic's press conference in New Orleans: 'Those individuals that have left the PGA Tour, to my knowledge, are still members of the PGA of America. There's a grace period involved there. I don't know the specifics.'

With this in mind, the PGA of America's chief executive, Seth Waugh, was emerging as a potentially significant figure. His organisation's primary role is to represent the interests of 29,000 club professionals across the USA. But the body also runs the US PGA Championship and the American side of the Ryder Cup. This was what the PGA was left with at the highest level of competition after the split of 1968 that led to the formation of the PGA Tour.

Waugh comes from a business background that included leadership roles at Merrill Lynch before spending 13 years with Deutsche Bank, where for a decade he was the company's CEO of the Americas. He is an accomplished communicator with an easy manner and a deep passion for golf. A long-standing friend of PGA Tour commissioner Jay Monahan, Waugh was an independent director on the PGA's board before taking over as CEO in 2018.

Regarding his captain's opportunity to pick LIV players, Waugh told *The Times* a few days later: 'To say he doesn't have the ability or right to do that would be wrong. If the captain decides a person can fit his team chemistry and gives the team the best chance to win, then we will talk about that. It's complicated.'

Talor Gooch, meanwhile, was taking another eligibility issue into the spotlight through the standard of his golf. When LIV left Adelaide it moved to a lower-key Singapore stop. There, Gooch powered to back-to-back wins by defeating Sergio García in a playoff. The 31-year-old American was clearly in prime form and was surely worthy of an automatic place in the field for his country's national championship, June's US Open in Los Angeles. But he was not because Gooch fell foul of a rule change by the United States Golf Association (USGA), one that could only have been made with the aim of deterring players from joining LIV.

The top 30 finishers on the PGA Tour's year-long standings earn a ticket to play the season-ending Tour Championship. The USGA give US Open places to those 30 players, but inserted a caveat that not only must they finish top 30, but they must also 'be eligible for the Tour Championship'. Gooch finished high enough in the 2022 standings but was not allowed to play the PGA Tour's finale because he had already joined LIV. 'Any time we make changes to our criteria going forward, it impacts somebody and that stinks,' USGA boss Mike Whan stated to the Golf Channel. 'But we can only look forward.'

This prompted a furious response from Mickelson, who has been a long-standing critic of the USGA, usually for the way it runs the US Open, the one major he has never won. 'Hey Mike, what about changing a rule and making it retroactive to exclude someone who has already qualified?' Mickelson tweeted. 'How can Talor Gooch not take that personal? It's a direct attack on him and his career. How does it benefit the usga or US open? It doesn't. Just a d!*k move.' Golf's oldest major winner went on: 'He qualified 9 months ago via Tour championship. 3 months ago Whan changed the wording on the qualifying criteria to take it away. Total d!*k move by Whan. He leads our governing body. Sad.'

Gooch, who had picked up individual prize money of $8m in two weeks, also seemed sadder than you might imagine following such a fantastically lucrative fortnight. It was not his US Open plight that irked him, but the fact that the Australian tax authorities raided his Adelaide winnings before they had even entered his bank account. 'It sucked that 47½ per cent was withheld for Australian taxes,' he told the *Fore The People* podcast. 'I am by no means complaining, but the four [million US dollars] once you cut it all up, let's just say that it's a lot less than four. It was a little bit disheartening.'

This helped stoke a 'greedy golfers' narrative that had been growing across social media and message boards ever since the arrival of big Saudi money into the game. It was another area where the chatter around golf had grown more fractious.

But behind closed doors, the peace initiative was continuing. On 26 April, Staveley's PCP Capital Partners made a slide show presentation to Jimmy Dunne and Ed Herlihy. It was entitled 'Best of Both Worlds' and proposed a long-term agreement between PIF and the PGA Tour. It included some startling ideas: that Tiger Woods and Rory McIlroy – deadly opponents of the Saudi Arabian intervention – should own LIV Golf teams and play in at least 10 events. PCP also suggested a LIV Golf-style team event with qualifying tournaments held in Saudi Arabia with a final week in Dubai, a global golf investment fund managed by PIF, and at least two PGA events sponsored by Aramco or the PIF, with one of those held in Saudi Arabia. Membership of Augusta and the Royal & Ancient Golf Club of St Andrews for Yasir Al-Rumayyan was also mooted.

The Woods/McIlroy proposal was swiftly rejected by the two men doing the PGA Tour's bidding but there was still enough of a consensus for negotiations to ramp up in the weeks that followed. On 11 and 12 May, Monahan was brought into the discussions. He flew to Venice in Italy, where Al-Rumayyan was attending the wedding of the daughter of Formula One boss Lawrence Stroll. The PGA boss was desperate not to be recognised because this was tantamount to consorting with an enemy he had vilified throughout the golf wars.

The PGA Tour delegation flew via England's Farnborough private airport. There was an initial meeting once Monahan arrived in Italy and the commissioner later said that he knew within 10 minutes that the PIF governor was someone with whom he could do business. Monahan was under intense pressure. Legal bills were mounting at an alarming rate, the inflated prize funds he was promising to compete with LIV were going to be tough to finance and the

Department of Justice were asking awkward questions about the tour's tax-exempt non-profit status.

Meanwhile, in the DP World Tour offices at Wentworth, CEO Keith Pelley and his executives were thrashing out with legal advisors their next moves after winning the arbitration appeal at Sport Resolutions. How would they now punish the 17 players involved? If £100,000 fines were appropriate for playing LIV events without consent – as the judge had ruled – then how steep could they make punishments for repeat offences? Should they introduce suspensions? 'I think they are facing four to six week bans as well as fines,' speculated one member of the DP World Tour's tournament committee.

Simultaneously, in Singapore, European Tour players now plying their trade on the LIV circuit gathered to decide how to proceed. There was no agreement. Some wanted to quit the DP World Tour to avoid further punishment, while others preferred to wait and see what Pelley would decide. And it was a tough call for the boss because Pelley knew he could be presiding over the end of several stellar careers on his tour. Equally, he felt he had to act 'to protect our membership' and there was a constant need to act in the best interests of their strategic partners from the USA, the PGA Tour.

When he delivered his verdict, His Honour Phillip Sycamore CBE, along with barristers Charles Flint KC and James Flynn KC, actually disagreed with the DP World Tour's rationale for arriving at £100,000 as the level of fine. But they did rule that it was an appropriate figure. 'It was explained that the level of £100,000 had been chosen as it represented a sum just lower than the prize money available to the last-placed participant in the LIV event,' the verdict documents stated. 'That does not seem to us to be a necessary yardstick. It is appropriate for the financial sanction to be set at a dissuasive level. In the context of a player incentivised to sign up for a rival event backed by the resources available to LIV, a fine in the order of £12,000 would seem trivial.'

Seventeen LIV players were affected and they had until 3 May to pay their initial fines. As April moved into May, the clock ticked ever faster without the fines being paid. Some had signed for LIV on the understanding that the new tour would cover the cost of any punishment. Sources indicated that on Tuesday

2 May, LIV finally deposited £800,000 with the DP World Tour, without specifying which pros' fines they were paying.

On the same day, three Ryder Cup legends – Lee Westwood, Ian Poulter and Sergio García – resigned their European Tour memberships, effectively calling time on illustrious Ryder Cup careers. Westwood played in a record 11 matches, García was the continent's leading points scorer and Poulter was a legend of the matches. The Englishman almost single-handedly inspired the 'Miracle at Medinah' in 2012, when Europe came from 10–4 down to beat the USA in one of the greatest Ryder Cups ever played.

Before quitting, García spoke at length with Ryder Cup skipper Luke Donald. 'Obviously I had to make some decisions when it comes down to the DP World Tour,' said the Spaniard, who had been tipped to partner Jon Rahm if selected. 'I wanted to see where I stood in regard to the Ryder Cup. Luke obviously is a good friend. I wanted him to be sincere and tell me the truth, and he pretty much told me that I had no chance. Obviously that made my decision a little bit easier.'

Realistically, none of the three was likely to play in Rome that September, but their departures from their home tour still stung many fans. It confirmed no future Ryder Cup participation for figures who had been front and centre of so much European success over the previous two decades. 'It has not harmed our team for Rome,' said one former captain to me. 'But it has robbed us three future captains and strong members of the backroom team.'

Westwood called it 'a sad day' and few would disagree. Indeed, in a statement the DP World Tour thanked the players for their contributions, before adding: 'The resignations, however, along with the sanctions imposed upon them, are a consequence of their own choices. As we have maintained through the past year, the tour has a responsibility to its entire membership to administer the regulations which each player signs up to. These regulations are in place to protect the collective interests of all DP World Tour members.'

Ironically, this was the week of the Italian Open and so the DP World Tour were at the Marco Simone Golf and Country Club, the home of that September's Ryder Cup. The illustrious trio were joined by the veteran Bland in walking away from the circuit where they had made their names. Bland later revealed in an interview with BBC Radio Solent that he was facing an eight-week suspension and fines totalling £675,000 if he remained a member. He also confirmed: 'LIV are taking care of the fines, so any fines we incurred for playing they would pay.' And those financial penalties would only come into force if he rejoined the DP World Tour.

Europe's captain, Luke Donald, was competing in Italy. 'It's sad we've got to this point, but this was always a possibility,' the skipper told me. 'I played with all three and they've been stalwarts of, and given a lot to, both the Ryder Cup and European Tour. . . . They've got a lot of history when it comes to the Ryder Cup. . . . Ultimately this is their choice and I wish them well. They feel like this was the best choice for them and now I've got choices to make that are best for me.'

Across the pond, McIlroy was playing in South Carolina, where he echoed his captain's sentiments. 'It's a shame that you've got the highest points scorer ever in the Ryder Cup and two guys, that when they look back on their career, that's probably going to be at least a big chunk of their legacy,' he said to reporters. 'For those three guys to not captain Europe one day, it's a shame. . . . But as the DP World Tour said in their statement, at the end of the day that was their choice and they knew that these were potentially going to be the consequences of those choices . . . and here we are.' Not much sympathy there.

The fines were paid by 16 of the 17 players. García was the exception and the DP World Tour threatened 'appropriate action'. Westwood, meanwhile, delivered a withering verdict on his former tour in an interview with James Corrigan of the *Telegraph*. 'I'm not great on stats but I must have played something like 600 events, won more than 20 titles, and three Order of Merits,' Westwood said. 'So no, I never would have believed it had ended like this and there has to be a bit of sadness, of course.'

Westwood's LIV contract was said to be worth more than $20m. He added: 'People say I knew exactly what would happen, but nobody told us the extent of the punishments. And they continue to do that. The way I view it is that, as a European Tour member, I was allowed to be a member of the PGA Tour without any problem for all those years. Tell me, what is the difference? Just because LIV is funded by the Saudis – a country where my tour used to play and where we were encouraged to play?'

The source of LIV's money was never an issue for the DP World Tour. As Westwood pointed out, it had happily jumped into bed with Saudi Arabia before the arrival of Greg Norman's enterprise. The English player's response, though, took no account of the fact that LIV had effectively rolled their tanks, uninvited, into the European Tour's back yard. Several of their venues, including the Centurion Club in Hertfordshire for that crucial first event, were in DP World Tour territories. At no stage have the PGA Tour threatened that local primacy in the way that LIV now do.

'I've been a dual member of the European Tour and PGA Tour,' Westwood continued in his *Telegraph* interview. 'But always said I was a European Tour member first and foremost and that I had fears about the US circuit basically being bullies and doing everything it could to secure global dominance. Check my old quotes, it's all there. But now, in my opinion, the European Tour has jumped fully in bed with the PGA Tour and even though Keith says he hates to hear it, it is now a feeder tour for the PGA Tour. The top 10 players on the tour, not already exempt this year, have a pathway to the PGA Tour – that's giving our talent away. That was never the tour's policy before this "strategic alliance". Sorry, I don't want to play under that sort of regime.'

Pelley's deliberations on how to punish the players who had played LIV and Asian Tour events without his tour's consent stretched into the following week. It was not until the evening Thursday 11 May that they were revealed. Fines ranging from £12,500 to £100,000 per event and suspensions of up to eight tournaments were imposed on 26 players.

Henrik Stenson was the first to join the four originals (Westwood, Poulter, García and Bland) in jumping ship. The man who started the year as Europe's Ryder Cup captain quit the continent's tour. 'It is sad that it has come to this,' the 47-year-old Swede told *Golf Digest*. 'But it is what it is and it certainly wasn't unexpected. They left me with no other choice so I have resigned.' Stenson estimated fines would cost him between $50,000–70,000 for each LIV event he had played. He also said he did not want to say much more because he did not want to make the situation any more 'infected' than was already the case.

Like the 50-year-old Westwood – a former world number one of remarkable longevity – Stenson was aware his best days as a player were disappearing in the rear-view mirror. In Westwood's case, it was little surprise and perfectly understandable that he was no longer eligible for the majors, but that was not the case for several of his LIV colleagues, who were losing status because LIV events do not attract world ranking points.

The next of the big four championships was the US PGA, which started on 18 May. It is often regarded as the fourth most prestigious of the quartet of majors. This is despite many a marketing plan to bolster its status – 'Glory's Last Shot' was its tagline when it used to be played in August.

If it does have a unique selling point, it is that it assembles the strongest competitor list of all the grand slam tournaments. One way or another, the PGA seeks to get the top 100 players in the world into its 156-man field. It remained true to that ethos for its first championship in the LIV era. There was no room for García, who was ineligible for a major for the first time this century, but Casey, who was down to 131 in the world, was invited before withdrawing through injury on the Tuesday evening of championship week.

It was clear that, unlike the USGA, the organisers of this major were less inclined to discriminate against LIV golfers – a tacit acknowledgement that the upstarts had some of the world's very best players in its ranks. Seth Waugh was in a conciliatory mood and less inclined to make pariahs out of the LIV golfers. He had seen that they had contributed significantly to the success of the Masters and in an interview with *The Times* praised the 'civility' that had prevailed. He also knew that it was vital for his major to have the strongest-possible field.

The non-discriminatory policy against LIV meant that the in-form Gooch could look forward to taking his impressive game to one of the sport's biggest stages. So too could Dustin Johnson and Cam Smith in the week after they had shared a playoff with Branden Grace, which was won by DJ in the LIV event at Tulsa. This was their first tournament where the true heavyweights of their circuit came to the fore with Koepka and DeChambeau also in the mix. With crowds estimated at 40,000, this was good news for LIV, although in some territories their TV partners, the CW Network, ended their coverage early, which was a more sobering development.

They were turbulent weeks in the golf wars after the Masters. After former PGA champion Martin Kaymer withdrew, Gooch, Johnson and Smith were three of 16 players from the new tour who headed to Oak Hill in upstate New York. They were going to try to win a major but their collective mission was to prove that LIV's encouraging showing at Augusta had been no fluke.

Elsewhere, a different kind of momentum was building. Jay Monahan had circulated a document detailing Saudi Arabia's Project 2030 to senior PGA Tour executives.

There was a flurry of crucial emails on 14 May, made public via the released Senate papers. Staveley's colleague at PCP, Mehrdad Ghodoussi, wrote to Herlihy and Dunne asking for a first draft of a potential agreement that week and suggesting 30 May 'would be an ideal time for an announcement'. He pointed out that this would also work well with 'His Excellency's trip to San Francisco'.

Herlihy emailed Monahan and Dunne.

Jay and Jimmy,
I spoke with Amanda and Mehrdad a short while ago. Very good conversation. Y [Yasir] told them today to get it done. They asked about agreements; we are going to move them along.
I said we'd speak tomorrow afternoon. They love the idea of Jimmy going to the Grand Prix in Monaco. They will be there for the first 2 days as well. They will speak to Y about it but they agreed it made sense for Jimmy and Y to be together and travel to San Francisco together.
Best,
Ed

Monahan replied:

Thank you Mr Chairman! Nice to hear that momentum keeps building. Jimmy in Monaco is pure genius on so many levels.

PGA Tour chief operating officer Ron Price was now part of the inner circle and replied on this 'Next Steps' email chain, saying:

Thanks, Jay! This is awesome and exciting!

Wheels were in motion and not just on the cars that race around Formula One circuits. The golfing circus meanwhile moved on to its next major, oblivious to potentially seismic changes that were afoot.

11

US PGA DIARY

Oak Hill, Rochester, New York

MONDAY 15 MAY 2023

Arriving at Chicago's O'Hare International Airport was the first chance to check the PGA of America's media site for an updated press conference schedule. Dustin Johnson and Brooks Koepka have been added to the roster and will give their thoughts on Wednesday. This is reward for their recent LIV showings in Tulsa and further evidence that the year's second major is true to its word in welcoming players from the breakaway league. They are not being treated as poor relations.

Indeed, there is a LIV presence on the small American Airlines jet that ferries us to Rochester. One player representative is eager to agree that there is real momentum about LIV at the moment. 'We had good crowds in Tulsa and the big guys really turned up,' he tells me while we wait at the luggage carousel. 'It was another good week for us.'

Volunteers populate the arrivals area in PGA uniforms ready to show this week's VIPs to their courtesy cars. Hoardings remind us that a big event has come to town and I can sense a local buzz for what promises to be one of the biggest weeks of the golf calendar.

No longer 'Glory's last shot', this PGA – with Masters champion Jon Rahm heading a field that includes in-form LIV recruits – feels more like a genuine world championship of golf.

TUESDAY 16 MAY

First into the interview area is Rory McIlroy. It is a cool morning, frost delayed early practice rounds, and his choice of a thick hoodie seems a wise option. There is also a distinct chill to his manner. He is no longer the expansive advocate for golf's establishment. It is becoming clear he is downing tools as an unofficial spokesman for the PGA Tour in its fight against LIV.

'Is it going to be a conscious thing for you going forward to try and sidestep that narrative?' asks the *Daily Mail*'s Riath Al-Samarrai.

'Yeah,' is all the usually loquacious McIlroy says in reply.

American writer Alan Shipnuck tries his luck and does not get anywhere either.

'We're coming up on the one-year anniversary of the first LIV Golf tournament. If you could look into your crystal ball three years from now, where do you think the professional game will be?'

'I don't have a crystal ball,' McIlroy replies.

'You don't want to speculate?'

'No.'

It does not bode well for the joint radio interview I'm about to do with RTE's Greg Allen. It is our usual pre-major arrangement, where we each are allowed three questions. Before we get our chance, McIlroy does two television interviews. Greg and I wait, slightly anxious, wondering what questions might elicit chatty answers.

We need not have worried.

Greg goes first and probes McIlroy over why he is stepping back from the prominent public role he has played on behalf of the PGA Tour. 'I would rather people be talking about me for my golf rather than stuff I am doing behind the scenes or a press conference,' he volunteered. 'I don't regret anything I have done because I think it will help the next generation of players, hopefully. But now the wheels have been set in motion, it is time to focus on me and trying to get back to winning ways.'

Then I weigh in, admittedly with some trepidation because I do not want to waste one of my three questions on what might be a curt reply. Deep breath: 'How much of a jolt was the Masters? Because we spoke to you on the eve of that and we all felt you were exuding a great deal of confidence and relish for what was to come?'

He could have batted it away with a couple of words, but the answer was vintage, headline-grabbing McIlroy. 'I was never so sure that I was going to have a great week at Augusta, never so sure,' he began, his eyes widening. 'And then that happens. And it was a great lesson for me not to put too much into the feelings or vibes. You know, I shot 5-under on the back nine on the Wednesday afternoon and felt great and, like, everything was in a good spot.

'But that's golf. You know, golf can be an imposter at times. That was the chat I had with [mind coach Bob] Rotella the night before – you know "I feel so good, how can I not get ahead of myself?" And the game can bring you back down to earth pretty quickly. But I think the best way to deal with that is to not let yourself get to that level of expectation so early, right?

'And that's what I'm now trying to do. Take what the golf course gives me, play good golf shots and just try and have a bit more acceptance. If I think back to Augusta and maybe the few months before as well, my level of acceptance probably hasn't been where it needs to be. And if I work on that and do the right things then I know I will start to play some really good golf again, pretty quickly.'

Phew. Now it is time to get those quotes on the radio, BBC Sounds and our website. Newspapers were eavesdropping and McIlroy's words to Greg and me will spread far and wide.

While the player has withdrawn from active service in the golf wars, the PGA boss Seth Waugh is continuing the diplomacy. 'What we're about this week is having the greatest field in golf,' he tells reporters. 'Everybody who's here this week is our invited guest, and we're happy to have them and we're going to treat them all the same. A lot of these folks [LIV players] are people that I've known for a long time that are friends that I still talk to.'

But he does add: 'We don't think division is in the best interest of the game. . . . I struggle and I have since the beginning, even before the beginning, with understanding how it's a sustainable business model.' He added: 'I'm not sure that it's a superior product [LIV] and I'm not sure that it's a sustainable business model because nothing has changed my mind about either of those things.'

And as an official wrestling with the issue of whether LIV's application to be awarded world ranking points should succeed, he reiterated: 'We've been, I think, very responsive to them in terms of their requests, and they've been responsive to us. It isn't some battle.' Very diplomatic on a very divisive issue.

Masters champion Jon Rahm is another looking to dampen flames. Asked about the vibe at Augusta when players from both tours came back together for the first time this year, he refuses to be drawn. 'I'm the wrong player to ask,' he says. 'I never got into the feud. I've never had any negative feelings towards any player that went over to LIV. In fact, I've mentioned many times, I still play with many of them . . . try to play practice rounds with Phil [Mickelson], played with Talor Gooch yesterday. Really doesn't make a difference to me.'

WEDNESDAY 17 MAY

It's freezing. Temperatures have plummeted. Security guards are wearing face scarves to keep warm. Jason Day – not feeling fresh off his first win in five years at the Byron Nelson last Sunday – wears a beanie and is rugged up as he chats with reporters. He reveals he will compete without playing a practice round. 'It sucks to not be able to prepare the way I want to,' he says. 'But having mental tiredness out there won't do me any good.'

The course is playing every inch of its 7,400 yards and there are fears of another delayed start tomorrow due to frost.

McIlroy's cold demeanour to the press yesterday makes headlines in the American media. The shift is noted, some reporters speculate that all is not well in Camp Rory, but the truth is probably less sinister. An insider mentions that his reserved and curt responses are because he is 'pissed off' at the way he was treated by reports covering his withdrawal from the Heritage a month earlier. McIlroy, for so long the darling of the golf media, is bearing a grudge, it is claimed. That might explain his more expansive mood with us broadcasters. In one of those interviews he revealed he has sought tips from Tiger Woods to help fix his two-way miss (hitting uncontrolled shots both left and right) when he struggled at Quail Hollow in his most recent tournament. Time will tell whether McIlroy has found a solution to his golfing woes.

US Ryder Cup captain Zach Johnson is asked whether he thinks his namesake Dustin is still among the top dozen players in the USA. In other words, should he be in the American team in Rome this September? 'Really difficult for me to judge that,' the skipper replies. 'I don't know the golf courses they [LIV] are playing. Never seen them. I'm not there on foot in person.' This answer shows disdain for the prospect of picking LIV players. Surely, if they were on the captain's radar he would be evaluating their performances. He also forgets that Dove Mountain, which staged LIV's Arizona stop, used to stage the WGC Matchplay and Sentosa in Singapore has been a regular venue for Asian/European Tour events in the past. He should know them pretty well.

On DJ, Zach Johnson adds: 'You're talking about an individual whose resumé is extremely deep and wide. He's certainly, in my generation, one of the best players I've ever competed against. But it's not fair for me to guess his true form or anybody's true form that I can't witness.'

And what about Brooks Koepka, after his runner-up finish at Augusta? 'I haven't really seen where he's at since Augusta,' Johnson admitted. 'He played really good that one week. But it's one week.' Not exactly brimming with enthusiasm for his chances of making the US team. 'There's still a lot of golf between now and then. One of the factors that we've looked at over the years is what kind of form are the guys in when it gets close to the Tour Championship. I think that would be wise for me to look at. I remember playing really well one spring thinking, "Man, I've got this, I'm a shoo-in," and I didn't make the team. There's a lot of factors involved.'

Away from Oak Hill, the *New York Times* reports on the latest developments as US authorities examine the state of the pro game. The paper says that the Justice Department's antitrust inquiry has included interviews with players, naming Phil Mickelson, Bryson DeChambeau and Sergio García. The investigation is also checking whether the PGA Tour sought to manipulate the labour market of men's professional golf and whether there has been collusion with the majors and official golf world rankings.

This comes at a time when many in the golf establishment continue to pin hopes on Saudi officials running away from being compelled to give discovery evidence in the PGA Tour's antitrust case against LIV. For both sides, significant skirmishes are being played out in legal corridors.

Meanwhile, the *Daily Mail* reports that Amanda Staveley, director of Saudi Arabia-owned Newcastle United, has been 'viewed as a potential peace broker for the controversial breakaway circuit in golf's civil war.' The paper also admits: 'It is unclear if her efforts have so far amounted to any progress at a time when the PGA Tour and LIV have been locked in bitter litigation.'

Jon Rahm and Scottie Scheffler are the bookies' favourites. The establishment would love one of their superstars to prevail in the way Rahm did at Augusta. Jordan Spieth completing the career grand slam would suit the PGA Tour perfectly and he declares himself fit after missing the Byron Nelson in his native Texas last week due to a wrist injury. DJ and Koepka dominate thoughts regarding LIV contenders. I find it odd that Cam Smith is not being mentioned. The Open champion is surely better than a 40–1 shot, isn't he?

THURSDAY 18 MAY

First light yields a scene fit for the front of Oak Hill's Christmas cards. As predicted, the course is coated with frost and the gates remain shut for early arrivals to 'protect the playing surfaces'.

Play begins nearly two hours late and Rory McIlroy is among the early starters. He may say he is concentrating purely on his golf now but he still looks preoccupied. His golf is imprecise and the course is unforgiving. At the second, his 11th, he is staring at the prospect of slipping 4-over-par before unexpectedly holing a putt up a severe slope from off the back of the green. It is a turning point and he covers the remaining holes in 2-under to finish with a 1-over-par 71. Nevertheless, he describes the round as 'messy'. He says: 'Just not at my best. I'm just struggling with my swing.'

Bryson DeChambeau becomes the first-day story. Many have likened this course to Winged Foot where the big-hitter won his lone major in 2020 and he appears at home. Fifth last week in the LIV event in Tulsa, DeChambeau looks the force of old in a 66 that will cheer the breakaway tour. 'It's a fantastic round of golf at Oak Hill,' he tells reporters. 'It's a prestigious place. Very difficult golf course. . . . I don't know how shooting under par is even possible out here on some of the golf holes.'

The conversation centres around his newly slimline figure. He has undergone a striking transformation. 'A lot of diet changes. . . . Carrie, my chef, she helps me out with that,' DeChambeau tells us. 'I took a Zoomer peptide test, which essentially tells you what inflames your blood when you eat it. I was allergic to corn, wheat, gluten, dairy. Pretty much everything I liked, I couldn't eat. I took that out. Started taking it out in August and over the course of time I've lost all this inflammation, lost a lot of fat and slimmed down like crazy.

'I lost 18 pounds in 24 days. It was crazy. It wasn't fat. It was all water weight. You know how I looked before. I was not skinny. So a lot of changes in that regard. Obviously having the hand injury was no fun and then learning to play golf again with a new hand.'

Apart from last week, his LIV results have not come close to justifying his rumoured $100m joining fee. 'The emotions have definitely fluctuated pretty high and pretty low,' he admits. 'Thinking I have something and it fails and going back and forth. It's humbling. Golf, and life, always has a good way of kicking you.' Hidden away on the LIV tour, DeChambeau has been off mainstream media for too long. He is missed. Always wacky, he remains one of golf's most quotable stars.

As the day goes on, LIV has more to cheer. Dustin Johnson finishes his 67 in the gloaming, as play is eventually suspended at 8.30 p.m. He sits alongside Scottie Scheffler, who was bogey-free in his 3-under-par round. 'It's just one of those places where you hit one shot maybe barely offline, and sometimes you can hit a good shot and end up in a place where it's pretty penalising,' Scheffler says to reporters. The man who replaced him as Masters champion, Jon Rahm, cards a surprising and miserable 76, where his putter was uncharacteristically cold. Talor Gooch signs for the same score.

By night's end, the chill has returned to refrigerate everyone at Oak Hill. This includes Tom Kim, the exciting young Korean who is potentially such an asset to the PGA Tour. In the interview area, his infectious smile helps him laugh off falling into a muddy swamp as he played his second shot at the sixth. He emerged covered in mud. The 20-year-old played the rest of his round with his trousers rolled up and his ruined shirt tucked away in his golf bag. Footage goes viral. Golf is developing a new character, potentially worth his weight in gold – or oil? LIV would surely love to have him on their roster.

It will be a short turnaround before the 11 groups still to finish their first rounds return to the course at 7 a.m. tomorrow.

FRIDAY 19 MAY

It is early, but it feels much more spring-like. The forecast rise in temperatures will surely materialise. Justin Rose finishes his round by chipping in for a 69 while overnight leader Eric Cole, playing only his second major, limps home by slipping from 5-under to 3-under. It means DeChambeau is out in front by a shot as the first round scores go into the books. Somewhere far away Greg Norman is purring.

'Grow the game' is one of Norman's great mantras. He believes that is precisely what his LIV enterprise is doing on a global scale, but others would argue that sort of work is done much closer to the recreational game. They argue the real heroes in spreading the golfing word are club professionals teaching beginners, helping lower handicaps and selling equipment and merchandise that ultimately leads to yet more money flowing into the pockets of top stars.

Michael Block is one such figure. A club pro from Southern California, he is one of 20 from the ranks of tee and ball vendors who have qualified to join the, otherwise, strongest major field of the year. Block is having the week of his golfing life. He cards a second successive level par-70 despite an awful shank on the fifth tee that led to a double bogey. The 46-year-old is mobbed by reporters seeking an early story on a day that is clearly going to be another grind for all concerned.

Block, who was inspired by constant shouts of 'You're one of us, do it for us,' obliges. At level par, he is currently beating the Masters champion Jon Rahm by six shots. 'Pretty cool, to say the least,' the club pro says, eyes welling. 'I wish those guys could come to my office and hang out with me and come teach with me on the back of the driving range with my students who are out there right now. I don't know why that makes me emotional, but it does. Sorry, Jon.'

Rahm is a later starter with fellow major champions Cam Smith and Matt Fitzpatrick. They are all in a battle to make the cut. The winner at Augusta is still afflicted by a cold putter but the ball striking is better as he cards a 68 to make the cut at 4-over-par. He will have another date with Smith tomorrow as the Aussie finishes on the same mark. But Fitzpatrick messes up the last and is on his way home.

Scheffler looks ominous even if his putting is still a little off. The Players champion adds an afternoon 68 and is joined at 5-under by

Canada's Corey Conners and the Norwegian Viktor Hovland – whose short game, especially from the bunkers, looks much improved.

Brooks Koepka has a fine afternoon after rains soften the course and the gusty breeze drops. He posts the day's low round, a 66 that leaves him three behind.

Handy.

DeChambeau bogeys the last for a 71, he's tied fourth, two off the pace. Also handy. 'It's been a few years, but it doesn't mean I don't know how to do it,' he says to reporters.

And McIlroy is still hanging around. There's no bounce, no joy about him – but he is battling. A birdie at the last has him puffing out his cheeks. It's a 69 that has him level par, within five at the halfway stage. 'Jeez, I need to be patient with the way I'm hitting it off the tee,' he says. 'I hardly miss a shot on the range, and then it's just trying to get it to go from the range to the golf course that I'm finding difficult.' Confidence is fragile, but he has a chance. Earlier in the week, he said: 'I've realised I often play my best when expectations are low.' He'll start round three on the same mark as Michael Block.

Along with Fitzpatrick, Gooch misses the cut.

SATURDAY 20 MAY

Why is Phil Mickelson wearing sunglasses? Those aviators are now his trademark look but it is dark overhead and rain is falling in stair rods. He is head to toe in black waterproofs and wearing two gloves to maintain his grip. Starting at 5-over-par, he made the cut on the mark and it is the 100th time the 52-year-old has made it through to the weekend of a major. That is an astonishing statistic. For all the controversy that has followed him through the golf wars, he remains an extraordinary figure for excellence and unparalleled longevity. 'It shows that I've had a lot of great experiences in the game of golf,' Mickelson later says. It'll be a soggy trudge today, though.

And it proves too much for world number one Jon Rahm, in the unfamiliar position of being out early on a major weekend. On the par-3 5th, he hits a poor chip and takes it out on an on-course boom microphone. At the par-4 8th, the burly Spaniard rounds on a TV cameraman. 'Stop aiming [the camera] at my face when I'm mad! It's all you guys do,' he says. A day earlier he was heard saying of the par-3 11th, 'Great hole, PGA. Great fucking hole.' It has not been a happy week for the Masters winner.

The rain is relentless. It will be hard but potentially lucrative work for the late starters. The PGA of America announce a $17.5m purse with $3.15m going to the winner.

On the first tee, as he emerges from underneath his Team USA Ryder Cup umbrella, Bryson DeChambeau is booed. He is preparing to tee off with LIV colleague Brooks Koepka, who also gets a mixed response from the crowd. 'It's not a big deal,' DeChambeau later claims at the press conference. 'They're gonna do that no matter what. Look, it's New York, you've gotta expect it here. And I appreciate the fans, and them doing that to me. . . . I've got no problem either way. If I'm loved, that's fantastic. If I'm not, then you know what? It's fine.'

DeChambeau shoots a level par-70 to remain 3-under-par, three behind LIV colleague Koepka. 'I think we have a common goal, growth of the game. We have franchises to focus on now,' says DeChambeau.

By day's end, Koepka fires another 66 to take a one-stroke advantage over Viktor Hovland and Corey Conners. Koepka's putter is inspired, including a bomb from long range on 17. 'I love New York,' Koepka says. 'It's always fun. You do something really well, they are going to let you know; and if you do something pretty poor, they are going to let you know, and I just love that. I love when the fans are on you, cheering for you, or you know, giving you crap if you screw up.' He insists he has learned the lessons of Augusta where he blew his two-shot lead going into the final round. He is eyeing a fifth major title and third PGA.

Meanwhile, the wholesome narrative generated by Michael Block continues. He holes a string of big putts in the company of Justin Rose to card a third straight 70 and he is tied eighth within six of the lead after

146

54 holes. The Californian club pro is caught on camera as the light fades. Reporters tell him he is paired with Rory McIlroy for the final round. He spins in utter disbelief. 'I'm living a dream,' he had told CBS viewers earlier in his round.

The dream continues.

McIlroy, meanwhile, has battled to another 69. He's not out of it despite being well short of his best. He's five back. 'I still don't feel like my game is in great shape,' he admits to reporters. 'I've held it together well.' Justin Thomas came from seven behind 12 months ago. I wonder if he has that in mind. 'If you had have told me on Thursday night that I'd be going into Sunday in the top five and with a realistic chance to win this golf tournament, I would have taken it,' McIlroy adds. The bookies have him at 20–1; they do not seem unattractive odds.

SUNDAY 21 MAY

It is a glorious day, one fit for the final round of a major. The course was softened yesterday, there are now clear blue skies and a negligible breeze. There will be birdie chances aplenty and a very realistic prospect of a LIV victory. That would mean the breakaway league simultaneously holding two of the four grand slam trophies.

The big question is whether Koepka can atone for squandering his two-shot 54-hole lead at the Masters last month. He called it a 'choke' and one he is determined not to repeat. He would never admit it but there is evidence to say he is prone to final-round slip-ups. Since his 2019 PGA win, he has entered the last circuit of a major in the top 10 six times – his scores: 68, 74, 74, 70, 74 and 75.

Interesting quotes on the Masters miss from Koepka's coach Claude Harmon surface in *Sports Illustrated:* He says his pupil was 'devastated' by his Augusta defeat because of how much he cares about winning majors. Harmon adds: 'There's this argument that everyone who went to LIV got the bag [money] and nobody gives a shit anymore . . . Guys don't one day just wake up and not give a shit.'

McIlroy stripes his drive down the middle on the first and then nearly holes his second. Tap-in birdie. Could he? At the second he bogeys from the middle of the fairway. No, he can't.

Another dropped shot at the fourth. His race is run.

Koepka birdies two of the first three holes. Jon Rahm is on a PR restoration mission after his earlier tantrums and joins the TV commentary team on CBS. 'He's like a shark in the water when it smells blood,' the world number one says of the championship leader.

Koepka is looking in control but Oak Hill remains a formidable test and Viktor Hovland's ball striking allows the Norwegian to constantly nip at the front-runner's heels like a tenacious terrier. Then a key moment at the long 13th. Hovland makes a textbook birdie after picking up a shot at the previous hole – he's charging. Koepka is out of position all the way through the par-5. He has around 13 feet to stay in front by a single shot. And he makes the putt. This is the moment we know his temperament is more than intact.

Hovland then finds the same bunker that did for Corey Conners the previous day on 16. Remarkably, we witness a similar outcome. Hovland piles his nine iron second shot into the lip and has to take a free drop for an embedded ball. It costs him a double bogey six and his chance of landing a first major evaporates. Koepka smells blood. Pounces. Sinks his teeth into the Wanamaker Trophy with a clinical birdie. Game over.

The course remains abuzz, though. Commentating for BBC Radio, the images I watch come from an iPad that is in synch with the feed being used by my fellow commentators back in England. Sometimes it can be hard to pick up the ball on the tablet screen. When Michael Block hit his tee shot on the short 15th we were discussing the top of the leaderboard, not a club pro who was out of contention.

He was not part of the conversation.

But I see his swing and follow the ball as best I can and then it disappears. I'm not sure where it has gone. Then I realise why, and I'm calling a massive moment. The ball has plunged straight into the hole for an extraordinary ace. Pandemonium! For all Koepka's brilliance, this is *the* moment of the 105th PGA. A club pro having the time of his life provides a much-needed reminder of the romance of the game. Mind you, it is noticeable that he is now wearing an official TaylorMade cap, compared with the tattier version of the previous day. A weekend on national television.

Ker-ching!

Koepka is a worthy champion. This is a win with ramifications as wide as his brilliant smile. Players now know they can win the biggest titles while playing LIV's lucrative shortened format. He must be a shoo-in for the American Ryder Cup team, no matter how uncomfortable that will feel for captain Zach Johnson and potentially some of his team members. 'They have to be careful with the Ryder Cup,' a former captain of Europe tells me. 'What if Europe win and America haven't picked their best team. For Rome we're not affected in playing terms, we've just lost future captains. The US team would be weaker if they leave out people like Brooks.'

Koepka, who rises to second in the qualifying table, might not want to be the only LIV guy in the line-up. A wildcard for Dustin Johnson? Maybe.

Frost returns to Oak Hill when Golf Channel pundit and arch Saudi critic Brandel Chamblee debates with colleague Brad Faxon whether Koepka should be included in the US team for Rome. Faxon, Rory McIlroy's putting coach, says: 'They're not playing for money at the Ryder Cup, Brandel, they're playing for their country.' Chamblee counters by saying: 'I think you make a reasonable point,' but in a sarcastic way that leaves no one in any doubt that he does not agree. 'They're playing golf,' Faxon says coldly, prompting one of those icy TV silences that seems to last forever. 'A stand-off here,' he laughs, slightly embarrassed, to end the awkward moment.

As Koepka is photographed with the trophy, PGA officials step in one by one to have a snap with the new champion. Seth Waugh is one of them and says something into the winner's ear that leads to a bemused look on Koepka's face. The PGA boss later tells Golf Channel's Todd

Lewis: 'I literally said to him, "I think they have four million pictures of me. They must have 24 million pictures of you. I've never seen one of them and I don't know if you ever have." He cracked up.' Waugh also said he had shaken Koepka's hand and told him how proud he was of him. 'Everybody is trying to make it into this LIV thing, which it's got nothing to do with.'

Koepka is not overly keen to draw parallels with LIV in his moments of triumph. He makes no immediate contact with Norman: 'I called my wife, and that's it,' the champion says in the post-tournament press conference. 'That's the only person I'm really interested in talking to.' He adds, fondly glancing at the Wanamaker Trophy, 'Yeah, it's a huge thing for LIV, but at the same time I'm out here competing as an individual at the PGA Championship. I'm just happy to take this home for the third time.'

He adds that what makes this really special is the way that it validates his battle back from potentially career-threatening injury. 'Pardon my language, but it's all the fucking shit I had to go through. No one knows. No one knows, I think, all the pain. There's a lot of times where I just couldn't even bend my knee. Yeah, it felt good. It felt really good.'

Meanwhile, Block is holding court in the player interview area. He reveals the PGA Tour have given him the last sponsor invite for their next stop, the Colonial in Texas. Block is already arranging flights. 'I'm looking forward to that, to say the least,' he says. 'I always had this thing . . . I always saw myself coming down the stretch with Tiger Woods. I was like, I'm going to do it, even if I'm 45 or whatever it is, I'm going to come down the stretch at an event with Tiger.

'It just happened to be that I was in the 2023 PGA Championship at Oak Hill, and I had Rory McIlroy in my group. I wasn't coming down the stretch to win, but at the same time, Sunday at a major with the crowd here at Rochester was unreal.' He had just given a tearful interview to CBS and it all comes down to his love of the game. 'The one thing in the world that makes me cry is golf,' he explains. 'If that puts into context as far as how much I love the game, you know now. It's everything to me.

'Obviously I love my family and everything else and my job and everything, but golf is my life. I live it, breathe it. I made sure of one thing in my life: that I was going to drive to a golf course every day, whether it was as a caddy or an onsite service kid or an assistant pro or a head pro or general manager, I was going to be at a golf course. I came to the golf course today at Oak Hill and played in the PGA Championship.'

He cannot stop talking. For cynical hacks covering a sport at war, his quotes are refreshingly open. A stark contrast from the carefully chosen non-committal prose that often flows into our notebooks. 'I was at the Pittsburgh Pub on Sunday night,' Block continues. 'Not one single person knew me. I'm going to go there in about an hour, and it's going to be on. We're going to have a crazy good time tonight, and I look forward to it. My life's changed, but my life's only changed in the better. I've got my family. I've got my friends. I've got the people that really love me and care about me here. It's an epic experience.'

One that money cannot buy.

But LIV are ready to party, too. Koepka's win is vital to their business model and injects energy for their upcoming tournaments in Washington, Spain and England. I'm on the bus back to my hotel, scrolling golf Twitter. Greg Norman is prominent in my timeline: 'Congrats @ BKoepka your comeback has been impressive. I am so proud of you. As for the @livgolf_league players they belong and the Majors and golf knows. 3 LIV Golfers in the top 10, 5 in the top 20, 11 made the cut.' The LIV irons are hot. It is, surely, time to strike.

12
DEAL DONE?

'Today is a momentous day for your organisation and the game of golf as a whole. . .'

Jay Monahan

Brooks Koepka was now being hailed as golf's most dominant figure of the post-Tiger Woods era. His five major titles put him ahead of Rory McIlroy in the pantheon of golfing greats. The only active player with more major titles is Phil Mickelson with six. It had become impossible for US Ryder Cup captain Zach Johnson to ignore the burly Floridian for September's defence of the trophy in Rome. 'Koepka's win forces the PGA of America to confront directly the toxic issue of LIV golfers' involvement in the biennial tournament,' wrote sports columnist Kevin Garside on the *Independent* website. 'There is nothing in the regulations to prevent selection. Exclusion would therefore amount to prejudice.'

Koepka's coach, Claude Harmon blasted the golf media for underestimating the standard of LIV Golf. He attacked critics who claimed that 54 holes was an insufficient test of a player's ability. He also heavily criticised the notion that LIV golfers' competitive instincts had been dulled by copious amounts of guaranteed money. The coach said to *Golfweek*: 'How you guys all thought that these guys just weren't going to show up and be great players is beyond me.'

If the three-times PGA champion was now nailed on to retain his Ryder Cup spot, the same could not be said of Europe's record points scorer, Sergio García. By joining fellow former teammates Lee Westwood and Ian Poulter in resigning from the European Tour, the Spaniard had removed himself from eligibility for selection. He held out some hope until he spoke to captain Luke Donald during that fractious spring. 'I wanted him to be sincere and tell me the truth,' García said when LIV arrived for their next event at the Trump National in Washington DC. 'He pretty much told me that I had no chance. . . . It was sad because I felt like not only because of my history but the way I've been playing, that I probably could have a chance.'

García's likely Ryder Cup partner, fellow Spaniard Jon Rahm, weighed in at the PGA Tour's Memorial Tournament. 'I'm going to miss him,' the Masters winner told reporters. 'We had a great partnership at Whistling Straits. . . . So it's a little sad to me that politics has gotten in the way of such a beautiful event. It's the best Europeans against the best Americans, period. And whatever is going on, who is playing LIV and who is not playing LIV, to me shouldn't matter.'

It looked as though Europe were heading for a potential disadvantage in Rome, unable to pick from a full deck of cards, unlike their American opponents. But more pressing for the DP World Tour's boss Keith Pelley was the search for an overall solution to the ongoing power struggle in the game. The diminutive Canadian, with a penchant for colourful eyewear, flew to San Francisco to become part of the tiny group of people aiming to complete what was still a top secret peace deal. This was the climax to the process, a meeting that once again brought together the PGA Tour with Saudi Arabia's PIF. LIV's hierarchy, meanwhile, remained oblivious.

Jimmy Dunne, Ed Herlihy and Jay Monahan were joined by John Wolf, who was a key figure in the commissioner's office at the PGA Tour. The officials busily set about agreeing their position as they flew on the tour's private jet from New York to California. They wanted to be ready for this vital gathering where, from the PIF, Yasir Al-Rumayyan was again joined by Mohannad S. Alblehed and Brian Gillespie. Amanda Staveley and Mehrdad Ghodoussi were also there from PCP Capital, as was Michael Klein.

This gathering between 28 and 30 May at San Francisco's Four Seasons hotel was crucial. Everyone present was there in good faith and all sides needed a successful outcome. The PGA Tour could not afford to continue to stump up vast legal fees for the ongoing litigation. The DP World Tour were dependent on their American partners remaining strong and Yasir desperately wanted Saudi Arabia at golf's top table as a legitimate force rather than renegade upstart.

In the run-up, at least eight drafts of a potential agreement were exchanged. The first was drawn up nearly two weeks earlier. The idea of staging a global World Golf Series event concluding in Saudi Arabia was thrown out. But a new for-profit entity combining the PGA and DP World Tours with PIF, known at that stage as 'NewCo' was at the heart of what was being thrashed out. Significantly, on 29 May, a broad 'non-disparagement' clause was added. It meant golf's establishment could no longer bad-mouth Saudi Arabia.

PGA Tour officials asked for a side agreement specifying that LIV Golf CEO Greg Norman and the public relations company that was in effect running LIV, Performance54 (P54), would not be retained. Norman and P54's dismissal should occur by a specific date. Covert discussions had already taken place over who would oversee LIV once Norman was gone. As emails released in the Senate hearing showed, in mid-May, Herlihy emailed Dunne saying, 'Jimmy, I raised the idea with Jay of you overseeing LIV going forward. He really liked it.' Dunne replied, 'You and me,' and Herlihy responded, 'Definitely. Meant to say both of us.' When this emerged, many observers interpreted it as a self-serving carve-up by the tour's two lead negotiators.

The rest of the golfing world had no idea. The news agenda was being set by Phil Mickelson taking a swipe at the world rankings for not including LIV events. Bryson DeChambeau was having to again defend his decision to take $125m of Saudi money, while 9/11 families protested at Donald Trump's course in Washington. 'You can talk about ethics, that's people's perception,' said the

2020 US Open winner. 'I completely disagree with [the criticism], but everybody has a right to their own opinion, and I'd say: "Was it worth it? Absolutely."'

DeChambeau's comments did not impress the local mainstream media. The *Washington Post* argued that LIV did not have 'legitimate events'. The paper said the tournament had 'a Trumpian feel' and that the tournament's positive messaging was trying to 'get people to believe that fiction is fact.'

Unbeknown to anyone other than those meeting on the other side of the USA, the people behind LIV were, in fact, potentially securing golfing legitimacy, which was Yasir's prime motivation. Fiction was about to become fact. A Framework Agreement was signed in the early hours of 30 May.

With the ink drying on his signature, Monahan departed for Jack Nicklaus' Memorial Tournament in Ohio. Nicklaus, along with Arnold Palmer, had been an architect of the breakaway from the PGA of America that created the tour in 1968. What had been agreed after seven weeks of covert negotiation was arguably the biggest development in men's professional golf since that era-defining moment 55 years earlier.

How to break the news was the next concern. Dunne wanted to wait until a complete agreement had been reached. There were still a considerable number of unanswered questions. He emailed his worries to all sides and Klein responded, as released in the Senate papers, saying: 'The announcement is too big to wait till the definitive.' The renowned global strategist insisted all sides needed to 'set the narrative of a true relationship and not to be reluctant combatants settling litigation [which was surely the more accurate interpretation].' Klein said this strategy had worked well in the past when a Saudi agreement with the Boeing aircraft manufacturers had been announced.

Both sides followed Klein's advice after a conversation between Monahan and Yasir Al-Rumayyan and on 2 June it was decided that the announcement of the so-called 'NewCo' would take place four days later either in New York or London. The commissioner needed to brief his board on the day before the scheduled announcement and he wanted (albeit in vain) to see Tiger Woods and Rory McIlroy to brief them in person. Klein wrote to Dunne and Herlihy, as released in the Senate papers: 'Hard to hold for this long but no leak yet and great that Jay and Yasir are aligned.'

155

Meanwhile, work continued among all parties, including the DP World Tour, to agree the wording of a press release and memo to the membership of both tours. They would drop on Tuesday 6 June.

A 'must-call' list was drawn up to inform key figures of what was about to be announced. Monahan would speak to McIlroy and Woods as well as key sponsors: Rolex, FedEx and RBC. The PGA Tour commissioner would also call other golf organisations and broadcast partners, including NBC and CBS. Keith Pelley also had Rolex on his call list as well as DP World, South African businessman Johan Rupert, Dr Pawan Munjal of the Hero MotoCorp, and the boss of the R&A, Martin Slumbers. Yasir contacted Greg Norman. It was the first the LIV CEO knew of it.

At 10.25 a.m. ET, players were intended to receive notification and a press release would be issued five minutes later with a pre-recorded interview involving Monahan and Yasir Al-Rumayyan to air on CNBC. It was a network selected because it was thought most likely to offer the most sympathetic line of questioning.

But they jumped the gun by half an hour.

It is not often that my jaw drops while reading a golf press release. I had just taken the first bite of a late lunch while I checked my emails on what seemed a quiet Tuesday afternoon. It was 3 p.m. UK time and as I opened my phone I could not believe what I was reading. In my subsequent reporting for a myriad of BBC sport and news outlets, I commented that it had felt as though I was reading some kind of April Fool's joke.

Publicly, the sides involved had been so far apart until this point. The rhetoric throughout the golf wars had been so bitter, so pointed against Saudi Arabia and from their side so antagonistic towards the golf establishment. Yet now the PGA and DP World Tours along with PIF were issuing an astonishing joint press release, announcing: 'a landmark agreement to unify the game of golf, on a global basis.' There would be a new, 'for profit entity' that will be collectively owned by the three organisations with PIF making a 'capital investment'. The release described LIV as 'groundbreaking' and there was a promise from all sides to 'grow team golf going forward.'

It was staggering stuff, not least the fact that they had 'mutually agreed to end all pending litigation.' There was also a promise to examine ways in which

LIV players could be reinstated to the established tours. Monahan, who had always taken the moral high ground against players who had accepted Saudi Arabia, was quoted, saying: 'After two years of disruption and distraction, this is a historic day for the game we all know and love.' For all those who had witnessed the outright hostility of those two years, it almost beggared belief to read Monahan saying: 'We are pleased to move forward, in step with LIV and PIF's world-class investing experience, and I applaud PIF Governor Yasir Al-Rumayyan for his vision and collaborative and forward-thinking approach that is not just a solution to the rift in our game, but also a commitment to taking it to new heights. This will engender a new era in global golf, for the better.'

Yasir added that PIF was 'proud to partner with the PGA tour' and bring the fund's 'innovation and global best practices' to the game. He claimed that the LIV approach has been 'positively transformative' for the sport and will continue to offer the 'highest-quality product' to new and existing fans across the world, while maintaining golf's 'storied history and tradition'.

The release stated that the Board of Directors of the new entity would oversee and direct its golf-related commercial operations, businesses and investments. 'PIF will initially be the exclusive investor in the new entity, alongside the PGA TOUR, LIV Golf and the DP World Tour. Going forward, PIF will have the exclusive right to further invest in the new entity . . . including a right of first refusal on any capital that may be invested in the new entity, including into the PGA TOUR, LIV Golf and DP World Tour. The PGA TOUR will appoint a majority of the Board and hold a majority voting interest in the combined entity.'

Although this was only a 'framework agreement' lines of demarcation were already in place and Yasir would join the PGA Tour's Policy Board while the DP World Tour and LIV Golf would continue to run their own schedules. Al-Rumayyan would become chairman of the new company with Monahan as chief executive. Ed Herlihy and Jimmy Dunne would serve as executive committee members. All the key architects, therefore, had already been assigned leadership roles.

Keith Pelley, meanwhile, was quoted in the press release, saying it was 'a momentous day.' Momentous was an apt description. When the press release was drawn up, not a single player had a clue what was in the pipeline. In total there were 1,032 words in the announcement, words that did not include Greg or Norman, but that seemed to change everything for the future of men's professional golf.

Monahan also sent a memo to his players. It began by stating: 'Today is a momentous day for your organisation and the game of golf as a whole,' before detailing the new partnership. This was supposed to be peace in our golfing time, but quickly it became clear it was anything but. The PGA Tour's media department anticipated a number of potentially hostile questions and drew up a list of responses to be used in subsequent interviews and news conferences on both sides of the Atlantic. The intent of the messaging was clear. 'Strong getting stronger', 'United Front' and 'Moving Forward' were key buzzwords in the preparatory documentation.

If pressed on Saudi Arabia's record on human rights, Monahan was advised to acknowledge concerns but to stress that they had met with policymakers, global experts on relations with the Kingdom, and sponsors and partners. This was to be presented as 'an opportunity to influence positive change and promote inclusivity in our own sport.' There was even talk of 'grow-the-game initiatives'. Such a briefing was not far removed from what the initial LIV recruits had been told to say by Ari Fleischer ahead of their first tournament almost exactly a year earlier. The irony was not lost.

Stunned observers were taking in the breaking news while CNBC's *Squawk on the Street* show aired the half-hour interview involving Monahan and Al-Rumayyan. It was extraordinary to see these two apparently sworn enemies now sitting chummily together in the New York Stock Exchange studios. The PIF governor insisted that the PGA Tour would retain control even if his body made bigger capital contributions to the new entity than the golf circuit. He also optimistically and erroneously claimed it would take only 'weeks' for the agreement to be finalised.

Already the narrative was moving towards this being a 'merger'. News organisations were running with the line that it was a coming-together of the PGA and LIV. This infuriated the DP World Tour, who were also signatories to what was nothing more than a Framework Agreement.

The European circuit were also aggrieved that their boss, Keith Pelley, was absent from the New York interview on CNBC. 'That was the most botched announcement I have ever seen,' a highly placed source told me. 'They were never meant to do an interview just the two of them . . . they released it half an hour early. And they release it as a merger! You're chasing your tail now.' One official called it 'a fuck up' and there was a strong feeling that Pelley – an astute media operator – would have steered the interview more effectively than Monahan.

Given all that had been said and done in the previous two years on both sides of golf's great divide, it was extraordinary to think that Greg Norman, Phil Mickelson, Tiger Woods and Rory McIlroy – the four biggest personalities involved – had all been blindsided by the move. 'A great day in global golf for players and fans alike. The journey continues,' Norman told his followers on social media. Mickelson tweeted: 'An awesome day today.'

Monahan, meanwhile, hotfooted to Toronto to brief players in a specially convened gathering at the Canadian Open. 'It was a tough meeting for both sides,' former US Open champion Geoff Ogilvy told NBC. 'Nobody knows what it's really going to look like in the end. One of the feelings here is the players just want the [PGA Tour] loyal players rewarded. . . . I don't know if it's all going to be happy families.'

The meeting, involving around 100 players, was heated. The lowly ranked Grayson Murray told McIlroy to 'fuck off' when the Northern Irishman suggested that the best way to improve his lot was 'to play better golf'. However, at the end of the meeting, relations were cordial between the two players.

Nevertheless, there was plenty of anger among rank-and-file PGA Tour members. Canadian star Mackenzie Hughes tweeted: 'Nothing like finding out through Twitter that we're merging with a tour that we said we'd never do that with.' Collin Morikawa, the 2021 Open champion, expressed similar sentiments. Weeks later, Monahan admitted he had been too hasty. 'My biggest regret was not being more patient on June 5,' he said at a news conference. He wished he had gone to Toronto to inform players prior to the rollout and sitting with Yasir in that New York TV studio.

In the immediate aftermath, up-and-coming Englishman Callum Tarren told the Golf Channel: 'The guys who stayed loyal to the PGA Tour, it's kind of a kick in the teeth to them. Obviously Rory [McIlroy] was a huge advocate of the

PGA Tour, and now it kind of looks like all his hard work and sticking up for the PGA Tour was left by the wayside.'

Golf's establishment, which felt it was on the right side of history until this deal was struck, was stunned and in some quarters furious. Former tour player and outspoken pundit Brandel Chamblee told Golf Channel viewers: 'I think this is one of the saddest days in the history of professional golf. I do believe that the governing bodies, the professional entities, have sacrificed their principles for profit.'

The deal also caused concern in the corridors of American power. Senator Chris Murphy, the Democrat representative for Connecticut, referred to his recent meeting with PGA Tour bosses when he tweeted: 'So weird. PGA officials were in my office just months ago talking about how the Saudis' human rights record should disqualify them from having a stake in a major American sport. I guess maybe their concerns weren't really about human rights?'

But the R&A, who run The Open, and Augusta National broadly welcomed the move. 'We are encouraged by the announcement,' said a statement from the Masters organisers.

After talking to his players in Canada, Monahan conducted a news conference over Zoom. 'I recognise that people are going to call me a hypocrite,' the commissioner admitted. 'Any time I've said anything, I said it with the information I had at that moment. And I said it on the basis of someone trying to compete for the PGA Tour and its players. And so I accept those criticisms. But circumstances do change.'

McIlroy had made this point to the commissioner. 'You've galvanised everyone against something and that thing that you galvanised everyone against you've now partnered with,' the four-times major champion told Monahan.

But the tour boss had to admit there were compelling financial reasons why the deal had to be done. 'We have significantly invested in our business in 2023. We're going to do so in '24,' Monahan said. '[But] we've had to invest back in our business through our reserves. Between our reserves, the legal fees, our underpin and our commitment to the DP World Tour and their legal fees, it's been significant.' In short, they needed Saudi money to sustain the expense of competing with LIV, who of course are funded by Saudi Arabia.

All sides seemed set to benefit. In earlier legal proceedings, a federal court had said Al-Rumayyan could not claim 'sovereign immunity' to avoid depositions requested by the PGA Tour, which would have been an awkward precedent for the Kingdom's ability to do business in America. And the tour were looking at legal bills running into hundreds of millions of dollars. 'With appeals it could have gone on for years and years,' said a well-placed insider. 'Now those bills go away.'

Speaking to reporters the day after the announcement was the most uncomfortable McIlroy had felt throughout a year in which, in effect, he had been the unofficial spokesman for the tour – against LIV. 'There still have to be consequences to actions,' he insisted when asked whether LIV rebels should now be welcomed back to the tour. 'The people that left the PGA Tour irreparably harmed this tour and started litigation against it. We can't just welcome them back.'

McIlroy admitted he still felt like a 'sacrificial lamb and feeling like I've put myself out there and this is what happens.' He was also unequivocal on his stance against Greg Norman's breakaway tour. 'I still hate LIV,' he said. 'I hate LIV. Like, I hope it goes away. And I would fully expect that it does. And I think that's where the distinction here is. This is the PGA Tour, the DP World Tour and the PIF. Very different from LIV.'

McIlroy revealed that it was Jimmy Dunne who had briefed him on the deal at the very last moment. 'He took me through the news,' the golfer said. 'What it meant for us. What it meant for the DP World Tour. . . . So I learned about it pretty much at the same time everyone else did. And, yeah, it was a surprise. I knew there had been discussions going on in the background. I knew that lines of communication had been opened up. I obviously didn't expect it to happen as quickly as it did.'

McIlroy added: 'The Tour felt they were in a real position of strength coming off of the back of the DP World Tour winning their legal case in London. It sort of weakened the other side's position. . . . And the way Jimmy described it, "Rory, sometimes you got 280 over water, you just got to go for it." And that's what they did.

'I think ultimately, when I try to remove myself from the situation and I look at the bigger picture and I look at 10 years down the line, I think ultimately this is going to be . . . good for the game of professional golf. I think it unifies and secures its financial future.'

McIlroy once told me that his interest in business was not just to feather his own nest, but rather to ensure an enduring relevance once his playing days are over. I am convinced this was his motivation for taking such a prominent role in the defence of his tour. But when it came to the crunch moment, he was left on the bench. In Canada, he summoned a typically statesmanlike and articulate response to golf's wildest week. But he was hurt by Monahan's about-turn on Saudi Arabia and by the fact that he was not involved in that decision.

Norman, meanwhile, was still in place and insisting – yet again – that LIV was still alive and kicking. 'The spigot is now wide open for commercial sponsorships, blue-chip companies, TV networks,' Norman told LIV staff on a conference call. 'LIV is and will continue to be a standalone enterprise. Our business model will not change. We changed history and we're not going anywhere.'

Elite men's golf was about to head to Los Angeles for its next major, the US Open. All the talk would surround this Framework Agreement, but it was clear there was still a long way to go before anything resembling peace and harmony would emerge from the golf wars.

13

US OPEN DIARY

Los Angeles Country Club, Los Angeles

MONDAY 12 JUNE 2023

Boarding the early flight from Heathrow to LAX, I bump into David Rickman, the R&A's chief of staff, who is also heading to the Los Angeles Country Club (LACC) for the US Open. We make small talk.

'So how are things?' he asks.

'Busy.'

'Indeed,' the genial Scot replies, and gives a knowing look. He does not need to say any more. The shock merger (if that is what it is) announced last week between the main tours and Saudi Arabia's PIF provides the main storyline heading into the third men's major of the year.

Sure enough, some 11 hours later, I emerge through US customs and check my phone for news from the initial press conferences at a venue that is staging the US Open for the first time. 'I thought it was kind of a joke that had come out,' said reigning Open champion and LIV convert Cam Smith. 'And then H.E. [His Excellency Yasir Al-Rumayyan] gave me a call and kind of explained what was going on. . . . I think there's still a lot of stuff to be worked out . . . there's definitely a lot of curious players, I think, on both sides as to what the future is going to look like.'

The defending champion this week, Matt Fitzpatrick, said at the championship's press conference: 'Are we signing with the PIF, are we not signing with the PIF? I have no idea . . . it's pretty clear that nobody knows what's going on apart from about four people in the world.'

TUESDAY 13 JUNE

It is 2 a.m., I'm wide awake. The eight-hour time difference has kicked in with a vengeance. But my alarm had been set early, anyway, because we are recording the first edition of our new podcast, *The Chipping Forecast*, to preview events at LACC.

The merger – as it is now universally known – is the other hot topic for presenter Andrew Cotter, DP World Tour player Eddie Pepperell and me. 'None of us knew and I was flying when the news broke last Tuesday,' Pepperell tells us. 'I opened up my phone and had 50 or 60 messages. It was crazy. I just couldn't believe it; in fact I nearly asked the pilot to turn around and just go back home.'

The player is a member of the tour's Tournament Committee and has been outspoken against the LIV project. He reveals that an hour's meeting between the committee and Keith Pelley on the night of the announcement yielded more questions than answers. 'I'm not sure he even knows where all this is going to go,' Pepperell says.

He speculates on the prospects of the deal being blocked and the implications of that. 'I would say with quite a high degree of confidence we should expect a couple of very high-profile players to jump ship to LIV. . . . If you're like me and want the established tours to continue to be the stronger tours in golf then you'd hope this goes through because I think if it doesn't there could be . . . another wave of top players who do actually go across to LIV.'

Pepperell reveals that in the early stages of the golf wars Pelley pushed for LIV to be given room in a global schedule and that such a move was blocked by the PGA Tour's commissioner. 'This does highlight Jay Monahan's hard headedness and frankly just terrible leadership throughout this whole process. . . . I can't really believe he's still got a job,' Pepperell adds. 'A bit of arrogance maybe on his part but certainly on someone's part to not to get round the table in the early days. For him to turn round and say that after sitting down with Yasir for 10 minutes he'd learned he could trust the guy, I mean you've had two years to sit down with this guy for 10 minutes. That's an outrageous thing to say, given everything that's transpired in the last 12 months and again it is an inability to look beyond the borders of the US to see what's happening in the wider world.'

It is strong stuff and the early start for the pod, which was recorded on Zoom from our respective locations, feels like it was well worth it. I was awake anyway!

Pepperell's speculation on potential defectors if the deal is blocked makes me wonder which players might go. LIV sympathisers on Twitter make hay with news that Jon Rahm is playing a practice round at the LA Country Club with Phil Mickelson. Then, at his pre-championship news conference, the Masters champion does not disguise his unease at the way the latest developments have been handled. He speaks of a sense of 'betrayal' and says: 'It's just not easy as a player that's been involved, like many others, to wake up one day and see this bombshell,' Rahm says.

'That's why we're all in a bit of a state of limbo because we don't know what's going on and how much is finalised and how much they can talk about, either. It's a state of uncertainty that we don't love, but at the end of the day, I'm not a business expert. Some of those guys on the board and involved in this are. I'd like to think they're going to make a better decision than I would, but I don't know. We'll see.'

McIlroy has cried off his media duties, but Rahm has filled the breach as far as the journalists are concerned. 'That'll do. When Rahm says "betrayal" you've got your story,' says a seasoned hack.

Further players enter the temporary interview structure as the day progresses. Each one tries to steer the conversation away from reacting to the merger and towards the upcoming major. It is obvious they are already sick of the story and the uncertainty. They prefer to contemplate what is traditionally the toughest test in golf, the often ghoulish US Open. That is their priority right now. I would never back a player to shun the media, but McIlroy's decision to give us a swerve looks the best thing he could have done. 'I said everything on the merger last week in Canada, what more can I add?' he confided to a trusted scribe.

Early evening and my heavy eyelids jump wide. An email drops from the PGA Tour's media department under the heading: 'Joint Statement from TOUR Commissioner Jay Monahan and the PGA TOUR Policy Board'. It says: 'Jay Monahan informed the PGA TOUR Policy Board that he is recuperating from a medical situation. The Board fully supports Jay and appreciates everyone respecting his privacy. During Jay's absence, Ron Price, Chief Operating Officer, and Tyler Dennis, Executive Vice President & President, PGA TOUR, will lead the day-to-day operations of the PGA TOUR with the assistance of the great team Jay has built, ensuring seamless continuity. We will provide further updates as appropriate.'

First reaction is concern for someone whom I have always found to be a warm and friendly individual. There are no details, but it is easy to conclude that he has been operating under incredible stress through much of his five-year tenure – not just the golf wars but running the tour through the Covid-19 crisis as well.

The second thought? Yet more uncertainty engulfs the game.

WEDNESDAY 14 JUNE

Like at the other majors, the organisation running the championship has its say. For the US Open, it is the United States Golf Association and they hold their traditional mid-morning news conference on the eve of the tournament. To be honest, it is often an occasion I will skip. It is always a state of the nation address that trumpets the USGA, its course set-up and the great inroads it is making in growing the game. All very virtuous but not very newsworthy.

This time there is no option but to listen to every word. This body is one of the four families that run a game currently in crisis. What is their reaction to the ongoing tumult?

From a reporting perspective, it proves another disappointment but not a surprise. In a 25-minute opening address, there is only passing reference to the story dominating the game. CEO Mike Whan wishes Jay Monahan well with his recovery and acknowledges the current turmoil by stating that he expects it to disappear into the background once 'we get balls in the air'. He means that the golf will be everything this week and the other stuff can wait.

When journalists are eventually invited to ask questions, that is his stock answer. Like so many people in the sport, the USGA boss is not prepared to put his head above the parapet. Why would he when there is so much – that word again – uncertainty? Why become a hostage to fortune?

McIlroy grants a short interview to the Golf Channel to say that his thoughts are with the ailing Monahan. No, he has not been in contact with the commissioner, that will happen after the championship, says the player, who seems an ever more reluctant tour spokesman.

The afternoon provides an opportunity take a proper look at this golf course, which is staging its first major. The club is as exclusive as they come; the undulating layout sitting snugly in Beverly Hills and views of the wider Los Angeles metropolis are magnificent.

The course is famously overlooked by Lionel Ritchie's sprawling home, the old Playboy Mansion sits behind the 14th tee, the clubhouse has its Reagan Terrace – named after the former US president – stretching down the side of the first fairway. It also overlooks the 18th green. The members insisted no grandstand should be built to obscure their view. Only 22,000 spectators a day will be admitted, 14,000 of whom are on corporate junkets.

The tentacles of commerce seem to invade every pore of this game.

The fairways are wide by US Open standards but contoured to repel errant shots into thick Bermuda rough. It looks a daunting prospect. The 11th is a 290-yard par-3, the closing stretch of three par-4s is the longest homeward slog in the game. Bunkers have thick eyebrows of broad-leafed, unruly, shaggy grasses that give these hazards a devilish look.

It seems like a place to concentrate the minds of the world's best. No wonder they do not want to be distracted by wider implications swirling around the game. It feels like a massive, muscular course that points to golf's other raging conflict – the distance debate.

The USGA and R&A want to rein back the ball for elite play. They say it flies too far. But players and manufacturers are, by and large, dead against the idea. At least Whan – who talks a lot without saying much – addressed this point. 'I think we can say that we and the R&A believe we cannot do nothing,' he stated at the earlier news conference. In normal times, this would be the argument that would dominate the golfing agenda.

These, though, are not normal times.

THURSDAY 15 JUNE

Balls are already in the air as I board the 7 a.m. bus from my Sunset Boulevard hotel. The hostelry's location is not as glamorous as its evocative address would have you believe but it is handy enough for the course. Unexpectedly, the streets are wet, there is light rain in the air and the marine layer of grey cloud hangs over the course, shrouding surrounding skyscrapers.

It is time for golf to break out and for Mike Whan's words to ring true that the fractious politics of the game are to be shaded by dazzling skills from the world's best players – whichever tour they consider home.

Rickie Fowler, who rejected strenuous and lucrative LIV overtures to remain loyal to the PGA Tour, is the first to deliver on Whan's promise. Once upon a time, this charismatic fan favourite was regarded as the future of American golf. Back in 2014, he finished top five in all four majors but recent years have not been kind. He seems resurgent today. Reuniting with legendary coach Butch Harmon has brought back the bounce that was the hallmark of his early years. Fowler posts a barrage of birdies.

We are commentating for BBC 5Live and wondering whether history is on the cards. Fowler has to settle for a par-5 at the 8th, a birdie would have put the first ever major 61 on to the agenda. In the end, he also pars his closing hole for a 62 to tie LIV's Branden Grace, the only other player to go lower than 63 in a major – at Royal Birkdale in the 2017 Open. Fowler has banked a record 10 birdies, but behind him Xander Schauffele is posting similar numbers.

This is supposed to be the US Open, where players are meant to be grateful for pars. But the moisture in the air has softened greens and the LACC is proving eminently gettable. Within 20 minutes, Schauffele has matched Fowler's birdie haul and his record US Open score. 'I think it made the greens sort of that more holeable speed almost, and then coming into greens you're able to pull some wedges back,' Schauffele says of the favourable damp conditions. 'And then the fairways are a little bit softer, too, because of that sort of overcast, and without the sun out it's not drying out much.'

Someone has calculated there have been more than 66,000 rounds of major championship golf and before today only one of them has been completed in 62 blows. Now we have had two in less than half an hour. It is a frantic spell of radio commentary.

There is no wind and the course continues to take a beating. Golf feels like it has been shifted from its normal axis. The LACC members cannot be enjoying seeing their pride and joy being brought to its knees.

Wyndham Clark, in form but no one's pre-tournament pick, cards a 64 and it is matched by LIV's Dustin Johnson. Rory McIlroy looks imperious hitting fairways and greens with ease. He is on course to equal those 6-under-par rounds but hits underneath the ball and fails to shift it from green-side rough at the last. He makes a brave bogey, his only dropped shot, and departs furious despite signing for a 65. He dodges the media. Rory's low-key approach remains intact. He is one of 13 players 3-under-par or better.

I defy anyone walking what looked a fearsome test a day earlier to have anticipated this birdie barrage.

FRIDAY 16 JUNE

Yet another cloudy morning and McIlroy is out early. Like Fowler and Schauffele yesterday, he is starting on the back nine. One glance at the pin sheet shows the USGA have tucked the hole locations to firm up the challenge. Inevitable after yesterday's scoring.

McIlroy makes a quiet, stuttering, start. The conviction of the previous day is conspicuously absent, but he finds his mojo by spectacularly matching his first-round 30 on the outward half – his back nine. As consistent as the morning cloud has been this week, the Northern Irishman is yet again in the mix at a major. His 67 contains seven birdies and he drags himself to the media tent. He is uncharacteristically curt and word has it that he has said he will walk out if any questioning turns to the ongoing debate over the future of the men's game. No one goes near it. It is birdies and bogeys and weather chat. He says he 'didn't see the scores being as low as they are'. He goes on that he thinks over the weekend the course will 'bite back', before exiting the tent ASAP.

Fowler adds a 68, which is a decent effort in afternoon sunshine that has made the course firmer, faster and trickier. The American seems averse to pars and now has a remarkable 18 birdies along with a fair sprinkling of bogeys in 36 holes. His halfway total of 130 ties the low 36-hole record posted by LIV's Martin Kaymer at Pinehurst in 2014.

People are starting to take notice of Wyndham Clark, observing that his first PGA Tour win came recently at a tough major venue, Quail Hollow in Charlotte, North Carolina. He has put in the prep having come in early to practise with a friend who is a LACC member.

Clark says his mate, PJ Fielding, is 'a good player' who 'really knows the golf course'.

Clark adds a 67 with only one dropped shot and credits the local knowledge gleaned during his early preparations. 'That 18 holes was the equivalent of probably playing 27 to 36 holes,' he says. 'He was telling me how certain putts break, how this one is faster than this, this plays this way . . . he was spot on.'

SATURDAY 17 JUNE

Opening the curtains reveals bright early morning sunshine for the first time this week. The June gloom, that marine layer of grey cloud, has been replaced by clear blue skies. The USGA will be as thrilled as they are with the stellar leaderboard. Drying conditions are crucial to ensuring the course is as firm and fast as possible. It will play tougher than at any other point this week.

Tom Kim has other ideas and destroys the front nine at the start of his third round, romping to the turn in 29. This is the gettable portion of the course. Rory McIlroy, who has eaten up this part of the course, will want another strong start. He smashes an imperious drive on the opening par-5 while playing partner Xander Schauffele finds the sand. He then needs three shots to escape while McIlroy makes a smooth birdie.

Dustin Johnson, one of nine LIV players to make the cut, is moving smoothly. Cameron Smith and Bryson DeChambeau are also showing up nicely but probably have too much to do to emulate Brooks Koepka's PGA victory. Koepka isn't a fan of this place: 'too many blind shots,' he contends.

It turns into a thrilling day. And it proves tough for the late starters who have to deal with crusty, crispy greens that become increasingly hard to judge. McIlroy battles to a 69 to move to 9-under-par, hitting fairways and greens without holing much with the putter. Rickie Fowler and Wyndham Clark look like major-winning veterans but are chasing a first title in one of the big ones. Their rounds end in gathering gloom as the marine layer finally shows up. The USGA's ridiculous decision to tee off as late as 3.40 p.m. looks absolute folly.

Fowler three-putts the last to fall back to 10-under – his par putt horseshoed out of the hole. Clark, who hit the pin with his approach, birdies to tie the lead. It means McIlroy, one stroke back, will play the final round in the penultimate group with world number one Scottie Scheffler, who is three shots off the lead. Johnson is five back but handily placed sharing sixth place with Schauffele, who battled hard in a ragged 73.

It is still a stellar leaderboard with stories all over the place. But will there be a fitting atmosphere? I doubt it. There are not enough fans here and too many of those in attendance are on corporate jollies. The spectacle is compromised. Defending champion Matt Fitzpatrick describes the atmosphere as 'very poor'. He adds: 'It's disappointing on the USGA side. They want a great tournament. From what I've heard a lot of members bought tickets and that's why there's so many less people. Hopefully it's not the same for other US Opens going forward.'

He later goes on Twitter to say he was not having a go at the USGA. The *Telegraph*'s James Corrigan joins his timeline to admonish the English golfer, telling him to 'own your words'.

SUNDAY 18 JUNE

The marine layer has not shifted, the final day of the 123rd US Open dawns with more battleship grey clouds and the Beverly Hills skyscrapers are shrouded in mist when the back markers begin their fourth rounds. Final-round stats on the PGA Tour this season make interesting reading for the lead contenders: Scheffler averages 67.7, Fowler 69.6, Clark 70.1 and McIlroy (who has suffered final-day fades in both of the last two weeks) 70.8.

I bump into a DP World Tour official. He says he saw McIlroy in the players' lounge and the golfer smiled with a reminder, 'Twelve years ago to the day.' Rory is remembering Congressional in Maryland and the 2011 US Open, where he landed his first major. It is an interesting insight into a confident frame of mind, just a short while before tee off. And he starts in that vein with an assured two-putt birdie at the first.

The course has yielded low early scoring. Tommy Fleetwood is tearing it up, but by the time he misses a shortish putt for a 62 on the closing green the putting surfaces have become treacherously firm. It is much more a traditional US Open test for the later starters and most struggle. McIlroy keeps creating birdie chances but cannot take them. He misses from short range at the par-5 8th. That could be a sign that things might take a familiar turn.

Wyndham Clark keeps his nose in front with gutsy par saves, the LIV challenge falters as Dustin Johnson and Bryson DeChambeau fade. But Cam Smith climbs the leaderboard without contending.

McIlroy makes a pig's ear of the par-5 14th – one of the few birdie holes on the back nine. He bogeys. It looks fatal.

Clark has daylight with a birdie at 14 but then bogeys the next two. It is a tense finish to a two-horse race with a 125–1 outsider just keeping his nose in front of the thoroughbred hope from Northern Ireland. At 17, McIlroy pars having launched his drive on to the adjacent second fairway. Behind, Clark holds his nerve.

To the last, where Europe's hope plays to the fat of the green. It is too far from the flag for realistic hope of the birdie he craves. McIlroy settles for par, meaning a four at the last will make Clark the shock winner. His approach creeps on to the green. It is a tough two-putt for glory but he is commendably up to the task and taps in to inflict yet more major agony on McIlroy. 'I feel like I belong on this stage,' the champion says and it is hard to argue. Another star is born in Hollywood.

For the man from Holywood, Belfast, it is another bitter tear-jerker. He says he will take a hundred of these days of bitter disappointment just to get his hands on another major trophy. Nine years and counting and just The Open to go in 2023.

This is now his overriding priority. He seems thoroughly divorced from that all-consuming role of trying to shape the future of a game still scrapping to determine a way forward. McIlroy is all about one thing and one thing only now: his own golf. 'I obviously never give up,' he says at a post-round press conference. 'And I'm getting closer. The more I keep putting myself in these positions, sooner or later it's going to happen for me. Just got to regroup and get focused for Hoylake in a few weeks' time.'

It has been a strange major. So much noise off the course, not enough on it. Compelling action watched by too few genuine fans on site. Two thirds of the 22,000 in attendance were on corporate jollies. Saturday's tee times were ridiculously late, to service US television. It feels like money is everything at every level of this game, and to its detriment.

This was the first $20m major. Clark pockets $3.15m. That is the inflationary effect of LIV. More money into the pockets of golfers who are among the portion of the population who need it least. How can that be an attractive look to the outside world?

14

REGRETS AND RECRIMINATION

'You know, a reputation that I spent 20 years putting together, I felt like it dissolved in one press conference here in London last year.'

Graeme McDowell

LIV came back to where it all started in the weeks that followed the US Open. And how the golfing landscape had changed in the 12 months since their initial launch at the Centurion Club in Hertfordshire. Driving into the same grassy field that served as the media car park brought back memories of their first event. Once again, the pristine grandstands, flags and tents were evident – just as they are at most top professional tournaments. Back in 2022, there was a sense that this was a new venture that needed to battle the controversy of its origins. But it was bold, brash and – internally – certain of its merits.

Now, that certainty was less apparent. There was a sense of vindication, although players and officials were reluctant to say it, but the environment did not smell of new paint, rather that knowing familiarity of second time around. And there was a hesitancy over what the future might hold.

The Framework Agreement and the fallout of the 6 June announcement brought a lack of clarity to the LIV message. Yes, officials and players kept stressing that they had assurances and that it was 'full steam ahead' but those messages felt rather less convincing. The sense of limbo that had enveloped the entire game included Greg Norman's circuit and there was nothing they could say or do to banish a feeling of irresolution.

Asked about professional golf's future, Graeme McDowell told me: 'I literally wish I had an idea what it looks like.' The Northern Irishman was in reflective mood. It was here that he had endured the most uncomfortable time of his otherwise stellar career. The hostile reaction to his news conference 12 months earlier, when he was interpreted as saying that LIV was sport washing for Saudi Arabia, still hurt.

'Obviously I took a leap of faith coming over here to LIV,' said the 44-year-old. 'And it was such a great fit for me and my stage of my career. I mean, obviously the financial benefits and the type of schedule that it was offering. There were so many positives to it, you know, and obviously we realised that it would be controversial to a certain extent, but I don't think anyone ever envisaged quite the fracture in the world of golf that it would create.

'I had no idea it would go to that extent. . . . I had long conversations with my sponsors and partners, my family. . . . I felt like I weighed up this decision very intelligently. You know, a reputation that I spent 20 years putting together, I felt like it dissolved in one press conference here in London last year.'

McDowell articulated better than most the sense of rancour that had gripped the game following LIV's arrival. 'Twelve months has really made me look very differently back at things,' he said. 'I feel like these tours of the world had to go after the weaknesses that were surrounding this product. And they had to try and expose them as weaknesses as best they could, because this was something that was compelling to the best players in the world. And they had to defend their turf and everyone had to defend their turf, you know? So all I did was try and represent a golf tour that was paying me. I wasn't trying to tell lies. I wasn't trying to make up monsters. I was just trying to do the best I could. And, like I say, in hindsight, it was an impossible situation.'

Cameron Smith had half an eye on his upcoming Open defence at Royal Liverpool. He was not part of the original line-up 12 months earlier having only joined LIV after lifting the Claret Jug at St Andrews the previous July. But the Australian was bullish about the future of his chosen tour. He explained at the pre-tournament press conference that their schedule of fourteen 54-hole tournaments supplemented by four majors was ideal. 'I really can't see LIV Golf going away,' Smith stated. 'I think team golf is here to stay, and if you asked every one of us out here, all the 48 guys, I think everyone has such a good time and everyone enjoys what they're doing out here.'

McDowell stood alongside the reigning major champion and acknowledged that the landscape had changed with the Framework Agreement. 'The PIF are going to become a very big investor in the global game of golf,' he said. 'I think that that's good for the sport to have that amount of money being directed . . . across the board. I think what's happened the last 12 months and the fracturing of the game is not something we ever, ever wanted. It's been said by players on the PGA and DP World Tours that if this money is going to be spent, let's work out how to all spend it together.'

Lee Westwood echoed the sense of uncertainty that was now gripping the world of golf. 'I have no idea how the peace deal will look,' he admitted to me. 'Obviously the PIF have made a huge financial investment into golf and they're doing it in other sports, as well. I think in golf they've almost forced a transparency from the other organisations, their finances and the way they run their operations, which has got to be good for golf really, to have it all out on the table and people be able to see how it all works.'

And that need for transparency took an uncomfortable turn for the PGA Tour because the following week, Jimmy Dunne and chief operating officer Ron Price were summoned to Washington DC to give evidence regarding the tour's deal struck with Saudi Arabia. The Senate Permanent Subcommittee on Investigations hearing was instigated by the waspish Democrat senator Richard Blumenthal. He began proceedings with a stinging rebuke. 'Today's hearing is about much more than the game of golf,' he said. 'It is about how a brutal, repressive regime can buy influence – indeed even take over – a cherished American institution simply to cleanse its public image.' He added that it was: 'A regime that has killed journalists, jailed and tortured dissidents, fostered the war in Yemen, and supported other terrorist activities.'

The near three hours of testimony was a bizarre combination of forensic questioning from and grandstanding by senators from both sides of the house. But it yielded some frank admissions from the PGA Tour officials who found themselves in the hot seat in the absence of their recovering commissioner Jay Monahan, who had been battling anxiety and was not back at his desk until the following week.

Clearly, the tour were desperate to conclude the proposed pact with the Saudi PIF, an entity that provided an existential threat if the agreement was not ratified. 'They have an unlimited amount of money,' Dunne admitted at the Senate hearing. 'I'm more concerned they'll end up owning golf if we don't do it.' He went on to say: 'If they take five players a year for five years they could gut us.' This frankness prompted fears among seasoned executives at the top of the game that the PGA Tour would lose vital leverage in future negotiations.

Price confirmed that the PIF investment being put forward was worth more than $1b, but Senator Blumenthal warned: 'You're not out of the woods.' Regarding LIV, the Connecticut representative added: 'They're going to continue to have this kind of bucket full of money and they're going to continue to wield the influence that they do . . . and whatever the good intention and rhetoric is now, you still have to reach a deal. My hope is that you will resist those buckets full of money.'

And the Senate hearing did nothing to quell growing disquiet among some of the biggest names. Quite the contrary, many observers believed the proceedings highlighted how the tour's leading officials were more interested in protecting themselves rather than improving the playing conditions of their members.

Adding to the unease was the resignation of the influential policy board member Randall Stephenson. The former chairman of AT&T, one of the PGA Tour's most loyal backers, served on the board for more than 12 years. In a letter dated Saturday 8 July 2023, Stephenson said the Framework Agreement: '. . . is not one that I can objectively evaluate or in good conscience support, particularly in light of the U.S. intelligence report concerning Jamal Khashoggi in 2018.'

Stephenson could not countenance jumping into bed with a regime that had been accused of what US authorities had concluded was a state-ordered murder of a *Washington Post* journalist. He added: 'I joined this board 12 years ago to serve the best players in the world and to expand the virtues of sportsmanship instilled through the game of golf. . . . I hope, as this board moves forward, it will comprehensively rethink its governance model and keep its options open to evaluate alternative sources of capital beyond the current framework agreement.'

Among the elite players, there was a growing sense of mutiny. They were also increasingly disenchanted with the leadership. 'As a player on tour, we still don't really have a lot of clarity as to what's going on and that's a bit worrisome,' admitted the world's top player, Scottie Scheffler, to press at the Scottish Open. 'They keep saying it's a player-run organisation, and we don't really have the information that we need.'

Scheffler is a mild-mannered, gentle giant. Despite becoming a major-winning dominant force, his public pronouncements are measured and respectful. He is not one to cause a stir when a microphone is put in front of his mouth. Nevertheless, there was no disguising a steely edge to comments that seemed to confirm disquiet among his peers. 'The players have all really stuck together and that's what's important to me,' he said. Forty-one of them, the elite of the PGA Tour, were about to write a letter to Monahan demanding change in the structure and running of the organisation. They wanted it to be truly run by the players, for the players.

Scheffler spoke the day after the Senate hearing, which was the eve of the Scottish Open, where Xander Schauffele was defending champion. 'If us players can stay together . . . stay unified and have the right goals in place for the future, then it would be less unsettling,' the Olympic champion told me during his pre-tournament news conference. 'Most of the players on the PGA Tour are together and want to be informed and want to have a say in what happens . . . these are just steps in the process to getting, I guess, not what we want but more transparency and getting a seat at the table. It's a for-members organisation and that's what it should be.'

Schauffele hesitated before heaping more pressure on the commissioner, who was about to return to work after his month-long absence. Doug Ferguson, of the Associated Press, is among the most respected golf correspondents and asked

Schauffele directly whether his trust levels in the PGA Tour boss had changed? The golfer hesitated and laughed.

'Thanks, Doug,' he smiled, buying time. 'Yes, yes, they have.'

'Care to elaborate?'

'We got a memo that he'll be back on the 17th [of July]. If you want to call it one of the rockier times on tour, the guy who was supposed to be there for us, wasn't. Obviously he had some health issues. I'm glad that he said he's feeling much better. But yeah, I'd say he has a lot of tough questions to answer in his return, and yeah, I don't trust people easily. He had my trust and he has a lot less of it now. . . . I don't stand alone when I say that.'

Three-times major champion Jordan Spieth echoed these sentiments. 'You talk to a lot of other players, it's been quite a shock from the get-go,' he observed to press. Spieth is another player who rarely courts controversy, but his unease at the cloud of uncertainty enveloping the game was more than apparent.

Spieth felt the forming of the Framework Agreement should have involved PGA Tour player input. 'It's a member-run organisation with a voluntary board that's supposed to look out for the interests of the PGA Tour players on the board. I don't believe that these decisions had to be made without involving players on the board and other board members.'

These three players – Spieth, Schauffele and Scheffler, all major stars of their sport – left little doubt about their frustration with the lack of communication prevailing over the future of men's professional golf. If they were prepared to go this far in public, how much stronger were the conversations going on behind the doors of the locker room? There is no doubt players were bitching and the PGA Tour's highly remunerated management were the target of their ire.

As Scheffler commented: 'What goes on behind the scenes, I don't share out here. It's not for y'alls' knowledge. It's for the players. I believe that the players are working together right now, which is exciting for me.'

Men's professional golf remained in turmoil as it headed towards its final major of the year, the 151st Open Championship at Royal Liverpool Golf Club at Hoylake in the north-west of England.

15

THE OPEN DIARY

Royal Liverpool Golf Club, Hoylake

SUNDAY 16 JULY 2023

It feels strange leaving the Scottish Open early but is has become my accustomed move the weekend before The Open Championship. It is tough to get much airtime while the men's final at Wimbledon is being played, so a better use of that Sunday afternoon is to acquaint myself with the environs of the final major of the year.

Except, except, except.

The forecast for high Sunday winds means they are teeing off early on the final day of the Scottish. And Rory McIlroy is leading. I'm in a quandary, but ultimately – like all the other national golf correspondents – I conclude I'm better off getting down the road to Hoylake for the big one the following week. I find a way to access PGA Tour Radio commentary, which keeps me company for the 200 miles south.

Compelling company.

Arriving in the cavernous media tent at Royal Liverpool, the giant screens were showing the denouement in Scotland. Bob MacIntyre's brilliant approach to 3 feet at the last looks like it might win the left-hander his home Open and, in all probability, a Ryder Cup debut.

But McIlroy has other ideas. He makes a late switch from four iron to two iron for a 202-yard approach into the wind at the final hole at Renaissance Club. Golf's politics are forgotten, now we are seeing just why the professional game is such a valuable commodity. It is nerve-wracking stuff. A birdie will win the title for McIlroy but if he fails this will be another agonising near-miss that will call into question his competitive nerve.

Victory will be the perfect set-up for The Open. He stripes the two iron with a sawn-off follow-through. His ball bores through the 25mph headwind and lands on to the putting surface, rolling to 12 feet from the cup. It is a brilliant shot. I digress. We should see more of those. How often do we see a pro hit a two iron into a par-4? Ordinarily, the ball travels too far, it really does.

Back to the action. After an age waiting for Tom Kim and Tommy Fleetwood to complete closing double bogeys, McIlroy steps up to strike his birdie putt. It is a similar distance to the final hole in Dubai in January – his most recent win. And it is the same outcome. He bends his back, looking and laughing to the skies. His first ever win in Scotland. Here in England at the home of the Royal Liverpool Golf Club we are left wondering what this means for the 151st Open that is just four days away.

MONDAY 17 JULY

We are expecting a McIlroy pre-championship news conference at 9 a.m. tomorrow. This will help set the agenda for the final men's major of the year. Is his drought at the biggest events about to end? Why has it been so long? Give us your thoughts on the LIV peace deal? Is there enough player power at the PGA Tour? Would you really retire if LIV was the only golf left? Tell us about your memories of your last and only Open win here at Hoylake? The answers to these questions would provide a banker narrative for the golfing media.

But I receive a WhatsApp from Greg Allen, my counterpart at Ireland's RTE. We usually double up for Rory's pre-major radio interviews. 'He's not doing a press conference,' Greg informs me. The R&A will be deeply disappointed, but McIlroy is following the same low-key policy he used in Los Angeles at the US Open.

This snub to the media does not seem right. Yes, McIlroy wants to avoid half an hour of cross-examination on the fallout from the Senate hearing. He does not want to spend that time also being reminded of his nine-year major drought. But he has a responsibility to the championship. He has just won the Scottish Open, he was the last winner here at Hoylake and – as his former caddie JP Fitzgerald once told him, he's 'Rory Fucking McIlroy'. The media are grumbling and some players are raising their eyebrows. One reporter gets a text from a golfer who says: 'Why does Rory always get treated with kid gloves?'

Meanwhile, what was once a quiet, intimate moment for the defending champion is now a commercial opportunity. The handing back of the Claret Jug becomes a branded photo shoot, but Cameron Smith admits he has to battle welling tears as he returned the famous old trophy to R&A boss Martin Slumbers. 'I didn't think I'd ever have to give it back, to be honest,' Smith tells me. 'It was a bit of a sad moment that crept up to me, I didn't know what to feel and what to think but it has definitely made me more determined to get it back. Once you have something as crazy and as great as that it's something you don't want to let go of.'

Earlier, he had told reporters at his pre-championship news conference: 'I think I'm actually a better golfer now than what I was last year.' He had added: 'I think golf is in a great spot. There's obviously a lot of things that are up in the air that no one really knows at the moment. I don't even think the guys that are trying to sort it out really know what this outcome is going to be like. Yeah, a lot of uncertainty, but I'm optimistic that LIV will be around in the future.'

Out on the course, PGA champion Brooks Koepka teams up with US Ryder Cup skipper Zach Johnson for a practice round. Another sign of thawing relations between those who broke away and the golfing establishment. It is now hard to imagine the US side without the five-times major winner.

It is announced that Matthew Jordan, a local DP World Tour pro who came through qualifying, will hit the first tee shot on Thursday. A nice touch from the R&A, who are always keen to start their major with as much momentum as possible.

I go and get a haircut – six weeks on the road has taken its toll – at Big Al's on Hoylake's High Street. Turns out Jordan is one of their most loyal customers. They are very proud of the local lad.

TUESDAY 18 JULY

The skies are threatening as I make my way into the course. It is a more leisurely stroll than it might have been given that McIlroy is not appearing for his 9 a.m. news conference. First up instead is major-winning LIV star Koepka. He is typically bullish about his chances and the career choices he has made but does admit he is spending time 'prepping' for fatherhood.

Once again, he reiterates there are no hard feelings between him and former colleagues on the PGA Tour. 'I've always been friends with all those guys,' he insists. 'Unless they're saying it behind my back. I don't know of anybody that's extremely mad at me. We've all been friends. We still see each other. I think everybody thinks just because there's a divide with LIV and the PGA Tour that the players are actually divided, and I don't think that's the case at all.'

And on playing alongside the US Ryder Cup captain, he makes out it is the most natural thing that could have occurred: 'It was fun,' Koepka says. 'We got to talk about it a little bit, just what's going on, I guess how the team is shaping up. It's kind of interesting.' Later he tells me that it is very hard to imagine a scenario whereby he will not be competing for America in Rome this September. He is in the team – that much seems certain.

Majors are great talking shops and behind the scenes there is much chatter regarding how men's professional golf will shape up after the Framework Agreement is thrashed out. One leading administrator tells me that LIV will run for another couple of years to make sure four-year initial deals signed in 2022 are honoured. He agrees we are destined for a world tour ultimately, but that process is fraught with difficulty for the established tours. They are members organisations and, unlike LIV, these are not companies who effectively employ their players. He predicts plenty of upheaval. 'I don't see how this gets done quickly,' he says.

One of the sticking points is likely to be how to compensate players who remained loyal to the established tours, rejecting Saudi millions. Jon Rahm has an interesting take on this. 'I wasn't forced into anything, it was my choice to stay,' he points out. 'Do I think they absolutely should be and there must be a compensation? No. I just stayed because I think it's the best choice for myself and for the golf I want to play. Now, with that said, if they want to do it, I'm not going to say no.'

This brings laughter from the gathered journalists, but Rahm is deadly serious. 'We all had the chance to go to LIV and take the money and we chose to stay at the PGA Tour for whatever reason we chose. As I've said before, I already make an amazing living doing what I do. I'm extremely thankful, and that all happened because of the platform the PGA Tour provided me. As far as I'm concerned they've done enough for me, and their focus should be on improving the PGA Tour and the game of golf for the future generations.'

It seems a classy response from the Masters champion. He clearly possesses perspective above the level of several of his playing colleagues.

The annual dinner of the Association of Golf Writers takes place in the evening. It is always a gathering of not just golf journalists but many of the game's leading administrators, agents and managers. We do not seem to attract many players these days. It feels as though they become more isolated from us with every year that passes.

Rory McIlroy sends a video message to thank the AGW for awarding him the Golf Writers' Trophy for his performances last year. In the past, he has turned up at the start of proceedings, but that was a step too far this time. Justin Rose does come along with his wife Kate to receive special recognition for his work in launching the Rose Ladies Series, but, as arranged, they leave before the food arrives. Thomas Bjørn stays for the evening to receive the Arnold Palmer Open Award for being good with the media.

I am Master of Ceremonies and it is always a nerve-wracking evening despite having performed the role for a decade. Tiger Woods sends a heartfelt video message to thank us for the Michael Williams (late golf correspondent of the *Telegraph*) Outstanding Services to Golf Award. It is richly deserved and Woods' near four-minute message steals the show. His manager, Mark Steinberg, is present and grateful on his behalf.

Steinberg also manages Rose and is delighted with the evening. In two decades covering the game, it is the first time I have ever had a proper conversation with him. He always operates at arm's length from most of the golf media, setting the tone for how many agents work in the modern era. Tonight, he is warm and friendly. But he remains a shrewd operator and is no doubt at the heart of much of the behind-the-scenes discussions about the future of the game. At the end of the evening, R&A boss Martin Slumbers makes a point of shaking his hand. It is clear they will be talking later in the week.

Much of the talk around the tables centres around how the Framework Agreement (not a merger) will play out between the established tours and PIF and, by definition, LIV. It is suggested to me by a well-placed PGA Tour source that LIV will continue to operate next year.

WEDNESDAY 19 JULY

The key pre-championship address comes from the R&A's chief executive Martin Slumbers, who has become an increasingly assured performer in front of the media. He is also a highly respected figure in the game, who will have a big say in how golf's future will shape up. 'We are waiting to learn more about the agreement announced by the PGA Tour, DP World Tour, and the PIF on June 6th and the implications for the wider game,' he tells reporters. 'We're not party to the agreement, and while we absolutely welcome an end to the disruption in the men's professional game, there is a lot still to be understood. We will await the outcome with interest.'

It is a canny tactic, warning us off a topic about which we have plenty of questions. He clearly is in no mood to provide any answers of substance. He admits a season-long qualification process to award LIV players spots in The Open is possible – but it is 'not the option that is top of my list at the moment.'

There will be 16 LIV players in the field this week. That number will dwindle if the status quo is maintained and Slumbers is on the committee that will discuss awarding official golf world ranking status to the breakaway league this week. He adds: 'The disruption being caused by the game is not good for the sport. It's tearing the sport apart. And as importantly, I care about what the perception of this game is around the world. I don't want it to be perceived as a game that isn't available to everyone, that isn't available to boys, girls, men and women.'

Slumbers reveals he watched the Senate hearing the previous week. 'I find it very unfortunate that our great game was in that situation. All credit, I think, goes to Jimmy [Dunne] and to Ron [Price], the way they handled themselves, and I was very impressed and glad I wasn't sitting in their shoes.' Tellingly, he continues: 'I do think that we have to have a sensible conversation about the long-term financial sustainability of golf.'

He will write a record cheque of $3m to this week's winner out of a total pot of $16.5m, which means the R&A are dipping into their coffers like never before. 'I think it is really important for all of us to not get too carried away with sums of money that can't be justified,' Slumbers tells me in a BBC Radio interview.

This takes us on to wondering whether The Open would ever entertain the prospect of accepting sponsorship from Saudi Arabia. He does not rule it out. 'I think the world has changed in the last year. It's not just golf. You're seeing it in football. You're seeing it in F1. You're seeing it in cricket. I'm sure tennis won't be that far behind. The world of sport has changed dramatically in the last 12 months, and it is not feasible for the R&A or golf to just ignore what is a societal change on a global basis.' Some interpret this to mean he is open to PIF money helping bolster their finances. Others believe he is being cautious. Who knows, current backers of The Open may have Saudi money behind them?

Nevertheless, it raises the question of the morality of the R&A potentially taking money from a country such as Saudi Arabia. 'I think human rights issues, wherever they are in the world and whichever country are at the top of a lot of people's agendas and must never, ever be forgotten,' Slumbers tells me. 'But we also, from a golf point of view, can't sit there and hold back what is a massive global societal change and there's a lot of political implications to this whole topic and I think that change will just continue.'

Players, meanwhile, go about their final preparations. Vast galleries swarm across the course and the crowd following McIlroy, Tommy Fleetwood, Tyrrell Hatton and Viktor Hovland is of a size you would expect if they were vying for the title on Sunday evening.

The sense of anticipation is palpable. Golf will do the talking for the next four days and the politics of the sport will slip into the background.

THURSDAY 20 JULY

'Forged by Nature' is the tagline of this championship. It, ironically, feels a manufactured concoction from the R&A's marketing department. The Open is the most natural of the majors, by definition, because it is played on seaside links courses. The message did not need tricking up and, in a further irony, it becomes apparent that the bunkers have been tricked up.

With bright, dry conditions, the newly flattened sand cannot prevent balls from running all the way to the revetted faces of these hazards.

188

Suddenly, already penal, sand traps become areas to avoid at all costs and those who do not take proper heed are punished.

Nevertheless, there is good early scoring as Amateur Champion Christo Lamprecht, a tall South African with an American drawl and size 13 feet, races to a 5-under-par 66, a score matched by local hero Tommy Fleetwood.

I'm out following McIlroy, Jon Rahm and Justin Rose, who tee off just before 3 p.m. All three would crave a similar tee time at the weekend because it would mean they would be among the leaders chasing the Claret Jug. Huge galleries follow and there is a sizeable entourage inside the ropes too with this grouping taking centre stage for TV, radio and the written media as well as an army of camera-laden snappers.

It is busy, very busy, as we all charge from greens to tees and the players are deprived of their usual unencumbered stroll. It shows that major championship golf is box office fare, even if the players in this group struggled to find their best stuff. 'I'm trying to walk and there's way too many people in my way,' Rahm complains after his opening 74. 'I can't go forward at my pace because they're in my way,' he says after finishing with a messy bogey six. 'I'm trying to deal with the unlucky moment on 18, and there's somebody with a boom mic on my ass keeping up with Rory's pace, and I can't go at my own pace. That's kind of the disregard that existed.'

Like Rahm, McIlroy's approach to the 18th had run up to the face of a steep bunker. He took two shots to escape but made a brilliant save for a level par-71. He is five behind but still in the hunt. 'These bunkers are just . . . they're really tough,' he tells Sky Sports. 'The ball doesn't seem to go to the middle and always seems to go into the face.'

The slimline Phil Mickelson fares much worse. The left-hander goes from bunker to bunker on the short 17th for double bogey before hitting his tee shot at the last out-of-bounds en route to a triple bogey eight. Wearing an unfamiliar-looking round neck sweater, without a collar in sight, he finishes with a ragged 77. Another lefty fares rather better with his afternoon round. Brian Harman picks up five birdies and a lone bogey on the 10th for a 67 that leaves the Georgia native just one stroke off the lead held by Lamprecht, Fleetwood and the late finisher, Emiliano Grillo of Argentina.

FRIDAY 21 JULY

One of the big attractions of golf to me growing up was that it can be a game for all sizes. Always one of the smallest at school, I could compete with a golf course that didn't physically stop me from trying to play as I wanted to. Football and rugby were a different story. This comes to mind as I watch the shortest player in the field usurp the tallest at the top of the leaderboard.

The 6 foot 8 inch Lamprecht does not repeat his first-round heroics but in the morning I witness the diminutive Brian Harman put together one of the finest rounds of golf I've ever seen. He reels off four front nine birdies in a row with a silky smooth putting stroke and determined avoidance of those pesky bunkers (they have been remodelled overnight to make the sandy surface concave to prevent balls from running up to the faces).

Harman finds just one of those hazards (on the 12th) and because he is left-handed he has no stance and has to play backwards on to the fairway. His third shot misses the green as well, but he chips in and maintains a blemish-free scorecard. At the last, he splits the fairway, then bypasses the bunkers guarding the green and holes an eagle putt from 15 feet to lead The Open by five shots. It was just the 23rd putt of his round.

'I love the golf over here,' he comments. 'I missed four or five cuts in a row coming over here, and I couldn't figure out why I wasn't playing well. Then the last couple years I had some good finishes and just kind of felt like, all right, now at least I feel like I love the golf.'

Indian star Shubhankar Sharma is also on the leaderboard and describes Harman's effort as 'amazing'. He says the American's 6-under-par 65 is like 'shooting 10-under on any other course.'

Tommy Fleetwood is Harman's closest rival heading into the weekend. There are no LIV players in the top 10, with Henrik Stenson best placed tied for 11th at 1-under alongside, among others, Rory McIlroy, who could not buy a putt in his morning round.

Defending champion Cam Smith eagles the last to make the cut in the evening gloom and world number one Scottie Scheffler raises his arms in mock celebration as he birdies 18 to make the weekend on the mark. It is a weird Open.

SATURDAY 22 JULY

Brian Harman is the dominant leader of The Open. Brian Harman! He is a largely unremarkable golfer, one of those names that sits on PGA Tour leaderboards but rarely causes a stir or makes headlines. He has had 29 top 10s since his most recent and second win on the US tour and has banked well over $20m in prize money. But despite encouraging recent results, few regarded him as a contender this week.

Indeed, you could get 200–1 on him in the build-up – absurdly long odds but he was always an outsider. Yesterday's press conference unearths his love of hunting and preparing his prey to be eaten. He is dubbed 'the butcher of Hoylake', which he prefers to being known as the 'Harmanater'. But for this weekend, is he the hunter or the hunted?

I'm out on the course commentating on his third round in the company of Tommy Fleetwood, who receives loud and passionate support. But the Englishman struggles to make an impression. Harman makes a nervy start, with two bogeys in the first four holes but then he gets on a roll. It is striking that he maintains an unfocused, narrow-eyed stare all the way round. He does not engage with the galleries and, apart from the odd word and smile with long-time caddie Scott Tway, the 5 foot 7 inch golfer shows zero emotion as he efficiently knocks off hole after hole. Idiots in the crowd shout abuse on tees but he remains unruffled. There are birdies at 5, 9, 12 and 13 and he avoids every bunker on the course in a superb 69. Still five clear, the hunter has the Claret Jug firmly in his sights.

So is a Ryder Cup debut.

The crowd, who wanted Fleetwood to prosper instead, have been hostile. Just like they will be in Rome this September, and Harman was inspired. 'You don't have the stones for this,' a spectator shouted. His message merely helped concentrate the mind of the American leader. This is the spirit his country will need in the Italian capital. US skipper Zach Johnson will surely take note.

Earlier, Rahm charged round in 63 to put his name on the leaderboard. 'Today was one of those days where I felt invincible,' he said after lowering The Open record at Hoylake by two strokes. 'I've been very comfortable from the tee, so it's easier to stay aggressive.'

McIlroy received great support and picked up three birdies in his first five holes before his putter went cold. He needed a low one and coming home in 37 for a 69 is not enough. His chances are all but gone with Harman at 12-under-par and the Northern Irishman trails by nine shots. He exits without talking to reporters. A theme is developing. Once the most eloquent, quotable golfer is now increasingly a reclusive figure as far as the media are concerned.

It makes me think how different it is in tennis, where players are contracted to speak after matches, win or lose. Maybe golf should adopt a similar policy? Or would we rather hear from someone when they are willing to speak openly? I don't know.

The Northern Irishman played with Max Homa, who was round in 70. A likeable character, he can be rather pedestrian with his pace of play and at times received 'Hurry up's from the McIlroy-supporting crowds. 'I kind of like the yelling because it makes me laugh,' Homa admitted. 'I had a guy yell at me, "Hurry up, no one is watching you anyways today," which I quite like, if I'm being honest.'

All eyes tomorrow will be on Harman, who will be in the final pairing with his closest rival, last year's runner-up, Cameron Young.

SUNDAY 23 JULY

I hate using the term 'journeyman' to describe a professional golfer who makes a fantastic living from the sport. Brian Harman is regarded as such, yet this week he is the 26th best player on the planet. Only 25 better golfers in the whole world; hardly a journeyman even though he has not won for six years. This week, he has not missed a putt from inside 10 feet and he has only visited two bunkers in three rounds.

It is gloomy; fine, saturating rain is falling relentlessly as the leaders tee off. By the time Harman has dropped shots at two and five, my feet are squelching and my socks are sodden.

He marches on, oblivious to the conditions. At the difficult par-3 6th, he fires a brilliant tee shot and converts it into a bounce-back birdie. One hole later, he picks up another. This at a time when the likes of Rory McIlroy, Jon Rahm, Tom Kim, Jason Day and Sepp Straka have been making progress.

Without Harman dominating, we would be witnessing an epic contest for the oldest and still most prestigious major title. The crowd want a contest; that is surely the main reason there is little enthusiasm for both of those birdies. Those successful holes keep the chasing pack at arm's length and Harman marches on, again devoid of outward emotion.

With the heavy rain, the wind drops. It makes his task easier – takes the teeth out of the treacherous 17th and 18th holes – although he does find a bunker at the last. By then, the result has long been a foregone conclusion. Naturally he gets up and down.

Escaping that bunker brings the first flash of emotion – a clenched fist. Then he drains the par putt – of course he does. Off comes the cap, his smile lights the gloomy skies, the galleries finally show some warmth in his direction and he throws his ball into the stands in celebration. Harman finishes at 13-under-par and wins The Open by six shots.

'Normally they do such a great job of letting you know where your golf ball is because the applause here is always great,' he said. 'They appreciate really good shots. But since everyone is holding an umbrella it's hard for everyone to clap. There was a couple times I got up there and I was like, oh, that's better than I thought it was. But the fans here have been incredible. My hats off to them. They packed the stands today. I damn sure wouldn't have been out watching golf today.'

It is a generous assessment, because he also endured plenty of brickbats on the way round from lone, drunken, idiotic voices that must be a concern for future Opens. Those unsavoury interventions left a sour taste.

Harman is the 10th consecutive first-time winner of The Open – proving, once again, the championship is what it says on the tin – open. Whoever finds their game in that single blessed week becomes the champion golfer of the year.

For the second major in a row we have an unexpected winner who we should have regarded as a threat. With hindsight, Wyndham Clark's US Open win made sense and so did Harman's, given the trend of his recent results. We in the media are sucked into talking about the big names in a sport where the talent pool runs far, far deeper than we credit. That is the nature of a sport where up to 156 players tee it up in a week such as this. It is much easier to control the narrative when there are only 48 starters, as is the case with LIV.

The breakaway tour celebrated Koepka's win at the PGA and Mickelson's stirring runner-up display at Augusta but this Open suggests we should revisit the question of whether LIV's format and calendar provides the best preparation for the biggest tournaments. Stenson, tied for 13th, is their highest finisher and Laurie Canter is their only other player to finish in the top 20. Cam Smith ends up alongside LIV colleagues Richard Bland and Patrick Reed in a share of 33rd place at 1-over-par, 14 shots behind.

How different might the golfing landscape look in 12 months when we reconvene at Royal Troon? There is plenty of scope for change and the final-day arrival of Yasir Al-Rumayyan at Hoylake with businesswoman Amanda Staveley does not go unnoticed. The *Telegraph* later reports that the PIF governor took the chance to meet with Martin Slumbers. The 'secret' talks, held in a hospitality box while The Open was being decided, were said to be 'more symbolic than substantive'.

Harman, meanwhile, celebrates with beer from the Claret Jug at a restaurant in the neighbouring town of West Kirby. He queues for a table at the American-style meat joint (how appropriate) and obliges fellow diners with a series of selfies. We witness it all because the BBC radio team are eating there as well. So is Matthew Jordan with his family. The Englishman, who started it all on Thursday morning, had finished in a share of 10th place to guarantee his spot in next year's championship at Royal Troon. That is one certainty for next year, at least.

16

BUILD-UP TO THE RYDER CUP

'I am honoured . . . we look forward to being at the table with [Commissioner Monahan] to make the right decisions for the future of the game that we all love.'

Tiger Woods

Jay Monahan returned to the commissioner's desk at PGA Tour Headquarters in Florida on Monday 17 July. That week the eyes of the golfing world were on Hoylake and Brian Harman's surprise Open victory. Monahan was looking at the future. He knew players from every strata of his organisation were unhappy. These included so-called 'mules', good enough to be a top 125 golfer on the PGA Tour but deemed insufficiently talented for 'Signature' tournaments, as they would be known from 2024, carrying the biggest prize funds. Even some of those who finished the season in the top 50, thereby guaranteeing their shot at these gargantuan prize funds, were annoyed at the way the tour had jumped into bed with Saudi Arabia. No one liked the fact they had been kept in the dark when the deal was being struck.

Indeed, one of the first items to land in his in-tray was the letter from 41 of his biggest stars calling for more player power and transparency. The commissioner had said little about the nature of his 'medical situation' that forced him to take more than a month away from his duties. He later told reporters he had been dealing with anxiety: 'To step away at that point in time was very difficult for me, but I needed to take care of myself and my family, and ultimately come back here stronger than I've ever been.'

There is no doubt the PGA boss had encountered some of the most stressful times in the history of the game, piloting the tour through the Covid shutdown before the challenge presented by LIV's arrival. 'With the support of my family and thanks to world-class medical care, my health has improved dramatically,' Monahan told his members. 'I am eager to engage with each of you – as well as our players, partners, fans and our PGA Tour family – to address any questions and protect the game we treasure.'

Golf's landscape was changing rapidly, but now it was time to borrow from the playbook of his predecessor. For much of his 22 years in charge, Tim Finchem recognised that in Tiger Woods his organisation possessed arguably the greatest name in sport. For most of his career, the 15-times major champion did not just move the needle, he was the needle. And Finchem knew it. Woods was the key asset when Finchem drove inflated television and sponsor deals, allowing prize money to explode in the late 1990s and 2000s. The season before Woods won his first Masters, Tom Lehman was the leading money-winner on the PGA Tour, banking $1.78m. Two decades on, when Finchem retired in 2016, Dustin Johnson took home nearly $10m. 'Tiger has been the instigator,' his arch rival Phil Mickelson told reporters at the time. 'He's been the one that's really propelled and driven the bus because he's brought increased ratings, increased sponsors, increased interest and we have all benefited.'

Woods was the most precious commodity in the game. When the superstar spectacularly fell from grace in 2009, as his secret and multiple infidelities became known, it was Finchem who orchestrated Woods' public rehabilitation.

In February 2010, the golfer made his first televised statement on the scandal in a carefully choreographed speech at the PGA Tour base in Ponte Vedra Beach, with Finchem among the very small number of people in attendance.

Woods had been protected in his biggest hour of need. He was nurtured and rehabilitated by a tour to which he has always been an ultra-loyalist. It is where his achievements lie, a record-equalling 82 wins. This legacy puts him among the very greatest to have ever played the game. Now in his late 40s he had a busted right ankle and an unresolved playing future. But, despite the scandal and multiple career-threatening injuries, he remained the Big Cat. One of the very few people in a divided game who could command universal respect. The Saudis had made an offer in the region of $700m to bring Woods on board long before recruiting Greg Norman, but the player flat refused. There are not many athletes who could turn down such riches, but Woods could and did.

By the summer of 2023 it was time for Monahan to do as Finchem had done and fully cash in the Woods chip. The commissioner needed to respond to the players' demands for more representation at the PGA Tour's top table. New governance and transparency measures were unveiled, promising players more say in future decisions – including approving the Framework Agreement with the Saudi PIF. Just as significant, Woods agreed to Monahan's approach to become a sixth player-director on the PGA Tour's Policy Board. He joined Patrick Cantlay, Charley Hoffman, Peter Malnati, Rory McIlroy and Webb Simpson. In effect, this gave the players a majority on the board.

'Tiger's voice and leadership throughout his career have contributed immeasurably to the success of the PGA Tour, and to apply both to our governance and go-forward plan at this crucial time is even more welcomed and impactful,' Monahan said in a statement announcing the move. 'I am committed to taking the necessary steps to restore any lost trust or confidence that occurred as a result of the surprise announcement of our framework agreement.' The commissioner still needed to fill the space on the board vacated by Randall Stephenson's resignation in protest at the tour's proposed involvement with Saudi Arabia.

But by bringing Woods into the fold, Monahan had recruited a voice that his members would respect more than any other. Some expressed surprise that the commissioner was still in a job, but this move seemed to make his position more secure, if less powerful. Three months earlier, he had felt entitled enough to strike a bargain with a perceived existential enemy; now, any move of any significance would need approval from his members and especially Woods. This, of course, included ratification of the Saudi deal.

'I am honoured,' said Woods in a statement. 'This is a critical point for the tour, and the players will do their best to make certain that any changes that are made in tour operations are in the best interest of all tour stakeholders, including fans, sponsors and players . . . The players thank Commissioner Monahan for agreeing to address our concerns, and we look forward to being at the table with him to make the right decisions for the future of the game that we all love. He has my confidence moving forward with these changes.'

Leading players were quick to welcome the move. Justin Thomas, who is Woods' closest friend on tour, pointed out that the greatest player of his generation could have chosen to hide away and 'live under a rock'. Thomas added: 'We've been dealt some roadblocks . . . I think he takes it seriously that he will be a part of paving the way for the future.' McIlroy also welcomed the appointment, describing Woods as, 'the player over the last 20 years that's left the biggest legacy on the game.' He added: 'For him to be involved in discussions around the future of professional golf and what that may look like, I think is very important.

'Tiger has stepped up for all of us on tour, and I think he realises that the players that are on the policy board were trying to play regular golf, and at the same time try to navigate all these different things . . . He's maybe got a little more time on his hands than we do. For him to step up and take a little bit of the load off us is very much appreciated.'

It was, perhaps, not too much a stretch to say that while Monahan remained commissioner, the real boss was now Tiger Woods. As McIlroy pointed out: 'He has a vote. Everything that goes through the tour has to be voted on and ratified, and he actually has a vote on what happens.' Some votes are weightier than others, he might have added.

By early August, the PGA Tour was heading towards its lucrative playoffs with the top 70 competing in the FedEx St Jude Championship in Memphis before the leading 50 played the penultimate event, the BMW Championship at Olympia Fields near Chicago. The highest 30 points scorers then contested the Tour Championship in Atlanta. In Memphis, Monahan was candid in his first meeting with reporters since his return. He said the 6 June rollout of the Framework Agreement had been 'ineffective'. Monahan admitted: 'As a result there was a lot of misinformation and anytime you have misinformation that can lead to mistrust. And that's my responsibility . . . I apologise for putting players on their back foot. But ultimately it was the right move for the PGA Tour.'

Monahan also addressed a tense player meeting at TPC Southwind at the Tennessee tournament. World number one Scottie Scheffler insisted the tour was still some way from resolving the crisis. 'You have the Framework Agreement, which nobody is entirely sure what that means, and then you've got whatever they're working towards,' Scheffler said. 'We still don't really have a great idea as to what is going on right now.'

Players were keen to know what conditions would be imposed on LIV players who want to return to the PGA Tour and how tour loyalists, who turned down potential Saudi riches, might be rewarded. Again, there were more questions than answers. Pro golfers do not like uncertainty and all Monahan could offer was 'confidence' that the deal would be done by the start of 2024. 'We have identified a framework to a future that has the PIF as a minority investor in the PGA Tour,' he said. 'We have the proper safeguards in place to protect our model from a governance standpoint and from a control standpoint. There are a lot of conversations that led to the framework. Admittedly, there's a lot more conversations that need to happen.'

Monahan had already taken a step likely to win approval from the majority of his players although, ironically, not Woods or McIlroy. In a leaked memo, the commissioner made it known that the PGA Tour would not support proposals to limit the distance golf balls could fly in the elite game. The R&A and United States Golf Association were nearing the end of a feedback period on the proposal to implement a Model Local Rule. In effect, it would mean recreational golfers could continue to hit balls that fly the maximum distance, while professionals and elite amateurs would compete using a ball that would have modifications that would reduce how far it could travel. In a memo to his members, Monahan said: 'There is widespread and significant belief the proposed Modified [*sic*] Local Rule is not warranted and is not in the best interest of the game.'

This was a big blow for the rule-makers and brought a schism to the golf establishment that had been as united as legally possible in its fight against LIV's insurgency. The R&A and USGA are convinced golf needs to limit its footprint and rein back the modern golf ball, which they believe flies too far. It is rendering traditional golf courses obsolete because of the distances leading players can achieve using today's equipment. Longer courses need more maintenance and irrigation and take longer to play. The two rule-making bodies run The Open and US Open respectively and have indicated they will implement a 'tournament ball' from 2026 onwards. The Masters also support the move while the PGA of America are aligned with the PGA Tour's stance. At this point there seemed there was a real prospect that three of the four majors will play with different ball specifications to those used in the rest of the pro game.

Of course, the companies that manufacture the golf clubs and balls that perform so efficiently resist any change. And they pay players handsomely to promote their gear. So it has been no surprise to see the likes of Justin Thomas and Patrick Cantlay vehemently argue against the proposals while sitting wearing branded Titleist caps. They reflect a majority view in the locker room – Woods and McIlroy being notable exceptions – and Monahan could ill afford to do anything that might further upset his membership. If the R&A and USGA's analysis on what needs to be done to protect the game was correct, it could have been argued that the health of the sport's future could become collateral damage in the golf wars.

'People forget how many courses can no longer host professional golf,' golf architect, blogger and commentator Geoff Shackelford told me. 'It was made worse by Jay's weakened position. This was something to appease those players who were clearly only ever thinking about themselves. It might be that he is doing whatever he can just to maintain his position and keep everybody happy. As a commissioner, though, you are in a position where you're supposed to do the right thing for the sport.'

In his *Quadrilateral* blog, Shackelford accused the tour of failing to anticipate 'every twist and turn' of the Saudi Arabian saga and was now adversely affecting the sport with its reactions to the R&A and USGA ball proposals. 'The hapless tour has bluffed, blundered and bungled the response to Saudi Arabia and, based on Wednesday's memo leak, they're not done yet making tough situations worse,' Shackelford raged.

R&A boss Martin Slumbers was more diplomatic. 'There've been a lot of really good points made,' he told me regarding the notice and comment period on the ball proposals that was coming to a close. 'But there are only three options for the game as we look at this. One is we change the ball for the entire game or we bifurcate – which is what we are in effect proposing – or we do nothing. And the R&A's guiding light here is that we are looking into the future and we fundamentally believe that doing nothing is not an option.'

The majors were over but the news agenda was unrelenting as the tour ploughed headlong into its playoff season. The first two of these three closing tournaments brought to a climax the race for the six automatic berths in the American Ryder Cup team. LIV's events were immaterial in this regard. Their players could only impress from afar and only if captain Zach Johnson was taking any notice.

Bryson DeChambeau fired rounds of 61 and 58 (just four shy of the magical 54 that would yield Yasir's promised $54m) to win the LIV event at Greenbrier by six shots. The unorthodox American collected 13 final round birdies, the sort of golf that is invaluable in the matchplay realm of the Ryder Cup. Brooks Koepka, meanwhile, was clinging on to his place in the qualifying positions, thanks almost entirely to his PGA win and runner-up finish at the Masters.

But at the BMW Championship in Chicago, the final event before the season climax at the Tour Championship in Atlanta, Max Homa and Xander Schauffele did enough to secure automatic spots in the American team. Koepka was edged out and needed a captain's pick. Suddenly, Zach Johnson would have to do something he had barely done throughout his tenure: acknowledge a player who had chosen to go to LIV. But it was an easy decision.

Koepka had missed out by relative loose change and the six automatic qualifiers – Scottie Scheffler, Wyndham Clark, Brian Harman, Max Homa, Patrick Cantlay and Xander Schauffele – were happy to have the LIV star as a teammate. 'He's very versatile,' Johnson said. 'Guys want to play with him. That's evident.' Koepka was joined as a captain's pick by the out-of-form Justin Thomas along with Sam Burns, Jordan Spieth, Collin Morikawa and Rickie Fowler.

LIV's supporters on social media were outraged that Dustin Johnson, who won five points out of five in the 2021 Ryder Cup at Whistling Straits, Bryson DeChambeau, Patrick Reed and Talor Gooch were all overlooked. None of them even warranted a call from the captain to say they were not included. 'They could have qualified; they had the majors,' the skipper told me before adding: 'They made their decision.' And as far as Zach Johnson was concerned, that choice was to opt out of the PGA Tour to play LIV and thereby sacrifice their best chance of qualifying. At no time in his captaincy did he lend any credence to the breakaway circuit. Performances there had no positive influence on their chances of being part of the Rome match in September 2023.

Europe were buoyed that their team would include the PGA Tour's most successful player. By winning the BMW Championship and then the handicapped Tour Championship (where the leader in the standings, Scottie Scheffler, received a head start by beginning the tournament a nominal 10-under-par), Viktor Hovland succeeded his Ryder Cup teammate Rory McIlroy as the FedEx Cup champion, banking $18m in the process. The Norwegian's total earnings for the season were a staggering $32.11m, relatively close to the $35.6m won by Dustin Johnson in LIV's inaugural 2022 season.

There was no doubt that the arrival of the breakaway circuit had brought huge pay rises on the PGA Tour. Scottie Scheffler won $23m, Rory McIlroy nearly $18m and Max Homa was eighth highest with $11.4m. The previous season on LIV, albeit from a maximum of eight tournaments, Pat Perez took home $8m as the eighth highest earner. The PGA Tour, with considerably more events and players, had become more competitive in terms of prize money.

Monahan called it 'a bridge year' that helped transition the tour to a calendar year-schedule for 2024 that includes eight 'signature events' each worth at least $20m. This concept had been introduced with the 'designated' tournaments that brought rapid prize money inflation but put pressure on future sustainability. 'We see that new stars have emerged, we have had iconic moments, we have had staggering performances, staggering comebacks,' Monahan told reporters in Atlanta. 'You look at the PGA Tour fan base, it's larger, it's more diverse, it's more youthful, and it's more engaged than it's ever been. PGA Tour-only broadcasts we've had 87 million unique viewers. When those viewers watch, they watch an average of 71 minutes per week, which is pretty extraordinary.'

Monahan also stated his organisation was moving forwards from a position of commercial strength. 'For 2024, we have $10 billion in committed sponsorship revenue, $5 billion in media rights revenue committed, both through 2030. We have 49 corporate partners who have been committed to us for a decade or longer. We have with the signature events companies that have stepped up to underwrite increased purse levels and to help us enhance those events.' And, of course, there was still the prospect of hefty and vital investment from Saudi Arabia's PIF.

Not that life at this stage was particularly comfortable for the governor of the Public Investment Fund. Senator Richard Blumenthal intensified his investigation into the proposed deal despite being rebuffed by Yasir Al-Rumayyan for the original hearing in July 2023. According to documents released by Blumenthal, the following month lawyers representing the Saudi boss wrote to the senator stating the governor was 'an inappropriate witness' because he is 'a minister bound by the Kingdom's laws regarding the confidentiality of certain information.'

'PIF cannot have both ways,' Blumenthal replied. 'If it wants to engage with the United States commercially, it must be subject to United States law and oversight.'

He called for Al-Rumayyan to appear at a further hearing in mid-September. 'If you continue to refuse to comply voluntarily the subcommittee will be forced to consider other legal methods to compel PIF's compliance,' the senator's response threatened.

It felt a lot less contentious in St Andrews as August moved into September, a month that promised a magical period of golf at its most captivating with the Walker, Solheim and Ryder Cups all being played. The Walker Cup pits the leading amateurs of the USA against those of Great Britain and Ireland. To mark a hundred years since the UK staged this historic match for the first time it returned to the home of golf. America fielded a clean-cut crew of 10 golfers, the vast majority with eyes on lucrative professional careers.

The US team was led by the big-hitting Gordon Sargent, who began his opening practice round by launching his athletic swing into a tee shot aimed at hitting the first green some 340 yards away. If ever there was an image of the direction of modern-day elite golf, it was this powerful action from a player regarded as the hottest prospect in the game. Nowadays, elite amateurs are able to accept representation and sponsorship before turning pro. They are full-time players in all but name.

But in this first week of September, all 20 players from both sides had only sporting glory on their mind. Not a penny or cent would change hands in pursuit of the famous old trophy – one of the largest in all of sport. The spirit was best summed up on the eve of the match when US player Austin Greaser said to reporters: 'I have the rest of my life to play professional golf. . . . I had this one opportunity to be a part of a Walker Cup team. Not only that, but to do it at St Andrews.' Greaser added: 'I'm from a small town in Ohio, and I'm not sure my dreams ever got to playing a Walker Cup at such a historic place. To be able to feel the nerves and the pressure and just the amazing opportunity to represent the United States of America, I don't care how many or what holes I play, I just want to play.'

It proved a thrilling contest as thousands of spectators wandered across the famous Old Course watching these young guns go head to head. GB&I were the heavy underdogs, but bucked expectations to take a three-point lead after the first day. They couldn't, could they? No, they couldn't, as it turned out, but it took until the final hour of an enthralling contest for the USA to retain the Walker Cup.

It was a refreshing reminder that golf can be about more than money and served as an excellent curtain-raiser before Europe's women defended the Solheim Cup against the USA in Spain and their male equivalents did battle for the Ryder Cup in Italy a week later when September rolled into October. It proved a captivating fortnight, with first the Solheim hitting the heights by delivering another thrilling match. The last home contest at Gleneagles went to the last putt on the final green before Europe won back the trophy, thanks to a decisive putt from Suzann Pettersen. Now, for 2023, the Norwegian was the continent's captain. And her team held their nerve magnificently to force a 14–14 draw, meaning they could keep the trophy for a record third match in a row. Carlota Ciganda, the only Spaniard in the contest, secured the crucial point for the home team to prompt jubilant scenes among European fans on the Costa del Sol.

For the Ryder Cup, Europe's Luke Donald announced his six wildcard picks the day after America had retained the Walker Cup. LIV players, who had resigned their membership of the European Tour, were ineligible, but none, bar perhaps Sergio García would have received any consideration anyway. Donald opted for Tommy Fleetwood, Justin Rose, Sepp Straka, Nicolai Højgaard, the out-of-form Shane Lowry and the young Swedish sensation, Ludvig Åberg, who the previous day had surged to his first professional win at the European Masters in Switzerland. He had only turned professional four months earlier. His debut win had come in his ninth tournament since going the paid ranks.

At 22, Højgaard was a year younger than Åberg and was thrilled with his selection. Donald phoned the young Dane on the eve of the announcement. He said: 'Good playing in the last couple of weeks . . . I'm going to cut to the chase. I want you in Rome. How do you feel?'

'Oh my fucking god!' was all Højgaard could summon in his initial response. 'I can't describe how this conversation feels! I've said all along and talking with [vice-captain] Thomas [Bjørn] about this all season, I said to him the biggest goal was to obviously get to Rome.'

Donald's selections left Poland's Adrian Meronk 'shocked, saddened and angered' at missing out on a Ryder Cup debut on the course where he had won Italy's national title the previous May. Meronk was edged out of an automatic spot by Scotland's Bob MacIntyre on the final day of qualifying.

But Meronk's omission and the decision to go with Lowry despite only one top 10 all year was the only contentious issue, as the English captain announced his team. LIV's Richard Bland stated on social media that the Pole 'deserves a pick over an out of form Shane Lowry in my opinion!' Another LIV player, Lee Westwood, said that Meronk was 'unlucky' but the Ryder Cup veteran pointed out to his followers: 'Someone always feels hard done to. If you don't qualify you can't really complain. Picking 4 rookies out of 6 picks would probably be a step too far for any captain.'

Donald and all of his wildcard picks appeared on Zoom press conferences throughout the afternoon of the announcement on Monday 4 September. At no point in the hours of questioning were LIV, rebel players or money discussed. The golf wars seemed to have been pushed aside for an event that was retaining its wholesomeness, despite the relentless controversy that had raged throughout the men's game for the vast majority of the period since the last Ryder Cup in 2021.

17

RYDER CUP DIARY

Marco Simone Golf and Country Club, Rome

MONDAY 25 SEPTEMBER 2023

Bleary eyes. Early morning flight from Málaga in Spain where Europe's women have just retained the Solheim Cup. Unforgettable stuff, with Carlota Ciganda securing the crucial 14th point to prompt those exuberant, joyous scenes in front of the King of Spain.

Like the Walker Cup, it showed how sport and, in this case, team golf can be so meaningful. Pure sport. I'm thinking this as I stand waiting at the luggage carousel at Rome's Fiumicino airport. My radio producer, Amy Scarisbrick, is with me and points out Ludvig Åberg waiting for his bags. The Swedish sensation was in the crowds at the Solheim. Now I realise he's travelled to his debut on Wizz Air. That he has travelled, as we did, on a budget airline feels reassuringly wholesome. But I suspect his future will not involve too many more luggage waits such as the one we are enduring right now.

My fellow 5Live commentator, Katherine Downes, shows me a video doing the rounds on social media. It is Rory McIlroy talking about the Ryder Cup. I'm cynically sceptical. I know these interviews can be pumped out to generate interest without much journalistic integrity. This one is different. McIlroy is confronted by his infamous quotes ahead of his 2010 debut for Europe. Then, he felt the Ryder Cup was nothing more than an exhibition. He scoffs at his younger ignorance. 'Those quotes could not be further from the truth,' McIlroy admits. 'It is the purest competition in golf. To me it doesn't get any better than that. You can't replicate that feeling of playing as part of a team.' He talks about the 'churn in his stomach' while watching teammates and the responsibility of trying to perform for them. Losing is 'the most disappointed you are ever going to feel,' says the man who was in floods of tears at the record 19–9 defeat in Whistling Straits two years ago. He says, 'it still makes me emotional.'

I didn't really need telling. The Ryder Cup is magical. I love it because there is no money at stake – not for the players anyway. They are in it for nothing more than the glory of the competition. Of course, they can enhance their reputations and make themselves more marketable by performing when golf's audience is at its greatest but that will not be the motivation this week.

For the DP World Tour it is a different story. This is their cash cow. What they make out of this week is sustenance for the next four years until they stage the next home Ryder Cup in Ireland. Arriving at the Marco Simone site, 17km outside Rome's city centre, is breathtaking. The size and scale smacks you in the face as soon as you walk into the main spectator area. 'It's a golfing Glastonbury,' Katherine remarks, as we wander across to the vast media tent.

It is all the more striking given the much smaller set-up at last week's Solheim Cup. Golf's gender gap is as wide as ever. The Ryder Cup shop alone would subsume the main spectator plaza at Finca Cortesin, where the precious crystal trophy was presented.

It took two hours to get through Rome's main international airport. It felt very much like Atlanta on that Saturday night before Masters week. Thousands of passengers swarming through Fiumicino, many wearing tell-tale attire. It was clear what event had brought them to Italy.

We arrived at the course 10 minutes before the first press conference. A gentle exchange with the two captains. Luke Donald and Zach Johnson are sensible media operators. The last thing they need is to stoke up controversy. Both stressed their determination to win in respectful tones. 'Very excited. It's been a long build-up,' Donald says, which made me smile. His tenure has been relatively short given that he took over only after Henrik Stenson was stripped of the captaincy in July 2022.

A penny for the Swede's thoughts this week.

Donald, though, has impressed with his measured approach during such turbulent times. His focus is the match and he is keen to temper expectations. 'I know it's going to be a difficult next few days, it really is,' he admits. 'The US are very strong. We know that. We are coming off our worst defeat ever in a Ryder Cup. US players are strong, high up in the world rankings and they have some great partnerships and have had a lot of success. We have our work cut out.'

There's little mention of how LIV is impacting this week, apart from an enquiry regarding Sergio García's reported attempt to rejoin the DP World Tour to be eligible to resume his Ryder Cup partnership with Jon Rahm. 'He resigned his situation five months ago, and once that happened, he was ineligible for me to even consider him,' Donald observes. 'I know there were some stories about him trying to pay off some fines and stuff. Obviously we know what the DP World Tour rules are, and once you resign, you cannot reapply for membership until the following year.'

The American team flew in overnight from Atlanta. All bar one of them. LIV's Brooks Koepka was coming from Chicago where he was playing the breakaway tour's latest tournament. Restrictions on flying slots made it difficult for the US PGA champion to hop from Illinois to Georgia to make the transatlantic crossing with the rest of the team. Indeed, Koepka arrived in Italy first but did not hang around to join the traditional team photo of disembarkation of 'Airforce Team USA'. Some media outlets attempt to make something of that, so desperate is the search for news lines.

While Europe's women were defending the Solheim Cup, Bryson DeChambeau was picking up $4m for winning in Chicago. Afterwards, the former US Open champion complained that he did not receive a call from Zach Johnson regarding his non-selection for the Ryder Cup. The American skipper is asked about this. He has a stock answer. I've heard it several times and know it off by heart by the time he reels it off once again. Basically, Johnson was working off the qualifying list and DeChambeau did not come close to qualifying. Therefore he was not a factor. His response confirms that the US captain had paid no heed to LIV tournaments throughout the qualifying process. End of.

TUESDAY 26 SEPTEMBER

Except it isn't. From Europe's perspective, the Sergio saga still has legs. Today, we have the first player news conferences. Each European golfer has 90 minutes of media duties. They do them on a rotation and today there are six of the team making appearances. They do various stops for interviews with Sky Sports, the Golf Channel, the European Tour's media channels and the BBC. They also spend 15 minutes in the main interview area where journalists give them a grilling. This is the arena from which most news lines are generated. The reporters are hungry for stories and with players ever more circumspect it seems a tougher and tougher task to generate headlines.

Jon Rahm cooperates though. The Spaniard has consistently championed the cause of LIV players – saying they should be eligible for the Ryder Cup. His successful partnership with García at Whistling

Straits, where they won all of their three matches together, left the Masters champion yearning for more action with his compatriot.

And he reveals that even though García cannot be here, he will have an influence, having spoken to him only yesterday. 'I did talk to him and ask for advice,' Rahm says. 'He did show me a lot of what to do at Whistling and obviously in Paris, as well. But I did have a little bit of a chat with him, and with Poulter, as well. Not that it's going to be easy to take on the role that those two had both on and off the golf course, but just to hear them talk about what they thought and what they felt is obviously invaluable information.'

For the first time since 1993 (the last time the continent suffered a home defeat), a home match for Europe will start with foursomes. 'I think we have an opportunity to send out four very strong pairings and hopefully grab an early lead,' Luke Donald says.

Donald also suggests to reporters that his team's statistical modelling system spat out data that indicated the USA might have been better to pick someone other than Justin Thomas. 'We kept track of all their stats . . . and they certainly could have gone a different way,' he discloses. 'But Justin Thomas has played two Ryder Cups, and obviously they feel like, despite some inconsistent play . . . that he brings a lot to the team room. Again, Zach obviously knows what he's doing.' It feels like a dig, dressed in diplomacy.

It emerges that world number one Scottie Scheffler has recruited English putting guru Phil Kenyon to try to improve his performances with the short stick. Kenyon advises a number of the Europeans, including Tommy Fleetwood. 'I'm glad that Phil has the opportunity to work with someone like Scottie,' the English player says. This is classic golf and its sporting ethos, something that could be threatened by the bitterness that enveloped the game during the golf wars. Mind you, Fleetwood does add: 'Hopefully [Scheffler's] putting takes another week to really get hot.'

Justin Thomas tells us he's in 'a really good headspace' and his likely partner, Jordan Spieth, addresses 30 years of American hurt on their

Ryder Cup travels and makes me feel old in the process. 'We've been made very aware of how long it's been,' the three-times major champion says. 'Over half the team wasn't born the last time we won over here. It's not something we really care about, to be honest.'

Europe certainly do. And they're desperate to take their unbeaten record into a fourth decade. That is the overwhelming sense I get from talking to their players at length. There is excitement, anticipation and, I suspect, a touch of trepidation brewing for all of the players involved. Europe, though, are desperate to avenge the hammering they received at Whistling Straits two years ago.

WEDNESDAY 27 SEPTEMBER

Another early start. We drive into Marco Simone at 7 a.m. A wise move: there are problems with the shuttle buses from our media hotel, a 25-minute drive from the course. DP World Tour media manager Briony Carlyon calls as I walk through the gates wondering if I've been affected by the bus not turning up. She is relieved I'm here because the European interview sessions start at 8 a.m.

It is the first time I have spoken at any length with Nicolai Højgaard. He is impressive and seems to have settled nicely in the week of his Ryder Cup debut. At 22, he is the youngest player in either team and has the potential to be a future superstar. The players come and go, exuding positivity. Justin Rose acknowledges that at 43 his chances of playing Ryder Cups are running out and admits he is noting the roles of the vice captains, implying that he is a likely candidate for such a role going forward.

Rory McIlroy is his usual eloquent self. 'Knowing that you're part of something that is bigger than yourself and you're playing for something bigger than yourself,' he says when I ask why these weeks are so special. 'That's what means the most to me. I want to go out there and win the Ryder Cup and obviously enjoy it for myself but I also want it for everyone else that I'm sharing it with this week.'

McIlroy warms to the theme. 'There's nothing contrived, nothing forced. It's good, pure competition and in a world where there's a lot of things that can be contrived I think it is a breath of fresh air. . . . I think it just reminds everyone of why we play the game and you cover the game.'

Back in the media tent, reporters have been banking on McIlroy to provide headlines. By his standards, the Northern Irishman has been unusually circumspect this summer, skipping those pre-championship interview sessions at the US Open and The Open Championship.

There is no escape today and his session with the mainstream media is vintage stuff. When asked about the absence of LIV recruits and former Ryder Cup stalwarts such as Sergio García, Ian Poulter and Lee Westwood he delivers the line of the week. 'It's certainly a little strange not having them around,' he begins. 'But I think this week of all weeks, it's going to hit home with them that, you know, they are not here, and I think they are going to miss being here more than we're missing them.'

One of the newspaper writers observes: 'He knows how blunt those words will look in print.'

Brooks Koepka is the only breakaway player here and seems to have little time for his LIV colleague DeChambeau bemoaning missing out on selection. 'Everybody had an opportunity to get her,' the PGA champion and Masters runner-up says. 'I had the same opportunity as every other LIV player, and I'm here. Play better. That's always the answer.'

Once again, Koepka notably rejects an opportunity to credit LIV or agree that he is their representative in this match. 'I'm representing the USA,' he says. 'That's what I've got on the front of my hat this week . . . We're just all one team, and that's the way we think. That's what I believe, and I'm pretty sure everybody else here thinks that.'

There's growing concern over unruly behaviour from golf crowds as Open champion Brian Harman encountered during his triumph at Hoylake. He is asked whether he will be advising his American teammates on how to cope with any brickbats flying in their direction this week. 'It's kind of like if you're trying to give someone advice if they're about to have their first child,' he replies. 'There's nothing you can tell them to get them ready for it. No, your life is going to change, it's going to be really hard, but you'll get through it. There's lots of people that have done it, and it's up to you how you handle it.'

As ever, McIlroy has an entertaining take on this issue. 'That's all part of the Ryder Cup . . . . Someone said to me once, if you want to be part of the circus, you have to put up with the clowns.'

US Open winner Wyndham Clark comes closest to antagonising the opposition when he defends the fact that nine of the US 12 have not played competitively since the Tour Championship concluded on 27 August. Rested or rusted? Clark turns it around, suggesting the fresher Americans can outlast potentially exhausted Europeans who have played events such as the BMW PGA and Irish Open in the intervening period. 'It's great that they got to play,' he says during the press conference. 'This is obviously a very intense environment and mentally challenging, and then also you put in a pretty physically demanding golf course being so hilly and up and down that maybe come Sunday they might be leaking oil and we'll be fresh.' Hmm, 'leaking oil': there's a quote with which the press can run.

Clark is right about one thing. This is an exhausting week. But it is also exhilarating. I can't wait for the opening ceremony – not for Tom Grennan's singing, nor the pomp and circumstance. I want to know the pairings and match-ups for the opening day's foursomes. The action cannot come quickly enough.

THURSDAY 28 SEPTEMBER

I've taken my time heading to the course, preferring a quiet morning prepping for the three days to come. When I arrive, Grennan is doing his soundcheck on a stage fit for the biggest of shows. He's good and at the end admits into his mic that he was thinking of Rory McIlroy while he was singing.

There is time to walk the back nine to complete my recce of the course. I was impressed by the first half of the layout when I walked it earlier in the week and the finishing stretch looks breathtaking. The level of infrastructure, the stands and giant screens is greater than I have ever seen on a golf course. The contouring looks fit to offer terrific views for more than 50,000 fans each day and the atmosphere could be electric. It feels seriously grand. I'd say it's the biggest golf event I've ever attended.

I catch up with the American team finishing their final practice rounds. They are signing mini footballs and throwing them to the crowds, clearly on a charm offensive. Europe have been playing the front nine and Viktor Hovland provides the highlight with a hole in one at the drivable par-4 5th. The '*Olé*'s are atmospherically in full swing for the Norwegian.

The opening ceremony is pretty slick and has moved on by light years from the stuffy, speech-ridden stodgy fare of yesteryear. The only set piece oration comes from the captains. The Italian equivalent of the Red Arrows, Frecce Tricolori, do an extra flypast spewing red, white and green trails across the brilliant blue sky. The second one interrupts Zach Johnson just as he tries to get into his flow amid choruses of '*Olé, Olé, Olé*' from the crowds. Poor bloke. Luke Donald stands up and starts in Italian. With gusto. And he nails it. The fans go wild. Europe one up.

And now the pairings. Johnson sends out debutant Sam Burns with world number one Scottie Scheffler. A dodgy driver partners a faltering putter against Europe's temperamental beast, Jon Rahm, and his equally combustible partner, Tyrrell Hatton. Ludvig Åberg makes his debut with Viktor Hovland in the unforgiving foursomes environment against Max Homa and Brian Harman. Shane Lowry partners Sepp Straka (they both use Srixon golf balls) against Rickie Fowler and Collin Morikawa. And the final foursome is Rory McIlroy and Tommy Fleetwood against Xander Schauffele and Patrick Cantlay – a blockbuster to end the session.

Around the media centre, American reporters grumble. 'Why pick JT [Justin Thomas] and not play him with his buddy Spieth?' says one. 'Where's Koepka?' says his colleague. 'He's left 11 major wins on the bench,' drawls another scribe. Koepka five majors, Spieth three, Thomas two and reigning US Open champion Wyndham Clark sit out Friday morning.

FRIDAY 29 SEPTEMBER

My alarm sounds at 4.30 a.m. I'm already awake. This is not a day to oversleep. This date has been circled in the calendar for a very long time.

It is chilly when I arrive at the first tee. There are already thousands of people gathered in the vast grandstands. The only empty seats are for those people who have paid extra for a guaranteed spot. Walking past the queues to get into those stands felt like a Saturday afternoon at a Premier League football match. It is 6.30 a.m. on a Friday morning and the singing has already begun.

European vice captains, notably Nicolas Colsaerts, emerge on to the first tee to orchestrate thunder claps and chants and whip fans into a fever. It strikes me that this is not far removed from LIV's vision of how the sport should be. Golf but louder. The thing is the people here care who wins.

They know it is the sport in its purest form. As McIlroy told me, 'There is nothing contrived.' He is certainly correct about the golf that will follow. The orchestrating of the fans might be edging towards contrivance, but there remains a natural joy and ebullience to make this feel very special.

I watch each of the four groups tee off and walk and commentate on the final match, which the Fleetwood Mac combo edges on the 17th green. They have never been behind and complete a comprehensive whitewash for Europe. The Americans have been rusty. The home team win all four matches and make their best start to a Ryder Cup.

The place is rocking as we head into the afternoon four-balls. These are much tighter contests apart from the one I commentate on. Matt Fitzpatrick one-putts the first six greens, never once looking like missing. He and Rory McIlroy romp to a 5&3 win over Collin Morikawa and

Xander Schauffele. In the other matches, Hovland, Rahm and then Justin Rose hole putts on the 18th to force halves – or ties, as the authorities would like us to refer to drawn matches. Rahm eagled two of the last three holes to snatch his unlikely half in thrilling fashion. It means America have failed to win a single match on the opening day. The crowds are ecstatic but some of us are fearing an anticlimactic rout.

When Rose holed his 10-footer to deny Max Homa and Wyndham Clark, the Englishman turned to his team, repeatedly and viciously shaking his clenched fist. His body was convulsed by the surge of adrenalin. My watch buzzed to fatuously warn me of a loud environment as I stood green side. As if anyone needed telling. It was pandemonium, a peak moment of joyful triumph. Rarely do you witness a golfer reacting in such a way, except at the Ryder Cup.

I get back to the hotel at around 8.40 p.m., exhausted. A former Ryder Cup player is standing outside and it turns out he is stranded. The bus that should have taken him to his hotel did not turn up, so he came to ours hoping to grab a taxi from here. There are no cabs. I have a hire car, so I drive him to his lodgings.

'When Rosey hit that putt, and all the other stuff that happened on that final green today, how do you think all those LIV players were feeling?' he wonders out loud as we trundle down the motorway. I get what he means. Do Saudi millions make up for not being part of moments like that? I have no idea. Nor does my passenger.

SATURDAY 30 SEPTEMBER

I've tried to sleep, I really have. But I was like a laptop that refuses to shut down because of an annoying program refusing to quit. In those few short hours of supposed shut-eye my mind whirs, refusing to switch off. I can't force quit, such is the all-encompassing nature of this Ryder Cup.

It is back to the course at 5 a.m. More stoking of the first tee crowd. This time they have a professional warm-up artist. Ryder Cup Europe seem to have thought of everything and their players are hellbent on building on a 6 ½ to 1 ½ lead from the first day. Again, they are straight out of the blocks and they take the foursomes session 3–1. Included is a record 9&7 defeat for the world's top player, Scheffler, and his partner, LIV's Brooks Koepka. They've been beaten by Viktor Hovland, playing only his second Ryder Cup, and Ludvig Åberg, who only turned pro in June. Scheffler is later seen head bowed on a buggy, distraught, in tears and being comforted by his wife, Meredith. Koepka's demeanour seems less distressed.

Rumours start to circulate that all is not well in the American camp. Sky Sports reporter Jamie Weir posts on X: 'Understand from several sources that the US team room is fractured, a split led predominantly by Patrick Cantlay. Cantlay believes players should be paid to participate in the Ryder Cup, and is demonstrating his frustration at not being paid by refusing to wear a team cap.' Weir also said Cantlay had, 'refused to attend the gala dinner earlier in the week' and, alongside his friend and partner Xander Schauffele, 'is sitting in a separate area of the team dressing room.'

It is bombshell stuff and word spreads rapidly. Fans are soon plugged in and let Cantlay know they are aware. As his afternoon four-ball with Wyndham Clark against McIlroy and Matt Fitzpatrick hits the back nine, fans start waving their caps in the air.

I see the players coming down the 16th. There are at least 10,000 people on that one hole, probably more. They are all waving their hats and singing. Initially, I thought it was a new expression of European jubilation; after all, Justin Thomas and Jordan Spieth had just lost a four-ball match together for the first time in their Ryder Cup careers on that very hole. But then it becomes apparent what the fans are singing. 'Hats off, for your bank account! Hats off, for your bank account!'

It was maximised derision for the notion that Cantlay wanted to be paid to play for his country and that he was baring his forehead as a protest. It was an extraordinary scene, the like of which I've never before witnessed on a golf course. The golfer at the centre of it all responds magnificently, birdieing 16 and 17.

In the scramble to the 18th fairway I'm tackled by a female steward trying to stem a tide of frantic fans breaking through the ropes to cross the fairway. I'm speaking live on air as my headphones go flying. Her forearm crashes into my head. Lord knows what it sounds like on the radio. It hopefully helps reflect the fevered chaos of the moment, but I doubt it.

The match is all square coming down the par-5 18th and on the home green Cantlay is 43 feet way in three shots. Both McIlroy and Fitzpatrick have significantly closer birdie putts. It is nearly dark. Somehow, the American picks the line and cans the putt. He goes wild in celebration. His caddie, Joe LaCava, raises his cap and twirls it to mimic the European fans. So do Cantlay's teammates and support staff standing by the green. It is a prolonged celebration and is met by a vociferous chorus of boos.

McIlroy is upset; we can see him having a go at LaCava before he and Fitzpatrick miss their putts. It is a potentially vital point for America, dramatically snatched against the most partisan home support. Europe lead 10½ to 5½ but the USA have a potential spark.

Cantlay is one of a handful of Americans who head straight to the media tent.

'Should you be paid to play in the Ryder Cup?' he is asked.

'It's not about that. It's just about Team USA and representing our country,' he replies.

'Can you answer the question?'

'That's all I've got to say about that.'

'Why no hat?'

'The hat doesn't fit. It didn't fit at Whistling Straits and didn't fit this week. Everyone knows that.'

Contrary to Weir's post, Cantlay had attended the Gala Dinner earlier in the week but left early after official pictures were taken. But both he and Xander Schauffele skipped the American team's pre-Ryder Cup recce to Rome. Their reasoning, attending a bachelor's party which had been arranged before the trip dates were known, did not seem as compelling as Jordan Spieth's, who missed it because of the impending birth of his second child.

Is the American team fractured? Who knows? It'll come out in the post-Ryder Cup wash. Meanwhile, social media lights up with footage from the Marco Simone car park. McIlroy is going mad, aggressively shouting in the direction of the mild-mannered caddie of Justin Thomas, Jim 'Bones' Mackay. McIlroy is waving his arms threateningly. Shane Lowry steps in to pull his teammate back. McIlroy's burly bodyguard also intervenes before Europe's star man is driven off to the team hotel. They are amazing scenes and they are going viral.

Earlier in that afternoon's match, McIlroy had crossed the eighth fairway to query a penalty drop taken by Clark. The US Open champion, who beat his opponent to win that maiden major title, asked McIlroy what he was whining about in a conversation overheard by a BBC colleague. The European felt the drop was being taken from the wrong place. 'I'm not whining, I just want to play by the rules,' McIlroy told him. Needle.

And now this extraordinary bust-up at close of play. It is what sets the Ryder Cup apart. That edge is vital to its allure. Real, authentic rivalry. Great sport. It is heartening that it has not become a cosy contest between mates who, predominantly, reside together in the USA.

What a day. I have to sleep.

Back in my room, I pour myself a glass – well paper cup – of red wine. Drink it and the head hits the pillow. Control, Alt, Replete.

SUNDAY 1 OCTOBER

This could go quickly. Europe only need four points and Luke Donald is sending out his big-hitters first to get the job done ASAP. Rahm, Hovland, Rose and McIlroy are his top four in the batting order. Rahm faces Scheffler, Hovland takes on Morikawa and Cantlay lies in wait for Rose. Frustratingly for those who wanted to see the American – who is being painted as public enemy number one – take on McIlroy, they miss each other by one place in the order. Sam Burns will be the Northern Irishman's opponent.

Some say the draw should not be blind. That the captains should have a system whereby they can choose the singles match-ups. To me, it would be an unnecessary contrivance. The established way of assembling two lists and putting them against each other works a treat. Captains can second- and third-guess their opponent's tactics, which adds to the intrigue. On this occasion, if it goes the distance it will come down to Tommy Fleetwood against Rickie Fowler or Bob MacIntyre versus Wyndham Clark in the anchor match.

I'm out with the top match – Rahm and Scheffler – and they depart amid tumultuous scenes on the first tee. Once again the crowds are in a frenzy, stoked not only by Mr Warm Up Guy but the drama of the previous evening. 'That 15 seconds of McIlroy going nuts, means everyone is interested. Not just golf fans,' Ross Mitchell, one of my 5Live producers, said to me on the way to the stadium surrounding the tee. 'My mum is even interested, and she hates golf,' he added.

The view from the back of the first green is breathtaking. The entire 445-yard hole is surrounded by crowds standing 10 deep, stretching all the way back down to the vast grandstands surrounding the tee. I do something I rarely do when I'm commentating and reach for my phone to take a quick photo.

This is genuinely golf on a different level, it seems massive, vibrant, vital and authentic. There's history to back it up, but this feels as though the game is breaking new ground. The crowds are relatively young, diverse, and despite a heavy UK bias, still cosmopolitan. Is this golf reaching its potential?

Rahm rolls in a birdie putt to send the home fans wild. It is the first blow in a stunning match that, for me, comes closest in rivalling that epic McIlroy/Reed contest of 2016. In that one, the fireworks came early and were more spectacular. This one slow-burns; Rahm goes two up early as Scheffler struggles with his putter. But the world number one gamely battles his demons and levels by the turn.

Scheffler then birdies 11 to go one up, and Rahm counters with birdies at 12 and 13 to move ahead again. It is a heavyweight slugfest, a tennis equivalent would be an epic Federer/Nadal grand slam final, such is the quality and intensity of the golf. The world number one birdies 14 and 15 and leads by one going to the last. There, Rahm conjures an extraordinary putt from all the way across the green for a conceded birdie that Scheffler cannot match. This classic contest ends in a hard-fought and glorious half.

Hovland has already won, Europe need just two and a half points to triumph and two of them are swiftly delivered by McIlroy and Tyrrell Hatton. But where will the extra half point come from? The rest of the board is a sea of red, but for a couple of slender European leads. MacIntyre misses a tiny putt and the European fans all around the course watching on big screens gasp and fret.

It is not until Fleetwood fires a glorious tee shot on to the 16th green after Fowler flays one into the drink that Europe can breathe easy. The Englishman moves two up with two to play. He cannot be beaten. It is a guaranteed half, the crucial half point that prompts scenes of unbridled joy among the thousands of European fans across the course. The half becomes a full point after Fleetwood fires his tee shot to close range on the par-3 17th and Fowler generously concedes the putt.

I'm still on the 18th, where I've seen Matt Fitzpatrick miss a putt for a half with Max Homa – America's stand-out player – that would have won the cup some time earlier. Sepp Straka was trying to do the same while Fleetwood's heroics played out on the 16th, but the Austrian succumbed to Justin Thomas.

Luke Donald is interviewed by Sky Sports and is in tears. I wait to speak to the skipper and my headphones are suddenly consumed with a buzzing noise. I cannot hear our programme. It turns out that there has been a major outage affecting all the broadcasters and we are off air. It is chaos around the green, which is surrounded by thousands of people, many of them eligible to be inside the ropes.

Fortunately our programme is back up and running by the time I interview Europe's triumphant leader. He is no less emotional than he was on Sky. It has been an extraordinary journey, having been initially overlooked for Henrik Stenson, who then decided to take LIV's millions.

Donald did a brilliant job. Insightful, intelligent and inspiring, he masterminded this triumph. I ask him if he dared to anticipate how he might feel at this moment of victory. 'No, I didn't,' he says, his voice cracking with emotion, his eyes misting with welling tears. It means so much to a man who was on the winning side in all four of his playing appearances.

It's been another extraordinary day. Zach Johnson says the defeat 'is on me' and that he wishes he could start the week over. Cantlay cracks a smile that truly transforms his face while he is quizzed again over 'hat-gate'. He seems happy for us to think he was just trying to improve his tan line ahead of marrying his fiancée in Rome tomorrow.

The American team do not appear to be hurting too badly. It feels as though they are taking comfort from making a contest of it by the end. Europe are jubilant, and rightly so. It has been a glorious week for them and for their sport.

18
MASSIVE DISCONNECT

'Greed has taken over now. In the past it was just underneath the surface and now everybody knows.'

James Corrigan, Telegraph *golf correspondent*

Europe celebrated their Ryder Cup success long and hard. From the jubilant scenes on the first tee, where the trophy was presented to captain Luke Donald, to their boisterous bus journey back to the team hotel, footage of the celebrations was plastered all over social media. Rory McIlroy lovingly clutching the cup belting out 'Europe on fire, America terrified', Bob MacIntyre renditioning walking '500 miles, and I would walk 500 more!', proclaiming Europe's triumph with unbridled joy.

This was more than a sporting victory. The thrilling nature of the final day reaffirmed the Ryder Cup's status as one of the pre-eminent sporting occasions on the planet. Those three glorious days in Rome captured the public's imagination across the continent. More than 270,000 people flocked to Marco Simone to witness the week's events. Social media impressions totalled in excess of 600 million and there were record-breaking viewing figures in the UK for the live Sky Sports coverage, up 38 per cent on the last match at Whistling Straits.

According to their official release, Ryder Cup Europe's platforms alone attracted 137,106,426 impressions, an increase of 117 per cent compared with the last home match in Paris, when Europe last won in 2018. The home side's early dominance and the inconvenience of the transatlantic time difference were reasons cited for lowered viewing figures in the USA. NBC Sports reportedly paid $440m over 15 years for the US rights – $55m per event.

What could not be denied was the increasing value of the Ryder Cup as a property within the game. It is a lucrative entity that the PGA Tour has long coveted. 'The one thing the PGA Tour always resented was that they let the PGA of America keep a major [the PGA Championship] and they never got their hands on the Ryder Cup revenue which is comfortably north of $100m every time it's played in the US,' Andrew Gardiner, whose ideas prompted so much upheaval, told me. 'And they always wanted it.' Ironically, the PGA Tour's closer alliance with the DP World Tour, prompted by the arrival of a breakaway circuit, could ultimately see the American tour gain a share of this prized commodity.

The continent's success came just a week after that thrilling Solheim Cup played at Finca Cortesin in Spain, which prompted such delirium among the home fans on the Costa del Sol as Europe retained the trophy. Those celebrations deserved due prominence, lasting far longer than the mere couple of days that transpired before being overtaken by the Ryder Cup.

That both matches were staged independently of each other showed how disjointed the overall running of professional golf remains. Stacy Lewis, the captain of the American Solheim team, claimed that 'an opportunity had been lost' by not strategically coordinating the marketing and staging of these separate Europe vs. USA encounters. It might prove beneficial that the Solheim now switches back to even years in the calendar going forwards, but the lack of joined-up thinking suggests the pro game is still very much everyman/woman for themselves, rather than an effective collective. As Gardiner noted: 'No one knows who owns what. This sport is entirely fractured and the sport is where it is because there has never been an ownership structure.'

Giles Morgan is head of sponsorship and partnerships at Howden Group Holdings and has 30 years' experience in the sports market. He wrote some of the biggest sponsorship cheques in golf's history when he held a similar role at HSBC, including the inaugural £1m first prize at the 2005 HSBC World Matchplay. Morgan believes professional golf is missing a massive trick by not uniting the forces of the men's and women's games. 'One hundred per cent,' he said to me. 'You'd stop the mad escalation of ego and price . . . It would be very engaging and demonstrate great skill, not in some kind of woke way, because golf should be the ultimate universal sport played by men, women, young and old.' And, by implication, increase its attraction to big business. He tried to capitalise on golf's mixed potential during his HSBC days but was thwarted by officialdom. 'I wanted to do it 17/18 years ago – but it was very clear no one was interested,' he said.

Nevertheless, last September's Ryder Cup proved that the match between the men of Europe and America remains golf's biggest noise. Pointedly, Europe's Ryder Cup director, Guy Kinnings, commented: 'The Ryder Cup is undoubtedly a unique and special event in sport.' The Wentworth-based executive noted the jubilant scenes on Europe's team bus that attracted 20 million impressions on social media. 'Those scenes captured what it means to play for something bigger than yourself.'

LIV would also argue that its recruits are motivated by its team format, but how much interest it generates is open to question. 'None of the LIV events are big events. They are PR stunts,' Morgan insisted.

There is widespread acceptance that those players who signed for LIV are playing on the breakaway tour primarily to bolster their bank accounts and in many cases by fantastic sums. 'That's why they went,' DP World Tour player Eddie Pepperell, who was a member of the circuit's tournament committee, told the *Chipping Forecast* podcast. 'If the money wasn't anything like this, none of them would have gone.'

When their players returned to Donald Trump's place at Doral near Miami for their season-ending Team Championship in October 2023, $50m was once again on the line. Talor Gooch had already secured the $18m bonus for being the tour's most successful individual player that year. His earnings from two LIV seasons were approaching $50m, nearly as much as two-times major champion and US Ryder Cup captain Zach Johnson won in his entire career. Gooch was not even considered for Johnson's team and headed into the 2024 season ineligible for any of the four majors. 'My feeling is that as a professional sportsman he is largely invisible,' Pepperell added. 'No one really knows who Talor Gooch is in the world of golf any more. Great, good on him. He's super rich, super wealthy, and he can buy whatever he wants to buy and that's absolutely wonderful. And that's his prerogative. But that's where it stops. He's got no legacy in the game; I don't personally see how LIV is going to grow to a point where their players can build genuine legacies . . . really these guys are not being seen.'

A week or so after the Ryder Cup, the official golf world rankings announced that LIV's events would remain ineligible for their points. It was another blow for their players, most pertinently Gooch, who needs OWGR rewards to climb the standings to be able to qualify for majors and the Olympics. Without official recognition, what do LIV events mean beyond making their already wealthy players even richer?

LIV stopped reporting their viewing figures in May 2023. This implied they were so poor on the CW Network that there was nothing to be gained from sharing the information. Coverage of their penultimate event in Saudi Arabia was shown on tape delay in the USA, where viewers are expected to pay for their YouTube coverage. Live action was available on the LIV Plus app for free worldwide, but its impact has been difficult to measure.

Daring to be different has certainly been one of the hallmarks of LIV Golf. Their team formats have yet to realise the investment envisaged to provide a return on the billions ploughed into the project. But the format has its merits and the end-of-season Team Championship provides LIV Golf, perhaps, with its most compelling form.

And shotgun starts. With players starting simultaneously all around the course, it shows it is possible to broadcast golf in a shorter, more manageable window. 'They were bold,' said former manager and tournament promoter Andrew 'Chubby' Chandler to me. 'I was remembering the late referee John Paramor.

In about 2008 he stopped us from having a shotgun start at the Belfry after a fog delay. He said, "that's not golf". Now shotgun starts are there aren't they?' The weather-affected Alfred Dunhill Links Championship in the autumn of 2023 was only completed because a shotgun start was used for what proved the third and final round at Carnoustie. That tournament was also shortened to 54 holes.

Chandler insists great opportunities were missed by the golf establishment when the offer of Saudi money first arrived. 'LIV should have been the European Tour with 10 designated events inside the tour,' he told me. 'They should have had ten $20m events on the European Tour and on the same week they should have played for two and a half million in smaller tournaments for the lads who didn't get in it. That would have worked. You could have had those 10 events in all the right places, like Australia.'

There persists a feeling that the bitterness and rancour could have been avoided if the main tours had been more receptive, starting with Gardiner's Premier Golf League proposals. 'In hindsight, one of the [PGA] tour's biggest mistakes throughout all this was not just to ignore the Premier Golf League group but to really go out of their way to not take a meeting,' leading golf observer Geoff Shackelford said to me. 'Had they done that, who knows, maybe something happens? Instead it opens the door for the Saudi element to lose patience.' He told me that by 'doing their own thing' it has been 'a disaster for the tours.' He added: 'They should have taken a meeting and they should have been more open to the franchise concept.'

Shackelford, whose coverage of Andrew Gardiner's efforts to transform the professional game has always been sympathetic, believes mistakes were made on all sides. He believes the franchise concept for team golf has been left in tatters. 'Andy's approach was to build slowly, start with players and then franchises,' the American blogger and podcaster told me. 'There would be an identity created in that team. But LIV comes along, takes the concept and gives these teams horrible names. And now I don't see the franchise concept being as attractive because of the way they forced it.'

Giles Morgan agrees. 'The way that LIV has done it looks very odd to me,' he said. 'I don't feel like I could belong to one of their teams. The commitment of the golfer to a brand [equipment manufacturer] is absolutely huge, and that's like motorsport. Fandom is like a feudal army, it's that you belong somewhere. Look at the Ryder Cup; it works. Give me something to hang my hat on.'

Yet Greg Norman insisted the team concept and their franchises are and will continue to become a big success. Having avoided the public spotlight in the months that followed the 6 June announcement of a potential deal between PIF and established tours, the outspoken Aussie broke his silence in Miami last October. Norman said it was the team concept that gave him confidence that LIV would survive any merger involving Saudi Arabia in the wider game. 'I knew exactly the investment into LIV and the long-term ability of the franchises and the valuation of each one of these franchises,' he told reporters at the season-ending LIV Team Championship. 'The money was always going to be invested in that. I knew LIV was always going to exist.'

Saudi Arabia's bludgeoning of golf's status quo is understandable, given its overarching objectives to diversify its oil-based economy. It is not just golf. The Kingdom is investing massively in football, recruiting the likes of Cristiano Ronaldo and a slew of Premier League stars from England, including international midfielder Jordan Henderson, who was booed by the Wembley crowds in his first home appearance after his 2023 move. Tennis is readying itself for offers of Saudi investment. The ATP Tour is said to be keen not to 'make the same mistakes' as golf has done.

Crown Prince Mohammed bin Salman remains fully committed to the policy deemed 'sport washing' and embraces the term. The billions will keep flowing from the Public Investment Fund into sporting coffers. 'If "sport-washing" is going to increase my GDP by way of 1%, then I will continue doing sport-washing,' MBS told Fox News in the early autumn of 2023.

'Project Wedge', as it was known, certainly made scores of golfers much wealthier, but it drove a huge divide through the sport. It continues to be a significant factor in the Kingdom's Vision 2030, a document they shared with the PGA Tour when the shock Framework Agreement was first mooted in the spring of 2023.

'Disruption is a strategy,' Professor Simon Chadwick reminded me. 'Golf has got global reach. Economically, socio-culturally, politically there is some capital to be generated through a presence in golf. There are economic opportunities that come with golf. Partly that is tourism,' added the professor of Sport and Geopolitical Economy. 'It is also worth remembering a lot of business deals are done on golf courses. There is a networking power within golf that still exists and is still powerful and still has economic and socio-political value.

'In 10 years' time there will be almost blind acceptance. It's almost as though legitimacy is synonymous with blind acceptance. "Let's go to Saudi Arabia to play golf," no questions, no suspicion, no doubts just a legitimate destination in exactly the same way as is the case with Marbella, Miami and Dubai.'

And, for now, that translates into billions of dollars pouring into the game. Is it mere coincidence that the notion of players seeking payment to play the Ryder Cup resurfaced during America's defeat in Rome? Did Patrick Cantlay's apparent 'hat-gate' protest signify that everything in the game needs to be done for monetary reward?

The last time this issue was so prominent was in 1999 when Tiger Woods was such an emerging force he was attracting more and more money to the sport. 'Every time there's a cash injection into golf it seems the Ryder Cup comes into the equation,' the *Telegraph*'s James Corrigan observed to me after last year's match. 'Never mind hat-gate, if you think about it now, the Ryder Cup is on the table in the merger negotiations. It is an asset of the European Tour and they have to put all their assets on the table. It's a massive money earner and the PGA Tour might want to get a bit of it because they've craved it for ages. So it is all up for grabs now. The players are just emulating what is going on.'

On a wider level, Corrigan, who has broken more stories about the so-called golf wars than any other journalist in the sport, believes its lack of soul has been laid bare. 'Greed has taken over now,' he told me. 'In the past it was just underneath the surface and now everybody knows.'

From the other side of the pond, Shackelford agrees. 'Initially this was a fun business story and an intrigue story,' the US writer said to me. 'And now you're starting to sense people are more and more fatigued with it and the money. There's so much greed and at some point that is just such a turn-off to fans. We're a wonderful niche sport. These players are not worth what they want to pay them.'

Shackelford's hunch is confirmed by Giles Morgan. 'The reason why I'm so glad I'm not at HSBC any more is that, knowing the bank, there is no way I could have got these big numbers through, but I wouldn't have wanted to,' he said. 'Would I want to be seen as the person feathering the pockets of 250 people maximum in the world? I don't think so.'

Some of the game's leaders fear for its future. One suggested the sport was potentially 'headed for a massive disconnect' and that the way it was going was 'simply unaffordable'. The majors have tried to keep pace, boosting their prize funds towards the $20m mark. Phil Mickelson insists this is short-changing the players, the stars of the show – who should be getting a much bigger share of the money generated by events such as the Masters, the US Open, the US PGA and The Open Championship. He posted on social media this message in the wake of LIV being denied world-ranking points last October.

But this mentality ignores what the proceeds of major tournaments finance and Morgan believes sponsorship deals that primarily benefit player bank accounts are increasingly unattractive to big business. 'The beneficiary is the golfer, not golf itself,' he said. 'If the money was being ploughed back into the sport for the good of the game, maybe thinking about the technological requirements to shorten the game, shorten courses, make it more environmentally friendly, make it more sustainable, to make the game more interesting to new audiences; if that's where the extra money was going then you could kind of justify it. That's golf reimagining itself for the future.'

Under Mickelson's player-focused vision, initiatives to grow the game would receive less and less resource because more and more money would be stuffed into the already bulging wallets of so many of the world's top stars. 'The four majors should collude and have a purse freeze,' Shackelford insisted. 'They give back to the game with the money they bring in at their tournaments. And nobody cares what the purse is at a major championship. Jon Rahm didn't care what he won at the Masters.'

And perhaps this is the key to golf's future. Its biggest prizes are not monetary. The tournaments that define careers with their trophies are all about moments rather than remuneration. Events such as The Open where, in 2023, we could celebrate an amateur first-round leader in South Africa's Christo

Lamprecht or the PGA Championship where club pro Michael Block lived his wildest dream with a hole in one while playing with Rory McIlroy in the final round. The Masters where Rahm revived the Spanish spirit of Seve Ballesteros or the US Open where Wyndham Clark conquered his demons to confirm world-class credentials.

The 2023 Ryder Cup was billed as 'pure sport' by Europe's captain Luke Donald and his talisman McIlroy. They were making perhaps the most significant point they could, in an era when almost everything else in the game seems to have a super-inflated price. Nothing had changed with the biennial dust up in Italy. It was the same match for the same prize.

Everything else around it in the game was in a state of chaotic flux, uncertain and fractious. The event itself felt all the grander and more important as a result. It brought natural sporting joy to anyone who watched and listened, and they did in their millions. That little pot of gold has never felt more precious. In fact, priceless.

EPILOGUE

That fortnight of team golf, when the Solheim and Ryder Cups portrayed professional golf in its most attractive light, provided occasions that stirred sporting passions in a way that is beyond most tournaments. Yes, the majors can be majestic, generating memorable moments aplenty and the same can be said of many tour competitions. They are all capable of yielding fairy tales and drama to sustain the golfing calendar, but rarely – if ever – can they boast the pulsating qualities of a Ryder or Solheim Cup, where golf is at its loudest. And the task of capturing the public's imagination week in week out is made more difficult when the best players are spread between competing tours.

LIV tournaments have shown they too can create a spectacle. The newcomers' first visit to Adelaide in the spring of 2023 proved the point with the revelry that greeted Chase Koepka's hole in one. Aussie fans – too often starved of top-level golf – celebrated their opportunity to watch some of the biggest names, including one of their own in Cam Smith, who happened to be the reigning Open champion at the time.

But all that is good and attractive is fragile and needs constant nurturing and protection. Just four days after the Ryder Cup, a hospitality stand at the Marco

Simone course became a raging inferno, casting a plume of thick black smoke across otherwise clear blue Roman skies. The blaze felt like a metaphor for the professional game with dark, foreboding clouds hanging over a sport set dangerously alight by unwelcome sparks.

While some would say these catalysts brought much-needed flashes of innovation, others argue the opposite was required in such a comparatively reserved and already wealthy pursuit. Regardless, a movement fuelled by the proceeds of Saudi Arabian oil had significantly altered the direction of professional golf as the calendar ticked towards 2024.

No one was hurt in the Italian fire despite the spectacular destruction of an imposing structure that only days earlier had been a vibrant hub for thousands of people. The Ryder Cup was a week of heroes and villains. Rory McIlroy basked in the glory of his best match in European colours and was nominated for the BBC's Sports Personality of the Year award. Jon Rahm and Viktor Hovland burnished reputations as continental warriors, Bob MacIntyre took on folk hero status, while his partner Justin Rose left no one in any doubt that he is as hard as nails. Ludvig Åberg confirmed the birth of a golfing superstar. For America, Patrick Cantlay attracted admiration for the standard of his golf under fire, but the suggestion that he would want paying to play for his country was regarded as criminal by many fans of these biennial jousts.

So much magic is lost when money becomes the key driver. The merest hint of greed acts as a touch paper to the volatile tinder of sporting glory. The best golfers have chased inflated earnings throughout history, but the professional game has always found a way to make it secondary to the lustre of titles. How many PGA Tour events has Tiger Woods won? Anyone with more than a passing interest in the game knows it is a staggering and record-equalling 82 victories. How much money has he won? Most observers would need to consult record books, although we are all aware it is an eye-watering sum. For the record, he banked just shy of $121 million on the PGA Tour in his first 27 years as a pro.

Yet in 2023 alone, FedEx Cup winner Hovland collected earnings nudging the $40 million mark. The popular Norwegian has yet to win a major. It is a sign of golf's LIV-inspired hyper-inflation that Hovland won close to a third of the legendary Woods' total PGA Tour income in a single season. And over on LIV, Talor Gooch – a US golfer yet to taste Ryder Cup action and currently ineligible for any of the 2024 majors – pretty much matched the spoils collected by Hovland.

Gooch's handsome LIV earnings are a mere rounding error in the account books of the Saudi Public Investment Fund. But they uncomfortably up the ante for the establishment, potentially to unsustainable levels. The PGA Tour, which has a significant stake in the future of Europe's DP World Tour, has been stretched beyond its means. This is why Jay Monahan took the meeting with Yasir Al-Rumayyan that set in motion the Framework Agreement aimed at ensuring Saudi money flows into PGA Tour coffers. But it soon became clear the tours also needed big money from elsewhere. This is why they were open to US investors such as the Strategic Sports Group (SSG), who are ploughing $3 billion into the newly formed, for-profit, PGA Tour Enterprises.

At the end of 2023, with a 31 December deadline to conclude negotiations with PIF fast approaching, Monahan wrote a memo to his players. 'As you know, the [PGA Tour Policy Board] unanimously directed management to pursue exclusive negotiations with SSG,' Monahan said. 'I am pleased to report that we have made meaningful progress.'

This is what the new-look Policy Board, with Tiger Woods at the helm, wanted after McIlroy surprisingly resigned to be replaced by Jordan Spieth in November 2023. The Northern Irishman said he wanted to concentrate on his playing career. But it became apparent he also desired freedom from the collective responsibility of board membership; to be liberated to say what he really thinks about the direction that golf is taking.

McIlroy soon let it be known that he had been involved in his own talks with Yasir in early 2023 to ascertain what the PIF governor really wanted from his involvement in the game. McIlroy urged his tours to talk to Saudi Arabia in the months leading up to the secret meetings that yielded the shock announcement of a Framework Agreement on 6 June that year. The fact that an apparent deal had been done so quickly was a surprise to him, but not the direction of travel.

The American government's reservations about the PGA Tour becoming so dependent on the Saudi state was another reason to do a deal to bring in domestic investors such as SSG. 'This dilution probably quells the concerns of some politicians who might poke around otherwise,' US sports attorney John Nucci told me.

This American-based investment group are a collection of extraordinarily wealthy individuals already well versed with the sporting world. 'SSG is uniquely positioned to ensure you hit a home run when you step up to the plate,' the organisation boasts on its website.

They are led by the Fenway Sports Group, the sports conglomerate that owns the Boston Red Sox, the Pittsburgh Penguins, Liverpool Football Club and a NASCAR race team. Other members of SSG include Arthur Blank, owner of the Atlanta Falcons; Wyc Grousbeck (Boston Celtics), Marc Lasry (Milwaukee Bucks), Tom Ricketts (Chicago Cubs), Cohen Private Ventures (New York Mets), and Gerry Cardinale, the managing partner of RedBird Capital Partners, which owns AC Milan and, perhaps significantly, has various interests in the Middle East.

Despite that looming 31 December deadline, talks to complete the Framework Agreement were delayed while Monahan and fellow executives discussed the SSG proposals. This pause prompted LIV to remind their potential partners of the power of the PIF. Their move was more than a shot across the bows: it was a laser-guided missile and it smashed into its target to prove hostilities in the golf wars were not quite over.

LIV courted the biggest name they could recruit: a Ryder Cup hero and a charismatic reigning Masters champion with global appeal. Jon Rahm had always shown disdain for LIV's abbreviated format and fields. He was a legacy guy, one of those motivated by trying to get as close as possible to the great Woods in the PGA Tour pecking order. But he had always been careful not to criticise players who had chosen to leave the tour. He remained close to former Ryder Cup partner Sergio García. Tim Mickelson – Phil's brother and caddie – used to be his coach and agent in Arizona. Rahm would frequently play practice rounds at majors with Phil and other LIV recruits.

Crucially, the Spaniard had also shown annoyance at being a loyalist kept in the dark ahead of the 6 June announcement. Remember what he said at the US Open staged the week after news broke of the potential Saudi deal: 'A lot of people feel a bit of betrayal from management,' he told us. 'It's just not easy as a player that's been involved, like many others, to wake up one day and see this bombshell. That's why we're all in a bit of a state of limbo because we don't know what's going on.'

These words suggested LIV could optimistically push at a door that might possibly swing open. Rahm did indeed have his price. It was an exorbitant sum, but the PIF could pay it without touching the sides of its vast reserves. The door did not just swing open, it flew off its hinges. Estimates of the package he signed in the first week of December 2023 range between $350 and $600 million. 'I made this decision because I believe it's the best for me and my family,' the 29-year-old Spaniard told reporters after completing the deal.

Rahm suddenly spoke warmly of the LIV formats he had previously derided and followed the pre-prepared lines on 'growing the game' that so many of their expensive recruits had previously followed. A jubilant Greg Norman told visitors to LIV's website: 'When I first met Jon at the age of 17, I knew then that the golfing world was about to witness the birth of a new star. . . . He's a generational talent who has proven his merit as a multiple major champion and tremendous ambassador for global golf by placing the game ahead of himself . . . We couldn't be more excited to welcome Jon to the LIV Golf family as the league continues preparations for a huge 2024 and beyond.'

When the Framework Agreement was first thrashed out there was a no poaching clause, but this was removed to satisfy anti-trust issues that might have led to the deal being scuppered by the US Department of Justice. Nonetheless, the spirit of the clause was followed after the 6 June announcement until the Saudis felt PGA Tour heads were being turned by other potential investors. 'I think the PIF came in and said "right we're going to get the biggest fish out there and if we can get him, we can get anyone,"' *Wall Street Journal* (*WSJ*) reporter Josh Carpenter told me.

It was a massive coup for LIV. With US PGA champion Brooks Koepka already on board, they now had two of the four reigning major champions. Norman was correct in his assessment that Rahm was box office. Arguably only McIlroy was a more significant figure in the upper echelons of the world rankings. 'It really strengthened the PIF's bargaining position,' New York-based lawyer

John Nucci told me. 'They are obviously in a much stronger position with the third best player in the world than they are without him. I do feel it was a play to force the PGA Tour's hand.'

Nucci, who has been a close observer of the golf wars, believes the Saudis were spooked by the establishment's courting of SSG. 'I think the PGA Tour may have been flirting with private equity a little bit too much,' the attorney stated. 'I think the PIF response to that was to continue to throw their money around and throw their weight around as a message to say if you're not going to negotiate with us in a manner that we want, then we're going to let you know we are not going anywhere.'

The PGA Tour was now under intense pressure, even with SSG investment seemingly in the bag. Their model for staging 'signature' tournaments to match LIV's purses was creaking, with sponsors being asked to plough in substantially more money to keep big events afloat. The American bank Wells Fargo called time on backing their competition in Charlotte, North Carolina. 'For these signature events they are asking for 25 million dollars a year – that's a ton of money,' said Josh Carpenter, who broke the story in the *Wall Street Journal*.

Carpenter made it clear to me that he believed Wells Fargo could afford the extra money. But he said it did not represent proper value if you consider the rest of the sporting market. 'Look at a company like Caesars [a Las Vegas-based hotel and casino chain], who have signed a deal with the Superdome in New Orleans,' he said. 'It was a twenty-year deal for maybe $140 million. The Superdome has concerts, NFL games, it has Final Fours, it stages big stuff year-round. Then look at a PGA Tour sponsor like a Wells Fargo. They have a connection with the tour that they can market year-round, but essentially it is one week only. And then it packs up and it goes away.'

It might be different if pro golf was increasing in popularity on a par with the boom experienced by the recreational game since Covid lockdowns. But that is not the case. 'It's not like they're paying that money at a time when television ratings are increasing threefold,' Carpenter contended. 'And you can't guarantee all the top players are going to be there. Even with the new designated, signature structure last year, Jon Rahm and Scottie Scheffler didn't play at Wells Fargo. So it's kind of hard to justify that kind of money.'

Nevertheless, the PGA Tour says it has contracted revenues worth around $10 billion through to 2030. Half of that comes in media rights despite subdued TV ratings in the USA. The Masters was golf's most watched tournament on US television screens in 2023, but was the year's 131st most viewed sporting event. 'You see agents say their golfer is worth [basketball star] Steph Curry kind of money,' Carpenter pointed out. 'I love golf, I eat and breathe it but it is a niche sport. It is not the NFL; it is not the Premier league soccer. PGA Tour final rounds last year on CBS and NBC averaged 2.2 million viewers. NASCAR races here in the US drew almost 600,000 more viewers, almost 3 million viewers per race. What NASCAR driver is getting paid four million dollars to win a race? Or is commanding 200-million-dollar contracts? None of them are.'

And LIV, who routinely pay that kind of money, languish in the backwaters of the CW Network with minuscule ratings. For all his money and potential value in resolving the golf wars, Rahm is likely to be playing much of his foreseeable golf in a largely unseen vacuum, although LIV could boast a new TV deal with Spanish broadcaster Movistar Plus in the wake of his signing. Nevertheless, he is not likely to generate great revenue either, certainly in the short term. LIV's takings for the 2023 season, reportedly, were less than $100 million – a sum comfortably smaller than what they paid Rahm to join.

But this is another example of how golf finds ways to punch above its weight in terms of the money it attracts. Days before LIV's third season began, Rahm's Ryder Cup partner Tyrrell Hatton was recruited for a reported $50 million. It is a scenario that can only continue while it remains a pursuit of genuine appeal to the biggest spenders – the likes of Saudi Arabia and people such as those who comprise SSG. 'These guys are billionaires, a lot of them are major team owners. They are successful businessmen and they've got a lot of money and all of them must like golf too, right?' the *WSJ*'s Carpenter contended. 'The PGA Tour has been the same for so long and so I think they see with their investment and possible investment by PIF as well . . . they see an opportunity for some change. . . . When private equity comes in they expect a return on investment very quickly, within three to five years something like that. I think Strategic Sports Group are viewing this as a long-term thing. They might not have a big ROI by 2030, maybe they are looking more at 2040.'

To maximise a return, the men's professional game needs to be united. When LIV schedule events against the biggest tournaments on the PGA Tour, they weaken the overall offering and divide the audience. The world's best golfers are not playing against each other in the same competitions and so the game is separated from its optimal state. 'We're already seeing it this year where LIV is putting some of their 2024 events up against some other big ticket PGA Tour events,' John Nucci, who has warned that golf could fall into a similarly divided world as professional boxing, told me. 'If that starts happening with competing events on different tours in the same weekend then it's just going to become a mess.'

McIlroy has always been a keen advocate of a unified calendar. 'My dream scenario is a world tour, with the proviso that corporate America has to remain a big part of it all. Saudi Arabia, too. That's just basic economics,' he told *Golf Digest* ahead of the Dubai Invitational, his first event of the 2024 season. But for that to happen, McIlroy envisages a much more international approach that would elevate tournaments such as the Australian and South African Opens as well as visiting fertile golfing landscapes including Singapore, Hong Kong and Japan. This is much more akin to LIV's more global schedule and counter to what has seemed an increasingly parochial America-centric PGA Tour ethos. That said, the tour knows that tournaments staged in different time zones far away from the USA are of considerably lower value to the networks who pay so much to cover their events.

McIlroy has come around to seeing a place for the upstarts. In his opinion – which still counts for a lot – the game could take a leaf from cricket's Indian Premier League and play LIV-style shorter-form team tournaments in certain windows of the calendar, say May and October. 'I could see that being fun,' he told former soccer star Gary Neville on the *Stick to Football* podcast at the end of 2023. He also admitted that he had been 'too judgemental' of players who accepted Norman's overtures and that LIV had exposed flaws in golf's status quo. 'Me making this whole LIV U-turn thing,' he later told reporters. 'Look, I still don't think it's doing anything for the game. But if it's done in a different way it could be beneficial.'

This still represents a significant change of mood, at the very least, from the man who doubled and trebled down when he vehemently told us in the summer of 2023 that he 'hates' LIV and that he would retire if it was the only professional golf left to play. Now he understands why Rahm and Hatton departed and furthermore recognises that their signings show unification is vital for the future of the game.

According to Carpenter, Rahm is similarly minded and probably sees his lucrative defection as a constructive move that is more significant than his gargantuan signing fee. 'He cares a lot about his legacy and I think he sees this as a legacy building move,' said the *WSJ* reporter. 'He sees this as "I'm going to LIV as a way to get the tours back together, to bring global golf back together." That's not based on anything I've been told, but if you read the tea leaves and look at some of the stuff that's happened since he moved to LIV, including Rory's comments . . . I think Jon can look back in a few years and say, "Hey I was the one who brought golf back together – and I have a few extra hundred million dollars in my pocket for it."'

Norman issued an upbeat assessment as LIV entered its third year of existence at the start of 2024. He highlighted Koepka's major success in the PGA Championship at Oak Hill and called Bryson DeChambeau's 'historic' 58 at LIV's Greenbrier event 'the best round I have ever witnessed.' His X (formerly Twitter) post also noted how LIV players Louis Oosthuizen, Dean Burmester and Joaquin Niemann collected five titles between them in co-sanctioned tournaments in South Africa and Australia around the turn of the year that also counted on the DP World Tour.

Norman stated that Rahm is 'the best and most important player in the world today,' promising 'more players to come.' He expressed hope that the Framework Agreement would come to fruition, saying it would be 'good for golf, players and fans' and concluded by saying that 'players now have a voice and influence over the future of the game.'

This had been one of his stated aims, two decades earlier, when Norman first tried to set up a world tour. Now McIlroy, who had vowed to be the 'biggest pain in the ass' he could be to the Australian, also seems in on the concept. He accepted that pro golfers should no longer be regarded as private contractors and instead should become employees of the tours to guarantee the biggest names for the biggest sponsors. This is another significant shift.

In Dubai, where 12 months earlier he had so dramatically beaten Patrick Reed in a win that meant so much because of the American's LIV affiliations,

McIlroy maintained his more conciliatory position. 'You can't ask these media rights partners and sponsors for as much money as we're asking them for and not be able to guarantee them the product they are paying for,' McIlroy told the *Telegraph*'s James Corrigan. 'Unless you want to regress and go back to playing for the money we played for 10 years ago. If the guys want to do that and stay independent contractors that's fine. But that's the alternative, because you've got sponsors that are either pulling out of the PGA Tour or are considering it, because of the numbers they're having to put out.'

McIlroy, who began 2024 by successfully defending his Dubai Desert Classic title, accepts he has moved with the ebbs and flows of the golf wars, telling reporters: 'For the last few years I've been trying to see this through very altruistic lenses. But I've just got to the point where I'm like, "I need to see the reality". If we want to make this thing sustainable, if you want to make the numbers that we're playing for sustainable, then we need to give something back.'

It is a pragmatic stance from someone who still resents the way that the golf ecosystem has been disrupted. 'I don't think this sort of upheaval in the game for the last two years has been great,' he said. "And people could argue that it takes two to tango. If somebody is willing to pay you more for your services than someone else, well, I understand that. But while I can understand it, I don't have to agree with it.'

The driver in all of this has been money and – like in so many other sports – cash from Saudi Arabia. Amid all the developments and machinations, concerns over the Kingdom's record on human rights have been shifted to one side. Those early days of hostile questions to Norman and the likes of Lee Westwood and Ian Poulter ('Who wouldn't you play for?' 'Would you play for Putin or in apartheid South Africa?') seem distant memories. The same can be said of trotted-out platitudes that in some way Saudi Arabia's greater international influence in areas such as sport will lead to greater liberties in the country. 'The success of their sports washing has actually emboldened them to crack down on human rights even further,' Felix Jakens of Amnesty International told me.

Jakens' organisation remains concerned, especially when high-profile sporting recruits claim living standards in the Kingdom are becoming more enlightened. 'They're not able to go into the specialised criminal court which uses torture and sexual violence against women to extract confessions for tweeting things like criticisms of the royal family,' Jakens insisted. 'If the situation of human rights was getting better we would say that but it is really not, it's getting worse . . . There are close to 200 executions a year now, many of them through beheadings . . . Being gay remains illegal in Saudi Arabia and potentially punishable by death.'

The campaigner believes sports taking Saudi investment need to brace themselves for when the Kingdom might become embroiled in a future atrocity similar to the 2018 murder and dismemberment of Jamal Khashoggi. 'At some point there probably will be a reckoning,' Jakens told me. 'The trajectory of Saudi is devouring sport at the moment, but at some point they could be accused of or actually do something which really does throw the spotlight back on them in a way that is going to embarrass these sporting organisations . . . I think these sporting bodies need to be careful about how they rely on this money.'

Saudi Arabia rejects such accusations, portraying itself as a dynamic, developing country that is becoming increasingly ready to thrive when oil revenues eventually run out. Having attracted some of the biggest names in football, Cristiano Ronaldo included, it appears the most likely venue to stage the 2034 men's World Cup. The Kingdom has its eye on tennis and signed a significant deal with Rafael Nadal in early 2024. It is increasingly influential in Formula One and boxing. It could be argued that Crown Prince Mohammed bin Salman has become the most influential figure in world sport. But his investment fund stretches far and wide. It has significant stakes in many global brands, the likes of Uber, Live Nation Entertainment, Meta, Starbucks, PayPal, Microsoft and Costco. Who are golfers to refuse the benefits from the riches of this almost bottomless pit of money?

And as Andy Gardiner identified two decades earlier, golf was ripe for change. It was stuck in its ways. Away from its prestige events – the majors and Ryder Cup – it needed to start behaving like other sports. Players should not be allowed to pick and choose where they play; instead they should go where their tours – their employers – tell them, if they want the wages they feel they deserve.

Greg Norman had a similar vision in the 1990s – he called it 'free agency', which is ironic because when he finally was able to recruit top names they had to sign up to play all of LIV's tournaments as well as Asian Tour events such as the Saudi Invitational.

A combination of Norman's and Gardiner's ideas and McIlroy's 'dream scenario' seem to offer a future blueprint for the men's professional sport. Who knows, the women's game may also benefit in the future and maybe Saudi funding will result in a narrowing of what has become an increasingly wide gender pay gap?

Certainly, administrators have plenty on their plate as Guy Kinnings takes over from the departing Keith Pelley as boss at the DP World Tour. The R&A also began a search for a replacement for chief executive Martin Slumbers, who leaves at the end of 2024. Pelley and Slumbers both played important roles in the years of upheaval that coincided with LIV's arrival.

Professional golf has always been open to slow and deliberate evolution. But it became increasingly vulnerable to revolution. So much of the rhetoric of the last couple of years has carried militaristic connotations despite the absence of physical victims. Some might say the biggest casualties were reputations and character as the greed of this oil-driven gold rush swept through during the period of the golf wars. Others will maintain that such collateral damage is an acceptable inevitability.

What is beyond question is that long-standing and historic bodies such as the PGA and DP World Tours have been changed forever because of golf's greedy and bitter infighting. To what extent it is altered is the final battleground.

Will LIV's so-called 'rebels' be allowed to return to the established tours? They must if the best are to play against the best more regularly. Should the establishment reward those players who remained loyal to their tours? 'A lot of people feel like they're owed something,' warned Xander Schauffele at a Hawaii news conference early in 2024.

The Olympic champion was speaking on the same day as two-time major champion Collin Morikawa addressed reporters. The 26-year-old seemed to sum up a pervading feeling when he said: 'I hope everything comes together and we're able to all play together at some point . . . Deals need to be made and we all need to get back to playing golf.'

This is a sentiment felt by so many of the pros who compete in what is still a pedestrian but attractive and idyllic sport. It was thrown into unprecedented upheaval, a process started when Gardiner began his scribblings. Two decades and billions of dollars later, we still cannot be sure where they might lead.

REFERENCES AND SOURCES

Statements from press conferences, press releases, social media, documents in the public domain and my own conversations are not referenced here.

Documents and exchanges released via the Senate hearing are identified within the text, and are fully referenced below.

1. LIV Origins

'Over ten years, the overall financial injection into the European Tour could reach $1billion': McEwan, M., 'How LIV Blew Up Men's Professional Golf, *Bunkered*, 20 February 2023.

2. Greg Norman: Born to Conquer

'There was no question in my mind . . .': Norman, G., *The Way of the Shark* (Ebury Press, 2006).
'By what he said, I felt sure that either Finchem or IMG had spoken . . .': *Ibid.*
'This is the biggest decision of my life . . .': Harig, B., 'Golf legend Greg Norman set to run competing tour that hopes to begin play in 2022', ESPN, 29 October 2021.

3. A Serious Business

'For me personally, it's not enough that they are sitting on hundreds of millions of digital moments . . . .': Huggan, J., 'Phil Mickelson says PGA Tour's "obnoxious greed" has him looking elsewhere', *Golf Digest*, 2 February 2022.
'At that point anything he tells me is going straight in the book...' McKellar Golf (podcast), 25 October 2023.

'On 17 February 2022, the writer used his *Fire Pit Collective* website . . .': Shipnuck, A., 'The Truth About Phil Mickelson and Saudi Arabia', *Fire Pit Collective*, 17 February 2022.

5. LIV Goes Live

'the four-times major winner promptly vowed "to make it my business now . . ."': Kimmage, P., 'Paul Kimmage meets Rory McIlroy – Part Two', *Irish Independent*, 4 December 2022.

6. Big Guns and Big Money

'Rory and Tiger took the PGA Tour's fight with LIV Golf into their own hands.': Shedloski, D., 'The night Rory and Tiger took the PGA Tour's fight with LIV Golf into their own hands', *Golf Digest*, 13 December 2022.
'If I'm willing to do this, so should you . . .': *Full Swing*, Season 1 Episode 8, 2023. Available at: Netflix.

7. The Trump Card

'Organisers declined to issue official attendance figures . . .': Graham, B. A., 'Golf takes back seat at Saudi-backed, Trump-hosted event', *Guardian*, 30 July 2022.
'I think it is very sad': Corrigan, J., 'Sergio Garcia: Rory McIlroy's lack of maturity ended our friendship', *Telegraph*, 23 February 2023.

8. Meetings, Money and Change

'on 8 December 2022, Devlin sent an email . . .': Released via: Permanent Subcommittee on Investigations, Majority Staff Memorandum to Members of the Subcommittee, *The PGA Tour-LIV Deal: Examining the Saudi Arabian Public Investment Fund's Investments in the United States*, 10 July 2023. Available at:
www.hsgac.senate.gov/wp-content/uploads/2023-07-10-PSI-Majority-Staff-Memorandum-Regarding-Preliminary-Information-on-Agreement-Between-PGA-Tour-and-Saudi-Arabian-Public-Investment-Fund-with-Consolidated-Appendix.pdf

'The *Sports Business Journal* reported that 24 per cent of US households . . .':
Carpenter, J., 'LIV draws 274,000 viewers for Tucson final round', *Sports
Business Journal*, 21 March 2023.

'Tour veteran Ryan Armour likened those left behind in full field events to
"mules"': Shedloski, D., 'PGA Tour rank-and-file criticize new system that
caters to the elite', *Golf Digest*, 9 March 2023.

'There is a shit-ton of money out here, and I already got a shit-ton . . .':
Shipnuck, A., 'Questions surface about LIV Golf's evolving business plan
in lively players meeting', *Golf Digest* via *Fire Pit Collective*, 20 March
2023.

'I think it's going to be more fun knowing that they hate us': Sens, J., '"They hate
us": Joaquin Niemann giddy for a PGA Tour vs. LIV rivalry at Masters', *Golf
.com*, 30 March 2023.

9. Masters Diary

'I came within touching distance on a few occasions . . .': Corrigan, J., 'Greg
Norman: If an LIV golfer wins Masters, we will celebrate on 18th green',
Telegraph, 2 April 2023.

'He "didn't speak at all"': Stutsman, D., 'Champions Dinner celebrates Masters
champion Scheffler and Texas as LIV-PGA feud quiets', *Augusta Chronicle*, 5
April 2023.

'"They're full of shit," he said of his LIV colleagues . . .': Babb, K., 'It's about the
damn money', *Washington Post*, 5 April 2023.

10. Fines, Bans and . . . Accord

'Masters 2023: LIV Golf is winning': Beall, J., *Golf Digest*, 8 April 2023.

'On 14 April, five days after Jon Rahm had won the Masters, he wrote to Jimmy
Dunne again . . .': 'Permanent Subcommittee on Investigations, *The PGA
Tour-LIV Deal*' [See Chapter 8 for full reference.]

'with a WhatsApp exchange with Yasir Al-Rumayyan . . .': *Ibid.*

'My mission was always to bring an event to Australia . . .' and 'The PGA Tour
come in and raped and pillaged for one tournament . . .': Gould, R., 'Greg

Norman says Australian states are lining up to host more LIV events', *Fox Sports Australia*, 11 April 2023.

'Somebody came in and offered competition to the PGA Tour and they didn't like it . . .': Gould, R., 'Norman reveals "incredible" list of "surprising" golfers set to join LIV. . . but one roadblock remains', NCA NewsWire, 18 April 2023.

'Maybe we should sit down and talk . . .': Corrigan, J., 'Greg Norman: "I have thick skin but am still surprised by the vitriol"', *Telegraph*, 19 April 2023.

'Staveley sought to maintain the momentum with an email sent on 26 April . . .': 'Permanent Subcommittee on Investigations, *The PGA Tour-LIV Deal*' [See Chapter 8 for full reference.]

'To say he doesn't have the ability or right to do that . . .': Broadbent, R. 'PGA of America chief: LIV Golf cannot keep burning cash', *The Times*, 11 May 2023.

'Any time we make changes to our criteria going forward . . .': Herrington, R., 'USGA CEO Mike Whan defends rules change keeping Talor Gooch out of US Open, LIV golfer pushes back again', *Golf Digest*, 3 May 2023.

'It sucked that 47½ per cent was withheld for Australian taxes': *Fore The People* (podcast), 28 April 2023.

'It was explained that the level of £100,000 had been chosen...', 'Golfers v PGA European Tour', *Sport Resolutions*, 6 April 2023.

'I'm not great on stats but I must have played something like 600 events . . .', 'People say I knew exactly what would happen . . .' and 'I've been a dual member of the European Tour and PGA Tour . . .': Corrigan, J., 'Lee Westwood: The Ryder Cup will lose so much experience – but it is time for me to move on', *Telegraph*, 5 May 2023.

'It is sad that it has come to this . . .': Huggan, J., 'Henrik Stenson resigns from DP World Tour following sanctions, says "they left me no other choice"', *Golf Digest*, 11 May 2023.

'praised the "civility" that had prevailed . . .': Broadbent, R., 'PGA of America chief: LIV Golf cannot keep burning cash', *The Times*, 11 May 2023.

'There was a flurry of crucial emails on 14 May . . .': 'Permanent Subcommittee on Investigations, *The PGA Tour-LIV Deal*' [See Chapter 8 for full reference.]

11. US PGA Diary

'the *New York Times* reports on the latest developments . . .': Blinder, A., Hirsch, L. and Draper, K., 'Mickelson Among Players Interviewed in Antitrust Inquiry Into Pro Golf', *The New York Times*, 17 May 2023.

'Amanda Staveley . . . "viewed as a potential peace broker" . . .': Al-Samarrai, R., 'LIV golf turn to Newcastle director Amanda Staveley in bid to broker peace talks with the PGA Tour . . .', *Daily Mail*, 17 May 2023.

'There's this argument that everyone who went to LIV got the bag [money] and nobody gives a shit anymore . . .': Herzig, G., 'Brooks Koepka's Coach Absolutely Goes Off on Media Over LIV Golf After PGA Championship Win', *Sports Illustrated*, 24 May 2023.

12. Deal Done?

'Koepka's win forces the PGA of America . . .': Garside, K., 'Brooks Koepka forces Ryder Cup bosses to confront the toxic issue', *Independent*, 22 May 2023.

'How you guys all thought that these guys just weren't going to show up . . .': Schupak, A., 'Brooks Koepka's coach blasts media, bashes Brandel Chamblee for treatment of LIV Golf players', *Golf Week*, 23 May 2023.

'In mid-May, Herlihy emailed Dunne saying . . .': 'Permanent Subcommittee on Investigations, *The PGA Tour-LIV Deal*' [See Chapter 8 for full reference.]

'The *Washington Post* argued that LIV did not have "legitimate events" . . .': Svrluga, B., 'Welcome to LIV, where the money is dirty and the golf doesn't matter', *Washington Post*, 31 May 2023.

'The announcement is too big to wait till the definitive.': 'Permanent Subcommittee on Investigations, *The PGA Tour-LIV Deal*' [See Chapter 8 for full reference.]

'Hard to hold for this long but no leak yet and great that Jay and Yasir are aligned.': 'Permanent Subcommittee on Investigations, *The PGA Tour-LIV Deal*' [See Chapter 8 for full reference.]

'Yet now the PGA and DP World Tours along with PIF were issuing an astonishing joint press release, announcing . . .' *and relevant quotations*: PGA Tour Press Release (6 June 2023). Available at: https://www.pgatour.com/article/news/latest/2023/06/06/pga-tour-dp-world-tour-and-pif-announce-newly-formed--commercial-entity-to-unify-golf

'It was a tough meeting for both sides . . .': NBC, 7 June 2023.

'The guys who stayed loyal to the PGA Tour, it's kind of a kick in the teeth to them . . .': Golf Channel, NBC, 6 June 2023.

'I think this is one of the saddest days in the history of professional golf . . .': *Ibid.*

13. US Open Diary

'None of us knew and I was flying . . .', 'I'm not sure he even knows . . .' and 'I would say with quite a high degree . . .': *The Chipping Forecast* (Podcast), BBC Sounds, 14 June 2023.

14. Regrets and Recrimination

'Today's hearing is about much more than the game of golf . . .': 'Permanent Subcommittee on Investigations, *The PGA Tour-LIV Deal*' [See Chapter 8 for full reference.]

'They have an unlimited amount of money': *Ibid.*

'You're not out of the woods': *Ibid.*

18. Massive Disconnect

'That's why they went . . .': *The Chipping Forecast* (Podcast), BBC Sounds, 17 October 2023.

'If "sport-washing" is going to increase my GDP by way of 1%, then I will continue doing sport-washing': Fox News, 20 September 2023.

Epilogue

'My dream scenario is a world tour . . .': Duggan, J. 'Rory McIlroy's "dream scenario," cleared mind and new plan to be sharp heading into the Masters', *Golf Digest*, 9 January 2024.

'I could see that being fun . . .': *Stick to Football* (Podcast), Acast, 3 January 2024.

'You can't ask these media rights partners and sponsors for as much money': Corrigan, J. 'Rory McIlroy warns fellow pros: Give up your independence or face prize money cuts', *Telegraph*, 10 January 2024.

ACKNOWLEDGEMENTS

Huge and heartfelt thanks to the scores of people who helped directly and indirectly in the writing of this book. To my literary agent Melanie Michael-Greer, thank you for having the original idea that 'there is a book' to be written on this unprecedented period for the game of golf. To my inspirational editors Matthew Lowing and Megan Jones and all at Bloomsbury, I am very grateful for your diligence and patience in equal measure. I am indebted to so many figures in the world of golf for making time to talk to me either for this book or into my BBC Radio microphone, especially: Andrew Gardiner, Andrew Chandler, Neil McLeman, Mike Clayton, Mitchell Platts, Geoff Shackelford, Professor Simon Chadwick, James Corrigan, John Huggan, Phil Casey, Giles Morgan, Josh Carpenter, John Nucci and Felix Jakens. Thanks to the media teams at the DP World and PGA Tours as well as LIV Golf for all their invaluable assistance while covering this extraordinary story. To all my brilliant BBC Sport colleagues, in particular editor Simon Foat, producer Amy Scarisbrick and fellow commentator Katherine Downes, thank you for putting up with constant 'book' chat as we made our way around the golfing world together. To Ken Jackson, thanks very much for lending your photographic skills. And most of all, I am grateful to Sarah and Ollie for their constant love, support and tolerance through the stresses, strains and long hours spent compiling the most compelling story I've encountered in two decades on the golf beat.